D0020658

W8-ASX-337

STRETCHING THE HIGHER EDUCATION DOLLAR

THE EDUCATIONAL INNOVATIONS SERIES

The Educational Innovations series explores a wide range of current school reform efforts. Individual volumes examine entrepreneurial efforts and unorthodox approaches, highlighting reforms that have met with success and strategies that have attracted widespread attention. The series aims to disrupt the status quo and inject new ideas into contemporary education debates.

Series edited by Frederick M. Hess

Other books in this series:

STRETCHING THE HIGHER EDUCATION DOLLAR

How Innovation Can Improve Access, Equity, and Affordability

Edited by

ANDREW P. KELLY AND KEVIN CAREY

Harvard Education Press
Cambridge, Massachusetts

Copyright © 2013 by the President and Fellows of Harvard College

All rights reserved. No part of this publication may be reproduced or transmitted in any form or by any means, electronic or mechanical, including photocopy, recording, or any information storage and retrieval systems, without permission in writing from the publisher.

Library of Congress Control Number 2013939176

Paperback ISBN 978-1-61250-594-7
Library Edition ISBN 978-1-61250-595-4

Published by Harvard Education Press,
an imprint of the Harvard Education Publishing Group

Harvard Education Press
8 Story Street
Cambridge, MA 02138

Cover Design: Steven Pisano
Photo Credit: © Gregor Schuster/Corbis
The typefaces used in this book are Sabon, Century Schoolbook, and Helvetica Neue.

Contents

Introduction

Andrew P. Kelly and Kevin Carey

In late 2012, an advertisement began running on commercial radio stations in the Washington, DC, metropolitan area. It was narrated by a middle-aged man, and he was talking about his daughter. She was in college, he said, his voice swelling with pride. But he was worried that, with the economy these days, he might not be able to keep sending her to school. Might have to tell her to drop out for a while. And she even made the dean's list last semester—the dean's list! Imagine that. No, he could never take his daughter's dreams away. Instead, he was going to go talk to the good folks at his local bank, who had financial products designed just for people like him. His little girl was going to stay in college where she belonged.

Paying for college has become one of the great parental obligations of modern life. In an unstable, hyper-competitive economy, higher education is understood to be the one sure path toward stability and prosperity. It's expensive, but, we are told, over and again, it's worth it—so much so that parents have been trained by their peers and their culture to accept extraordinary financial sacrifices in exchange. If you love your children, you will do what it takes to get them through college, even if it means borrowing large amounts of money from a commercial bank. (At the time of the radio advertisement, the bank was offering student loans for 9.6 percentage points above variable interbank lending rates, or a fixed rate of 12.25 percent.[1])

But in the last few years, the implicit compact between families, colleges, and society has begun to crumble. When protesters occupied Wall Street in 2011, their rage against economy-destroying financiers quickly expanded to include the banks and lenders to whom many of them owed tens of thousands of dollars in student loans. A Federal Reserve estimate that total outstanding student loan debt had exceeded $1 trillion—more than total credit card debt—quickly entered the roster of conventional wisdom, a jolting number that could be summoned in a moment to bolster critiques of higher education and the financial industry that supports it.

1

Lingering unemployment sent many new college graduates home to live with parents whose savings had been depleted by ever-larger tuition bills.

Meanwhile, the popular press, with its bias toward counterintuition and finely tuned antennae for stories that shock the bourgeoisie, began running articles questioning whether higher education was truly "worth it" after all. With the late-2000s real estate bubble and resulting catastrophe still fresh in the public mind, iconoclasts like Silicon Valley investor Peter Thiel advanced the thesis that the next bursting bubble would be higher education.

In part, this idea was fed by declining short-term job prospects among college graduates and highly publicized research from sociologists Richard Arum and Josipa Roksa, whose 2010 book *Academically Adrift* found limited or no evidence of learning among many college graduates.[2] But the overwhelming driver of public ire was price. After three decades of published tuition rates steadily increasing faster than inflation, the brutal arithmetic of college pricing has become impossible to ignore. Even as median family income declined, four years of tuition, room, and board at the private colleges offering entrance to the ruling class soared past $200,000, with a half-million-dollar college bill looming in the distance for parents of the young. Elite public universities that had long offered coveted degrees at low prices were rapidly privatizing in response to state budget cuts, adjusting their tuitions to match. That left open-access public universities and community colleges struggling to keep their doors open and their faculty employed in the face of similar cuts, or for-profit colleges offering suspect programs financed by outsized loans.

As Thiel said, "Education may be the only thing people still believe in in the United States."[3] Where, parents wondered, with mounting anxiety, were they supposed to find the money to make good on that belief? What if the good folks at the bank wouldn't lend them the money? They'd have to take away their dean's list daughter's dreams, which would make them, by the rules of modern society, the worst parents in the world. It didn't used to be this way. College wasn't always so expensive. What should they do? Who should they blame?

To these basic and increasingly dominant questions, traditional colleges and universities have offered few satisfactory answers. Like most terrible problems, the current state of affairs has many causes, not all of which flow from indifference or bad faith on the part of university administrators. By the late 1990s, one prescient state policy analyst was already observing that higher education budgets were caught between two forces: rising demand for college driven by demographic and economic changes, on the one hand, and the growing cost of providing health care to the aged and prisons for the incarcerated, on the other.[4] In the past, the author noted, higher education appropriations had been used as a kind of fiscal balance wheel, dropping precipitously in bad financial times in order to keep other budget lines intact. It was likely they would be used so again.

This proved true in the 2001 recession, and calamitously so in the Great Recession of 2008. By 2011, inflation-adjusted state spending per student had declined to $6,290, a 22 percent drop from 1986, even as college enrollment reached all-time highs.[5] Over the same time, tuition revenue per student nearly doubled. When states pass the buck to colleges, colleges turn and pass it right along to students and their parents. As the Delta Cost Project has documented, students are paying for a larger percentage of their higher education across all sectors and types, public and private, two-year and four-year, undergraduate and doctoral alike.[6]

At the same time, the education that students are paying a larger share of has, itself, grown in cost at an alarming rate. This distinction is crucial: states are spending less even as colleges are spending *more,* with students and families making up the growing gap between the two in tuition that is increasingly financed by debt. To be sure, spending patterns vary widely within the industry, with private research universities far outpacing the field in their endless quest for much and more. But even lesser-known public institutions have doggedly increased spending, dreaming perhaps of reaching the promised land of research funding and selective admissions.

Damningly, the money hasn't even been spent on the students picking up a larger share of the tab. Instead of hiring more tenured professors, colleges brought legions of low-paid adjuncts on board. In 1975, most instructional faculty were tenure-track or full-time. By 2009, that percentage had dropped below 40 percent.[7] At the same time, the ranks of university administrators swelled. Anecdotes of universities building elaborate recreational facilities featuring lazy rivers (these having replaced climbing walls as emblems of excess) are commonplace, as are money-losing sports programs, aggressive new building plans, and other expenditures that belie any sense of financial restraint.

College leaders will cop to these and other offenses, if you press them. But, they insist, the true cost drivers in higher education are structural, even eternal. Whole books have been written arguing that spending on higher education must inevitably grow, due to an economic phenomenon commonly associated with the economist William Baumol.[8] Higher education, it is argued, is a labor-intensive service not susceptible to the technology-driven productivity increases found in sectors of the economy such as manufacturing. Economic growth in those areas drives up the price of labor, which colleges must pay despite realizing no corresponding productivity increases of their own. Thus, the labor productivity of higher education is destined to decline over time, resulting in college cost and price increases that simply must be borne by some combination of students and society, if the quality of learning is to be maintained. Howard Bowen advanced the counterthesis to Baumol, arguing that colleges increase costs not because they must but because they can, and want to, as they wage eternal positional status battles with their peers. While there is likely truth in both claims, a recent analysis suggests that "for every $1 in Baumol cost effects there are over $2 in Bowen cost effects."[9]

Yet both diagnoses are, in different ways, fatalistic. Neither offers any credible hope that college as we know it will ever be able to seriously restrain spending and prices. Industry organizations have been quick to point to the concept of "net price," using recent data to argue that the amount of money students pay out of pocket for college after accounting for grants and tuition discounts is both substantially lower than published tuition rates and growing more slowly over time.[10] But price discrimination via tuition discounting is essentially a one-time strategy for revenue maximization that many colleges, seeking to reduce their discount rates, have apparently already reached. And the recent unprecedented surge in federal grant aid depressing net prices (the annual cost of the Pell Grant program has grown from $15 billion to nearly $40 billion in less than five years) will be difficult to maintain, and will under no plausible scenario continue to grow.

This presents a grim future, one in which colleges and universities shrink into enclaves of wealth and privilege. Instead of serving the egalitarian purpose of access and upward mobility, ever-more-costly colleges will play a contrary role, reserving higher education and the credentials that go with it to the fortunate few. The creeping privatization of public institutions that is already under way will likely accelerate in such a scenario, as a resentful public further withdraws support from institutions that offer it little in return.

Can this fate be avoided? Can the Baumol/Bowen pincer of structural productivity loss and rampant status seeking be broken somehow? Is there a way to meet the surging demand for higher learning in a time of constrained public resources? Can policy makers, educators, and other stakeholders "bend the cost curve" of college sharply and quickly enough to forestall a collapse of confidence in higher education? This book is designed to answer those questions.

Even a few years ago, such a discussion would have been largely theoretical. After the 2008 recession, colleges reacted to budget cuts largely as they had in the past: raising prices, freezing salaries, cutting services, and generally hunkering down to wait out the passage of the storm. Technology, the great driver of productivity gains in other sectors, seemed to have left traditional academic norms unscathed. Most institutions had simply added technology costs to their budgetary bottom lines—indeed, it is not uncommon for university leaders to cite technological changes as a *cause* of ballooning costs and prices, rather than a cure.[11] While the number of students taking online or so-called blended courses that mix in-person and online instruction has grown significantly over the last decade, encompassing nearly one-third of all college students by 2010, most of these classes were offered by traditional institutions charging standard tuition rates (often adding an extra "technology fee") or by newly incorporated for-profit colleges charging substantially more than typical public institutions.[12]

But the last two years have seen a ferment of activity among entrepreneurs, technologists, educators, and higher education leaders, all circling in different ways the possibility that higher education dollars can be used in far more productive ways. In his 2011 State of the State address, Texas Governor Rick Perry charged the state's public institutions of higher education with developing bachelor's degree programs that would cost students no more than $10,000—total. Pundits dismissed the idea as sloganeering from a politician who lacks a reputation for intellectual heft. Critics called it "preposterous" and "absurd."[13] Yet by the end of the following year, ten state universities had rolled out $10,000 degree plans employing a variety of approaches, including competency-based assessments and crediting high school and community college learning.[14]

More famously, 2011 saw the rise to prominence of Massively Open Online Courses, or "MOOCs." Kicked off by news coverage of tens of thousands of students flocking to a free online artificial intelligence course taught by Stanford professor and Google roboticist Sebastian Thrun, MOOCs grew by orders of magnitude in size and attention. In Cambridge, Massachusetts, the historical seat of American higher education power, Harvard and MIT announced a joint nonprofit MOOC venture called edX. The flagship campuses of the University of California and University of Texas joined edX soon after, along with a handful of prestigious liberal arts colleges. Thrun himself took the traditional Palo Alto approach, which involved references to *The Matrix,* resigning his Stanford professorship, and raising millions of dollars from venture capitalists to found a tech startup lacking an obvious revenue plan.

Other Stanford professors split the difference by founding the for-profit Coursera, which offers individual courses taught by professors at colleges with luminous brands. Coursera launched its first handful of courses, in computer science, statistics, and cryptography, in March 2012. By December, it reported enrolling 2.1 million students, far more than most American colleges and universities have ever enrolled over decades or even centuries.[15] Its slogan is "Take the World's Best Courses, Online, for Free."

The world's best courses have been available somewhere in the world, to a select few, for thousands of years. Online courses have existed for over two decades. The tantalizing elements of Coursera's invitation, and that of edX, Udacity, and MOOC providers sure to come, are the openness of the proposition, and the "free." The higher education price problem has always been defined using inflexible parameters of family income, government subsidy, and capital and labor cost. What happens if radically smaller numbers are suddenly thrown into the equation? What happens if one of those numbers is zero?

The chapters in this volume all wrestle with this and similar questions, in a variety of provocative ways. The book is roughly divided into four sections, beginning with a pair of chapters that make the case for reform and pinpoint why the cost structure of higher education is difficult to change. The second section identifies opportunities for improvement at existing colleges and universities, while the third explores the promise of an unbundled model that features multiple pathways to college credit. Finally, the volume concludes with a pair of chapters that discuss the implications of all this innovation for higher education leaders and policy makers.

The book begins with an overview and sharp critique from Anya Kamenetz, the technology journalist and *Fast Company* writer whose 2006 book *Generation Debt: How Our Future Was Sold Out for Student Loans, Bad Jobs, No Benefits, and Tax Cuts for Rich Geezers—And How to Fight Back* (Riverhead) prophetically described the cohort of disillusioned millennials who hit the barricades on Wall Street five years later. Her second book, *DIY U: Edupunks, Edupreneurs, and the Coming Transformation of Higher Education* (Chelsea Green Publishing, 2010) again presaged an emerging shift in modern society, this one at the intersection of technology and higher learning. Kamanetz makes the case for moving beyond the limitations of Baumol's hypothesis, toward a higher education ecosystem that is far cheaper, customizable, and responsive to student needs. Kamanetz's critique is followed by Centre College emeritus economist Robert E. Martin's diagnosis of why traditional colleges and universities seem unable to stop themselves from increasing prices. Martin describes a deeply rooted, intertwined system of higher education governance that not only makes cost containment difficult, but also pushes rational institutions in the opposite direction.

This does not mean, however, that such actions are impossible or that no institutions have tried to implement them. Indeed, in the third chapter Tulane University economist Douglas N. Harris argues that higher education institutions can become more productive, but only if leaders take a hard look at cost-effectiveness when making decisions. To get them started, Harris lays out a framework for this kind of analysis and then uses it to evaluate a number of popular policies, including the use of part-time versus full-time faculty, improved student services, and remedial education. In chapter 4, Ari Blum and Dave Jarrat of InsideTrack, a student services counseling firm, examine how more effective student services can save colleges money in the long run. Colleges, Blum and Jarrat explain, often provide student services poorly and expensively. By applying technology, leveraging economies of scale, and using data to drive decisions, they argue, colleges can save money while increasing student learning, retention, and other academic outcomes.

The fifth chapter, written by former *Chronicle of Higher Education* editor Jeffrey J. Selingo, tackles the cost containment problem from the perspective of management consulting. Numerous campuses have hired Bain & Company to analyze their cost structures and recommend improvements. Bain has identified millions of dollars in potential savings, yet has been faced with skeptical university employees and a strict mandate to leave the academic side of spending alone. This chapter shows what happens when people from outside the academy arrive on campus, what they typically find in budgets and management structures, and the kinds of changes they recommend.

Having examined college costs from within traditional institutions, the last three chapters show how different the cost equation can look from without. In chapter 6, Internet entrepreneur Michael Staton begins with a new taxonomy of what, exactly, colleges are providing to students, and how vulnerable each discrete element of the college experience is to competition and disruption from people like him. Staton's conclusions are sobering for those counting on college prices staying high for the foreseeable future: many institutions are spending their limited resources on parts of the learning experience that are *easiest* to unbundle and provide at scale. Staton provides examples of startup and educational technology companies that are hard at work finding ways to compete with different parts of the conglomerate college business model.

Veteran higher education journalist Ben Wildavsky provides a new perspective on the instructional side of online higher education by examining how three providers of large-scale Internet instruction have designed and operate their courses—and how much they cost to develop. The University of Maryland University College has been in the distance education market for decades and is the rare public institution that competes at scale directly with for-profit providers for adults looking to learn online. In contrast, the University of California's UC Online and Sebastian Thrun's Udacity are much younger and have developed unique production and delivery models of their own. Following Wildavsky's look at online course delivery, Paul Fain and Steve Kolowich, journalists for *Inside Higher Ed* and the *Chronicle of Higher Education*, respectively, use chapter 8 to explore the emerging world of "prior learning assessment" and nontraditional methods of granting college credits. For nearly a century, college credits have been awarded by institutions for time spent learning at those institutions—the "credit hour." Fain and Kolowich document a new movement toward less expensive modes of certification like competency-based exams, portfolio assessments, and MOOC certificates, and they discuss what these advances may mean for existing colleges' traditional control over credentialing power.

Having described how the different components of traditional higher education are being broken into pieces by technology-driven innovation, the final two chapters discuss how they can be put back together again in new and interesting ways and how public policy often serves to hinder such entrepreneurial approaches. Paul J. LeBlanc, the president of Southern New Hampshire University, describes how his institution has become one of the biggest providers of online higher education over the last decade, as well as the university's nascent effort to offer a radically low-cost, competency-based associate's degree. Burck Smith, founder and CEO of the online higher education company StraighterLine, concludes with a bold set of recommendations for comprehensively changing the higher education policy environment. Smith argues that the current regulatory and financial structure was established to subsidize and sustain a single organizational model of higher education—the college—and that these outdated rules are now preventing new organizations from providing students with high-quality learning experiences at low prices.

In total, the chapters in this volume paint a picture of traditional higher education on the verge of dramatic change. The huge run-up in college spending and commensurate increase in college prices that has occurred over the last three decades has left academe in a perilous position. At some point, sooner than many seem willing to acknowledge, the combination of government subsidies, student tuition, endowment earnings, and other revenue sources that fuel the higher education spending machine will simply run short.

As the initial chapters in this volume demonstrate, we are not lacking in theoretical explanations for this problem, nor solutions that colleges and universities can implement, if they choose, to stretch the higher education dollar. We may, however, be lacking in political will, institutional urgency, and time. As the later chapters amply demonstrate, if traditional institutions are unable or unwilling to change the way they set prices and use resources on behalf of students, a whole range of new technology-driven competitors stand ready to take their place.

From Baumol's Cost Disease to Moore's Law

Bending the Cost Curve in Higher Education

Anya Kamenetz

As a nation, we must dramatically reduce the cost of postsecondary education. There's an economic imperative to do so, to allow the United States to fully recover from the past five years of economic stagnation and resume a fighting stance. There is a moral imperative to do so, to restore the promise of the American Dream that has been darkened for an entire generation. And there's a third reason, what you might call the innovator's imperative: we have tools available to us today, as we've never had before, to deliver the key benefits of top-notch higher education, and what's more, at a much lower cost than was imaginable just a few years ago and in a manner befitting all the new ways we access and share knowledge. This chapter will outline the adverse economic and social consequences of the runaway growth in tuition over the past thirty years, explore the underlying reasons why college has become so expensive, and hint at the possible solutions to come in the rest of this book.

STUDENT DEBT: A NATIONAL (PRE)OCCUPATION

On November 21, 2011, in the newly cleared and heavily patrolled Liberty Plaza in downtown Manhattan, a group of Occupy Wall Street activists, dressed in caps and gowns made from garbage bags and draped with paper chains, announced the official launch of the Occupy Student Debt campaign. They urged those struggling with student loans to sign a national pledge of "debt refusal," seeking safety in numbers by stopping payment on their loans once the signatories reached 1 million.

The Occupy Wall Street movement helped bring the cost of college and the attendant increase in student loan debt to the national forefront in 2011 and 2012 like never before. News networks covered the issue nightly; online petitions attracted hundreds of thousands of signatures; Congress had a showdown over student loan interest rates; President Obama and his opponent, Mitt Romney, spoke about the issue from the campaign trail.

The Millennial protesters were connecting the right dots between the rising cost of their education and an economy parched for opportunity. Whatever your political leanings, it's easy to understand that a country with an outstanding $1 trillion in student loan debt (outpacing credit card debt), where over half of recent college graduates are either unemployed or underemployed in jobs not requiring a bachelor's degree, and where average tuition at public universities has risen 827 percent since 1980, is a place where hard work and talent no longer result in a fair shot for young people.[1]

HOW RISING COLLEGE COSTS HURT INDIVIDUALS AND SOCIETY

In the past seven years, crisscrossing North America as a journalist and advocate investigating generational economic issues, I've encountered countless students who have had to drop out and put their dreams on hold because of a divorce or a job loss in the family. Parents no longer able to contribute to their children's education because of a home foreclosure. Adult students exhausted from the demands of raising a child and holding down one or more jobs while trying to progress in their coursework. Graduates stuck in a catch-22, whose debt makes it difficult to find employment. The cost of college—and the attendant high student loan debt—has adverse consequences that ripple throughout our society: economic, social, cultural, and even emotional.

Student Loan Debt and the Prospects of a Generation
The burden of student loan debt has come to define a generation's prospects and promises. Many of the social conditions associated with the Millennials' extended adolescence can be traced directly to economic factors such as the changing job market, the cost of living, and the cost of college. Graduates with high debt burdens, a threshold crossed when monthly payments total more than 8 percent of disposable income, are more likely to move back home with their parents.[2] Recent grads are more likely than ever to accept family support for housing, food, health care, college loan repayments, and car payments.[3] They're more likely to file for bankruptcy, less likely to save for retirement, and more likely to delay marriage and buying

a car or home.[4] Heavy student loan debtors are more likely to choose the first job they can find, not the job that is the best fit—a tendency that can depress individual incomes for years to come, and one that depresses productivity on an economy-wide basis.[5] In one survey they even reported higher levels of anxiety and sleeplessness.[6]

In the professions, student loan burdens are much higher than for undergraduates, and the impact is pervasive. Doctors, who graduated with an average of $145,020 in debt in 2010, are struggling in poverty during their residencies and gravitating to high-paying specialties over primary care.[7] Lawyers, who owe over $100,000, choose white-shoe firms over public interest law, when they can find jobs in the first place; some have resorted to suing their alma maters for misrepresenting graduates' employment rates.[8]

In a Kafkaesque twist, student loans, by themselves, can have an adverse impact on job seekers. Sixty percent of employers routinely check applicants' credit reports, which typically include student loan debts.[9] After Latoya Horton lost an accounting job due to her high debt-to-credit ratio, caused by her student loans, she started a petition that garnered forty thousand signatures, asking TransUnion not to sell job seekers' credit reports to employers.[10] But it's not really the employers' fault, or even the credit bureaus'. It doesn't take an accountant to tell you that something doesn't add up when an education forces you to take on such high debt that it disqualifies you for the very job you're preparing for.

The Dream Deferred

We hear so much talk about the key role of education in the American Dream. Perhaps the most damning indictment of the education system is the large number of young people in America who are giving up on that dream. In poll after poll, Americans insist that college is important, yet large majorities believe that it is too expensive for their families. In one nationally representative survey conducted by Rutgers University in 2012, 40 percent of recent graduates expressed a belief that their generation will be less successful than the one that preceded them.[11]

Although high school graduation rates have inched up in the past few years, young people by and large need postsecondary degrees to secure jobs above poverty wages. The lowest performing rich kids, from families in the top quartile of income, are more likely to attend college than the highest performing kids in the bottom quartile.[12] Stubborn effects like these make a mockery of the idea of meritocracy. As long as college is widely perceived as being reserved for the rich, it actually deters students in lower-income communities from enrolling in the competitive classes that will prepare them for college, making it a self-fulfilling prophecy.

What's desperately needed is an open dialogue about the cost of college and possible solutions. Yet a lot of the dialogue about the value of higher education is conducted with a thumb on the scale, or in outright bad faith. Those who tout the payoff for student borrowers, the average 70 percent higher earnings for those with a BA rather than just a high school diploma, leave out a huge part of the story. What about the students who lag behind or fail to finish their degrees? Only 56 percent of entrants at four-year universities manage to graduate within six years.[13] Dropouts add to the percentage, which in 2011 spiked to 8.8 percent, who default on their loans within two years after leaving school.[14] Or what about those whose degrees don't happen to match up with what the market rewards? Or the ones who graduate into a recession, like the one we've been in since 2008, and face lower earnings for a decade or more?[15]

Young people are universally told that if they want to succeed, they have no choice but to go to college. They graduate only to find out that while the diploma may be a necessary condition for success, it is by no means a sufficient one. In May 2012, a nationally representative survey of those who graduated college between 2006 and 2011 found that just over half were working full time.[16] Only four in ten had found jobs that actually required their four-year degree. And 40 percent of the graduates of the past three years had yet to pay off any of their debt. It's hard to tell them, at least in the short term, that it was worth it.

But the toll from our collective failure to control the rising cost of college doesn't just fall on these individuals. Educational stagnation contributes to economic stagnation generally.

Education and Economic Growth

The relationship between education and economic growth has been a major area of study for economists at least since the nineteenth century. There are robust findings over many decades that individuals increase their earnings by 10 percent for each additional year of schooling.[17] On a nation-by-nation comparative basis, adding an average year of education to the adult population is correlated with a long-term increase in economic output of between 3 and 6 percent.[18] In the mid-twentieth century, the GI Bill sent 8 million Americans to college, marking the height of our prosperity with a giant bet on education. It's been estimated that for every dollar spent on sending servicemen to college, seven were returned to the public coffers because of higher lifetime earnings for the graduates of the 1950s.[19]

Unhappily, the United States can draw the converse example from its more recent history. The economic dominance we enjoyed for much of the twentieth century went into decline starting with the 1973 oil crisis and recession. It was also in the 1970s, with the onset of a demographic "birth dearth," that college enrollment actually fell for the first time, following the great expansion of public higher education with the 1965 Higher Education Act and placing a new economic pressure on colleges.[20] Facing stagflation, states withdrew support from public universities, and tuition started to rise faster than inflation.[21] For the first time in history, America began to lose ground in the education level of the population (falling from most educated nation for the whole of the twentieth century to thirteenth most educated today, by the most common measure).[22] And in 1972 President Nixon created the student loan marketing agency Sallie Mae, marking the beginning of the modern student loan market.

Today, even in the midst of faltering recovery, business owners perceive a shortage of graduates with specific skills. With the unemployment rate still at 9 percent, 40 percent of owners of fast-growing private companies in the fall of 2011 cited the inability to find qualified workers as the biggest factor holding back their growth.[23] And manufacturers, in particular, struggled to fill six hundred thousand vacancies, mostly of workers with specialized technical or administrative skills, even with over 13 million Americans unemployed.[24]

If we look at the likely sources of economic growth in the decades to come, there are few paths forward for us as a society that do not include a significant increase in the average education level of the population. Indeed, both President Obama and much of the nonprofit leadership in the field have called for doubling the numbers who graduate with a postsecondary degree in the next decade.[25] And yet there are no projections that the United States will actually succeed in doing anything like this, nor is there any serious public proposal or commitment to get us there. Higher education is roughly a $320 billion enterprise in the United States already.[26] Finding another few hundred billion dollars in state and federal budgets, philanthropic coffers, or family pockets seems highly unlikely at this juncture. The only logical assumption is that something has to change. But what?

THE REAL PROBLEM: COSTS, NOT JUST PRICES

As the author of 2006's *Generation Debt*, one of the first books to document the current student loan crisis, I've spent most of the past eight years speaking to faculty, administration, and especially students about the toll that high tuition and high loan debt takes. I think we're finally arriving at a tipping point with regard to tuition, as a Moody's investor report concluded last year.[27] The ability of colleges to continue to finance growth by depending more and more on tuition has reached its natural limit. Families and students are fed up, and they're searching for lower-cost, higher-quality alternatives.

During the time that I've been immersed in this topic, the dialogue has progressed. Mostly gone are the days when pundits, usually those in possession of several hundred thousand dollars' worth of education, simply point to the vaunted $1 million increase in (average) earnings over the (average) lifetime of the (average) BA and explain patronizingly that college is a good value no matter what. Thinkers of all political stripes are taking this issue much more seriously today, and looking at the details.

However, some of the conclusions they're drawing are incorrect. I've come to realize that the entire framing of the current public debate over the cost of education and the growth of student loan debt is misconstrued. We talk about making loans more affordable or stretching out the payments instead of cutting tuition. We talk about reducing tuition and reducing costs as if they were the same thing, when tuition is only one of many revenue streams at nonprofit institutions. We lump together all financial aid rather than looking at the difference between need-based and merit-based aid and how each might contribute to making college more accessible.

And the most fundamental error of all: we focus more on affordability— the price to the student—than on transforming the underlying cost drivers in higher education. When we do talk about cost drivers, our focus is often on the wrong ones. It's popular to blame professors' salaries when in fact the percentage of college budgets that goes to teaching has been in decline for twenty years, and when it is benefits, not salaries, and administrative positions, not teaching positions, that are responsible for the rise in labor cost at most institutions.[28]

Reducing the cost of student loans through further subsidizing the interest rates, providing more repayment plans, or any other scheme that depends on pouring more federal student aid dollars into the system, does nothing directly to change the underlying cost structure of higher education, except to continue to influence it to grow in the wrong direction. As we've seen over several decades, loosening the federal student aid spigot actually fuels the growth of tuition in the long run. The answer to college costs needs to go deeper, to how colleges actually operate.

WHY IS COLLEGE SO EXPENSIVE?

To understand how to make higher education more affordable in a real and lasting way, we have to understand first the factors that make it so expensive to deliver in the traditional fashion. This requires looking at the work of the university in two ways: the interactions between professors and students in the classroom, and the ever-increasing number of functions that take place outside the classroom.

The Story of the String Quartet

The leading explanation—or perhaps one should say the leading excuse—for why college costs tend to rise faster than inflation comes from the 1966 paper *Performing Arts: The Economic Dilemma* by economists William Bowen and William Baumol.[29] Why is it, they asked, that certain endeavors have resisted the pull of the automation, efficiency, and globalization that allowed the price of so many goods to come down in the twentieth century? Well, take a string quartet, for example. You can't save any money by cutting the cello player; you'll suffer a serious reduction in quality if you replace the skilled players with novices; you can't save money by playing the music more quickly; and you can't outsource the quartet to China if you want a live concert in Chicago.

The authors concluded in a series of papers that certain highly skilled, labor-intensive industries, including the performing arts, education, and health care, would always see basic costs rise faster than inflation. They dubbed this phenomenon the "cost disease." There is a kernel of fundamental economic truth to this. Inflation is simply an index of prices of both goods and services, and the prices of goods have tended over the decades to be more amenable to modification than the prices of services (i.e., labor costs).

But the assumption that higher education is synonymous with—or even deeply analogous to—the experience of sitting in a room passively enjoying a live performance is, above all, fundamentally flawed. It's being tested, and disproved, every day by the new models you will hear about later in this chapter and this book. Suffice it to say at this point that stretching the higher education dollar requires curing the cost disease.

Four Factors That Lead to Higher Tuition

Let's look in a little more detail at the other common reasons cited for the rise in college tuition. I'll deal with them more or less in ascending order of importance, which differs whether they predominantly affect private universities, which charge higher tuition, or the public institutions where most students enroll. The factors, as we'll see, include out-of-control spending, various measures to squeeze more money out of students (as opposed to other sources of revenue), labor costs, and the impact of student aid itself.

The climbing wall. At private nonprofit universities—according to the Delta Cost Project at the American Institute for Research, which does detailed research in these areas—most of the rise in tuition is driven directly by a rise in spending. And spending on student services—everything from counseling to recreation—has increased at a faster rate than spending on instruction.[30]

The most visible part of this spending has to do with marketing. These colleges compete nationally for students, so they hire brand consultants, build dorms that look like luxury condominiums, and offer gyms with rock-climbing walls and Olympic-sized pools.

But a lot of this spending has very little to do with appealing to students at all. Traditional colleges and universities owe their existence to a variety of stakeholders who derive status and economic benefits from being associated with the project of educating the next generation. This list includes religious, community, political, and business leaders; wealthy alumni and donors; faculty; and staff. Among the stakeholders who financially support the university, most of that money arrives with earmarks attached. Students, although necessary to justify the university's existence, are rarely involved in founding or running one. This explains why universities direct so much money to all sorts of projects that have very little to do with educating students.

In thrall to wealthy alumni, colleges are beholden to produce highly visible capital projects that donors can put their names on, instead of, let's say, an improvement in online course offerings. In response to public pressure and regulation—much of it with laudable aims—over the last forty years, colleges have been pushed to spend lots of money outside their core missions of teaching and research on such things as complying with ever-growing accreditation regulations, sponsoring a full complement of women's athletics under Title IX, adding mental health and diversity counselors, making courses accessible to those with a variety of learning disabilities, fielding a broader and broader list of student activities, increasing their orientation programming and support, improving campus security, creating luxurious study-abroad experiences . . . and the list goes on. There seems to be no end to the responsibilities taken on in loco parentis in the age of helicopter parenting.

And in pursuit of their own prestige, college administrators throughout the centuries have sought to climb the status ladder in higher education. They add graduate and research programs with little demand so they can rebrand themselves as "universities" rather than "colleges." They support professional-level sports teams that lose millions of dollars a year.[31] They pay consultants to tell them that "Beaver College" is not a good name for their school.[32] They add staff in their fundraising offices even as they cut the budget for teaching. As Robert Martin describes in chapter 2, colleges' financial behavior can be described by something called *Bowen's rule* (not the same Bowen who authored *Performing Arts: The Economic Dilemma*)—that is, they raise all the money they can, and spend all the money they can raise.

From the students' point of view, all of these actions fall into the category known in the military as "mission creep" or what Clark Kerr calls "the multiversity . . . all things to all people."[33] If colleges were able to finance all of this activity independently, we might say more power to them. But unfortunately, undergraduate students, sometimes seeming like little more than the excuse for the institution's existence, have been asked to shoulder more and more of the cost of all this caravansary.

The great cost shift. At public universities over the past two decades, the Delta Cost Project found, tuition increases were directly due to declines in state subsidies, more than any other cause. The Project reported that "between 1995 and 2006, the dominant revenue pattern across public institutions was the growing dependence on tuitions as a primary source of revenue." Spending grew, and students simply paid more of the price of their own education. The University of California, the nation's largest public system, is an extreme example. Between 1990 and 2010, the state's contribution declined by 51 percent per student. Students went from paying 13 percent of their educational costs in 1990 to 49 percent in 2011–2012.[34]

Cost shifting occurs across teaching programs as well as outside them. Freshmen in two-hundred-person lecture courses pay the same tuition as seniors in ten-person seminars. Literature majors, whose programs require little more in the way of materials than paper and a few books from the library, pay the same as photography majors who require a darkroom and agriculture majors who need an entire cattle ranch.

In addition to raising undergraduate tuition, colleges squeeze more money from students by creating cash-cow graduate programs like executive MBAs and various trendy and narrowly targeted master's and one-year graduate certificate programs where almost everyone pays full tuition; and, following the example of airlines, they've broken more costs out into fees, making it harder for students to calculate the total bill before they are already enrolled.

Enrollment management. A key reason colleges raise their asking prices sky high is so they can practice *enrollment management*, a new category of professional activity that has exploded in the past ten years. I've discovered in my campus visits that it's even possible to get a master's degree in the science of enrollment management. What it prepares you to do is maximize revenue from students who are able to pay full freight, particularly by marketing your college to wealthy, out-of-state, and international students—all of which activity militates against the stated commitment of public and nonprofit institutions to support their communities and equalize access to knowledge.

Setting higher prices, meanwhile, gives colleges room to bargain, offering financial aid packages full of discounts (labeled "grants") to entice students who have higher test scores or supply diversity to their class. The discounted price for the most coveted students might still be higher than the fair market rate for that education. This, in turn, raises the apparent quality of the college as judged by the qualifications of the entering class, which improves the marketing materials still further.

And in some cases, raising tuition can be a selling point in itself, a crude reckoning of the category in which a college places itself—which, in the absence of real information about a college's performance, becomes a proxy test of quality.

Colleges practice enrollment management for a simple reason: if they didn't, then cost shifting wouldn't work. Public four-years used all of the preceding techniques to increase net tuition revenue per student by 39 percent between 1999 and 2009.[35]

Health care and pensions. At both private and public universities, compensation, including both salaries and benefits, accounts for between 60 percent and 70 percent of all spending for the entire operation.[36] Most of that, it should not surprise you by now, does not go directly to the classroom—60 to 70 percent of that compensation is for noninstructional roles (everyone from the president, to athletic coaches, to enrollment management specialists and development officers who help generate more revenue for the college, as just described).[37] In fact, colleges have gotten very good at cutting costs for instruction by simply having more part-time teaching assistants and low-paid adjuncts in the classroom, many of whom are literally working for poverty wages.[38]

The rise of compensation at public universities is driven largely by the rise in health care and pension costs for the remaining tenured faculty and the growing administrative staff.[39] Remember, public university employees are, first and foremost, public employees with all the lifetime retirement and health care that implies. Both my parents, who retired from Louisiana State University in excellent health after thirty years on the faculty, get this type of benefit, and I'm very glad for selfish reasons. On a national basis, however, it becomes an intractable problem. By 2009, one in four compensation dollars at public universities was spent on benefits alone.[40]

THE PROBLEM WITH FREE MONEY

If you look at each of the main reasons why tuition is growing so horrendously you won't find villainy. What you see is a collection of more or less well-meaning and self-interested people responding rationally to a messed-up market, with consequences both adverse and unintended. And what's mostly messing up the market is subsidies, especially federally subsidized student loans.

There are solid reasons for taxpayers to subsidize universities, ranging from a better-educated citizenry to large universities that drive innovation and new research. That said, because of unrestrained spending bloat on the part of universities, combined with the many other competing priorities for government in an era of historic revenue crunch, the relationship between many states and their colleges has become dysfunctional. Giving state universities more money no longer expands access for students.

Gross and Net

Apologists for the out-of-control college cost spiral never fail to point out that about two-thirds of undergraduate students enrolled full-time receive grants—effectively, tuition discounts—that reduce the actual price of college. In addition, many states and institutions grant tuition waivers to groups such as dependents of employees, veterans, or teachers.

Between 2006 and 2007 and 2011 and 2012, average published tuition and fees at public four-year colleges and universities increased by about $1,800 in 2011 dollars, an annual rate of growth of 5.1 percent beyond inflation. Yet the *net* average tuition and fees paid by in-state students, subtracting grant aid, tax credits, and deductions, increased less than a tenth as much—$170 in 2011 dollars, an annual rate of growth of 1.4 percent beyond inflation.[41]

But this net effect doesn't get public universities off the hook. The way aid is disbursed means that it doesn't go to the students who have the greatest need, and therefore it doesn't erase the adverse social effects of the rising cost of college. Besides the basic unfairness here, the problem for many students is that they have no way to plan or understand exactly how much they'll be paying. The financial aid office, not the student, holds all the cards. As long as the office follows federal guidelines, it has no incentive to disburse its funds to the group of qualified students with the greatest overall financial need, and instead it practices enrollment management by extending discounts to the students it wants to recruit. The lack of transparency disrupts the functioning of a normal market.

Part-time students are far less likely to receive any kind of grant aid.[42] So are students at for-profits, where institutional scholarships are almost unheard of. So, therefore, are many older and working students. The students who get the biggest discounts, then, are some of the ones who need them the least. The same misallocation is true at an institutional level.

Student Loans

It's widely acknowledged that the major driver for the run-up in housing prices prior to the 2008 crash was the availability of easy credit to home buyers. By 2008, half of all mortgages in the United States were guaranteed by Freddie Mac or Fannie Mae, both government-sponsored entities, and most of the rest were implicitly underwritten by the promise of a federal bailout—the idea that banks writing these loans were "too big to fail."[43] This gave confidence to investors around the world, who poured more and more money into these loans, which in turn enabled people to pay more for their homes, which fueled the bubble and eventual bust.

The student loan market of today has many similarities with the mortgage loan market of the mid-2000s. Eighty percent of student loans are federally guaranteed and the remaining 20 percent private or alternative loans an implicit federal guarantee—no bankruptcy protection, so they remain collectible until the borrower dies.[44] Anyone who is accepted by any accredited institution may be eligible for up to $57,500 in federal loans, depending on age, the cost of the school, and other circumstances; private loans can go much higher, into the tens of thousands, and parental PLUS loans have no set limits.[45]

The availability of all this credit is the secret enabler of every other cost factor on this list. Financing makes families less sensitive to price, allowing colleges to layer on special perks, reap the most money possible from each student through enrollment management, and cope with the decline in state support by practicing cost shifting. Student loans have delayed the day of reckoning on college prices year after year. But now that time may be drawing to a close.

I predict a somewhat softer landing for the student loan market than we saw in mortgages. As this volume's coeditor Kevin Carey has pointed out, you can't flip a college diploma, nor can you foreclose on or repossess someone's education. However, I think it's only a matter of time until the federal government, for both ethical and pragmatic reasons, starts to let the air out of the bubble. The July 2012 student loan deal, which preserved the 3.4 percent interest rate for an additional year while removing the six-month grace period and subsidized loans for graduate students, is a step in that direction.

Conservatives will call more and more insistently for raising the cost of borrowing, as the long-term liabilities of the federal budget continue to grow, and progressives continue to call for sanctioning private loan lenders and reinstating bankruptcy protection for private loan borrowers. Both fronts of reform will tend to have the effect of restricting access to student loans.

If this happened next year, it would mean that far fewer students could enroll in college, which would be a disaster both for individuals and society. But in the long term, something has got to happen to shrink the student loan program, because ever-higher student debt is itself a disaster for individuals and society.

THEY JUST DON'T GET IT: COLLEGES AND COST CONTROL

In my experience, the administration and, even more so, the faculty at traditional colleges assume a defensive crouch when confronted with the reality of mounting tuition and student debt. They would like for state funding to go up, but they don't want any other part of the equation to change. In May 2012, as part of a series on the cost of college, the *New York Times* ran a story with the online headline "Colleges Begin to Confront Higher Costs and Student Debt."[46] Lawrence T. Lesick, who, as vice president for enrollment management at Ohio Northern University, is one of the architects of revenue maximization and cost shifting, was quoted sounding the right notes. "We know the model is not sustainable," he said. "Schools are going to have to show the value proposition. Those that don't aren't going to be around."[47]

However, the remainder of the article didn't breathe a word about improving the value proposition of this publicly established and funded institution by lowering tuition, serving more students with the money they have, or even controlling increases. Instead, we heard about the millions to be saved at Ohio State, where tuition is $24,630 a year for out-of-state students and the president makes $1.6 million, by consolidating orders for office supplies among branches of the state institution.[48] Really? That's cost control 101. The folks at Dunder Mifflin, the paper company on the American sitcom *The Office*, could tell you all about it.

Lesick's phrasing about a "value proposition" is a telling one. Clearly he sees this as a sales challenge, not a fundamental threat to the college's way of doing business. Traditional colleges continue to operate by Bowen's rule; their response to any perceived need is to ask for more money.[49] The responsibility is on policy makers, states, and the federal government to break this cycle.

Back to the Drawing Board

If we were to design and fund the higher education system from scratch to meet the broadest conception of the public good, two major things would have to change. Money would follow the neediest students, and institutions would be organized to serve the largest number of students in the best way possible with the most efficient use of resources. It's time to challenge the assumption that it's impossible to provide quality education at a cost that's truly affordable to students.

From Baumol's Cost Disease to Moore's Law

When I started covering higher education as a journalist, I naturally turned for answers to the knowledgeable sources at think tanks, government agencies, and existing colleges and universities. Yet it was quite difficult to find critical discussions about the basic finances and operations of higher education, particularly among the laureled scholars and gilded experts whose livelihoods were so often dependent upon the status quo. Upton Sinclair's maxim comes to mind: "It is difficult to get a man to understand something when his salary depends on his not understanding it."

So I reached out for new sources. I started talking to those who had experience with digital innovation and disruption in industries like movies, music, and journalism. Recent history has a lot to tell us about what radical transformation looks like. Clayton Christensen, the Harvard Business School professor who coined the term *disruptive innovation*, has made a special study of higher education over the past few years, and his observations have informed mine.[50]

I've become convinced that what we need is an application of Moore's Law to higher education. This is the observation of Intel's Gordon Moore that there's been a doubling of the number of transistors that fit on a silicon computer chip every eighteen to twenty-four months—which has held true since the 1970s.[51] When you go back to Moore's original paper, you realize the true insight here: chips are getting better and faster because they're also getting cheaper. The reason you can have a smartphone in your pocket that's as powerful as a desktop from thirty years ago is because unit cost has continued to drop as manufacturing became more and more efficient.

What Technology Hasn't Done—Yet

For the vast majority of higher education providers, technology hasn't yet been yoked to the economic imperative to produce true innovation. Traditional institutions have spent millions to install high-speed Internet in their dorms and digital whiteboards in their lecture halls, hire IT staffs, and contract with enterprise software providers that offer feature-laden, buggy software packages called "learning management systems."[52] Blackboard, by far the dominant provider in the industry, scores as the second most-hated software company after Microsoft in user surveys.[53] And for all this, IT professionals often tell me that it's a struggle to get faculty members even to post their syllabi online, making the systems less useful than a cork bulletin board.

All this effort is duplicative. None of it is following an economic imperative to find efficiency or replace labor, the largest cost in a university budget. Quite the opposite—it requires more workers and creates more work for faculty, who aren't generally rewarded for incorporating technology into their teaching and thus, reasonably, tend to see it as a burden or something to do in their spare time.

The mainstream online higher education providers have yet to take full advantage of the possibilities of technology either. They largely preserve the same faculty/student ratio as a brick-and-mortar university, depending on passive knowledge transfer through video and written materials.[54] And they haven't radically cut the cost: for-profits charge upward of $14,000 per full-time enrollment per year, and nonprofits tend to charge the same tuition for their online programs as their offline ones, if not a premium for convenience.[55] When I asked the dean of one private graduate school that had implemented a live, video-based, online version of its program about efficiency, she bristled at the question of cost savings. "I don't know if I'd use that word—efficiency," she said. "We actually haven't sat down to do a one-on-one cost comparison. If you want a [PRIVATE U] degree you have to pay [PRIVATE U] tuition."[56]

It's clear that technology isn't a magic formula for education. It must be used in truly innovative structures that respond to demand from learners. And above all, it must be used with the mandate to cut costs or use existing resources more efficiently. Happily, we can already see indications of how that's going to work.

Better, Faster, Cheaper

I've found that students are looking for three main categories of benefit from a college or university: *content*, the acquisition of skills and knowledge; *socialization*, the process of personal maturation through relationships with peers, mentors, and oneself; and *accreditation*, the assessment, diploma, or degree that provides a signaling effect in the job market. Radical solutions to the college cost problem are still emerging. But what's clear is that a path toward change means unbundling each of these component benefits so we can examine clearly how they can be offered.

For knowledge transfer, efficiencies develop in the transfer from the live lecture to the digital sharing of video, audio, and text, where the marginal cost of delivery drops to zero. Socialization comes to scale through the use of networks, a greater reliance on peer roles in learning, and experiential learning that embeds students in the world, drawing on local communities and businesses to take a greater role in fostering learning. Accreditation will open up to include peer assessment in online communities, self-assessment through portfolios and community assessment from badges, student participation in communities of practice, as well as improved computer assessment using machine learning and artificial intelligence techniques.

The era where every college attempts to be all things to all people is ending. The promise of the future is technology to complement the parts of the job that can be done only in person: tools to leverage the power of peers and communities to improve quality while also reducing cost. These experiments need to rely increasingly on the specific benefits rendered by tools such as video delivered over broadband, the application of data to continuously improve teaching and learning, online social networking, and automated feedback. The roles of existing personnel must coevolve with these tools, and new ones as they emerge.

Here are some possible directions for change. Top-tier research institutions with robust endowments and high costs could bear the torch of knowledge production. They can support faculty to create and publish multimedia courses, including assessment and social features, for millions of learners around the world to absorb, whether or not they are attached to a formal program. The prototypes are Coursera (Stanford, Berkeley, Michigan), Udacity (Stanford), and edX (Harvard, MIT). These platforms capture fine-grained information about how learners learn, allowing for continuous improvements in the presentation of knowledge. The federal government should support this vital work and mandate that its fruits remain open and free to all.

Once a full curriculum of high-quality, video-based courses is created, streamed, and continuously updated, that's when the fun begins. Close-to-the-ground, teaching-focused institutions like community colleges could build programs around this content, leveraging their limited resources—an average of about $10,000 per student—to counsel, tutor, support, and motivate students face-to-face. They would go hyperlocal, building bridges with employers and community groups, and convening cohorts of peers onsite at internships and volunteer placements to ensure that programs serve their students' needs. People who succeed with online courses do it with support from friends, family members, or robust social networks. Imagine libraries, community centers, high schools, and workplaces like

Starbucks hosting small meetups of students who work together over a few laptops or mobile devices, with a support person in the room to help them and keep them motivated. Paul LeBlanc of Southern New Hampshire University (and author of chapter 9 in this volume) is helping make that vision a reality.

Government could do a lot to encourage such innovation, since it holds the purse strings. I've been advocating for years to restore bankruptcy protection on federal student loans, which would ultimately restrict access to the pile of easy credit that allows tuition to inflate year after year. The "gainful employment" rule, which ends eligibility for federal aid if too many of a college's students default on their loans, should be extended from for-profits to all institutions, to force the issue of whether they offer reasonable value for money. Pell Grants don't work to increase lower-income students' access to college because their distribution is controlled by college financial aid offices, and the amount is tied to the tuition charged by that institution. Imagine what would happen if the grants were awarded to students directly on the basis of need, to be spent anywhere the learner saw fit? Institutions would be competing to serve the neediest students and offer the best value for money.

Finally, states could find new economies of scale if they revised the old "master plans" to mandate the kinds of collaboration on curricula that new platforms make easy, so that a course designed at the flagship institution could be offered with modifications for accessibility at every community college.

Each of these approaches has the potential to improve the learner's experience through increased individual control and greater relevance to the methods and modes of knowledge required in the twenty-first century, and at the same time to reduce costs. It is improvement on both dimensions, performance and cost, that Moore's Law describes; and it is improvement on both dimensions that our students and our nation demand.

There's a lot to do, and survival is not guaranteed to anyone. Change is coming to higher education whether it comes through the doors of the ivory tower, steamrolls it, or bypasses it altogether. Those who make it through this time around will be those who recognize that the means and tools at our disposal have changed—while the mission has not.

2

Incentives, Information, and the Public Interest

Higher Education Governance as a Barrier to Cost Containment

Robert E. Martin

The network of incentives driving higher education's economic performance is not properly aligned with public interest.[1] This conclusion follows from two discouraging trends in higher education. First, college affordability has declined among an increasingly large share of middle class households.[2] Second, a growing body of evidence suggests that the quality of undergraduate education is also declining.[3] The public might tolerate rising cost accompanied by rising quality, but rising cost and declining quality is a dangerous trend that cannot be continued. But the news is not all bad: higher education responds to economic incentives. Get the incentives right, and economic performance improves.

The objective of this chapter is to identify the incentive network within and around higher education; this network drives cost higher and leads to lower quality. Understanding the incentives reveals opportunities for reform. But reform will demand more than simply "getting some of the incentives right." Indeed, the governance problem is analogous to the legendary Gordian knot: attempts to unravel the knot are defeated since pulling one strand merely tightens the knot elsewhere. By this property, the famous knot defeated all its challengers' attempts until Alexander the Great famously cleaved it in two with his sword. Now, I am not suggesting that Alexander's brute-force solution is appropriate in this case, since there are many things that are right with America's higher education system. Rather, the wisdom offered by Alexander's solution resides in attacking the problem as a whole, not wasting time pulling individual strings that are quickly offset by incentives that pull in the opposite direction. In practice, this means reform must reveal the current network's core architecture and then realign the complete incentive structure so it is more in line with the public interest.

In the end, the higher education financial problem is not too little money. Indeed, a good case can be made that *too much* money relieves institutions of the need to use resources efficiently (fundraising in higher education is like giving addicts more of the same substance they abuse). The governance structure itself is the problem, functioning as a barrier to cost containment.

WHY ARE COSTS HIGH . . . AND GETTING HIGHER?

The higher education cost literature contains four theories that seek to explain rising cost: (1) government regulation, (2) bundling services previously not supplied with higher education, (3) Baumol's cost disease, and (4) Bowen's rule.[4] Together, the four theories are a complementary network, with each one identifying factors that contribute to rising cost. These theories are the pillars on which the adverse incentive structure rests. After touching briefly on the first two theories, I'll focus my attention here on Baumol's cost disease and Bowen's rule.

Government Regulation

Government imposes unfunded mandates on higher education that can have adverse consequences on cost and sometimes on quality. Title IX, which banned gender discrimination in athletic programs, is a federal mandate that increased cost. Regulations regarding learning or physical disabilities force similar cost increases. But these costs are often accompanied by social benefits. In other words, government mandates are not necessarily all dead weight loss. Sometimes regulation can solve an economic coordination problem, where individual institutions have little incentive to adopt a new policy even if widespread adoption would provide considerable social benefit. Well-designed government regulation can help to solve such coordination problems, while at the same time increasing costs for an institution.

Bundling Services

Colleges and universities provide a variety of services to both students and the public beyond simple classroom instruction. They provide housing, food service, entertainment, travel, health services, and insurance. Beyond this, there is an increasing array of special-purpose institutes and off-campus community outreach programs. These services are bundled into a single package and presented to students as the "college experience." When observers invoke extravagant campus facilities to explain rising college costs, they identify a broader concept from economic theory: the efficiency of bundled services.

In addition to increasing the price of two goods, elite colleges and universities practice price discrimination by tying other services to the primary service, exclusive education. In order to have access to the exclusive good, consumers will pay more for both the bundled good and the exclusive good than they would be willing to pay for the two goods sold separately. For example, an exclusive institution builds luxurious new residence halls and elaborate new dining facilities and then requires all students attending the institution to live on campus and eat at the new dining hall. This eliminates local competition for both housing and food service. The rationale given is that living and eating on campus is an essential part of the college experience. Notice that this policy reduces students' ability to control the cost of their education, as they are not allowed to choose which part of the "experience" they want or can afford.

Baumol's Cost Disease

The two most significant cost theories are Baumol's cost disease and Bowen's rule. Baumol argues that service industries are subject to fixed-proportions production—that is, producing more requires increasing costs by a proportionally equal amount. This limits a service industry's ability to substitute capital for labor in production because it will not effectively lower costs. A common example is a string quartet, which will always require the same amount of labor (four players). Another example is the requirement that each classroom of thirty students have a teacher; an increase in the overall number of students enrolled in a school does not decrease labor costs because the number of teachers required is directly tied to the number of students enrolled. When labor costs rise, the institution cannot substitute cheaper capital for more expensive labor. The result? Costs tend to rise as productivity remains the same.

Many other industries, however, *do* experience rising productivity; this translates into an increase in real wages paid to productive workers, which forces wages up for workers economy-wide. This puts the service industries in a bind: they must pay higher real wages or risk losing good employees. For industries that experience increased productivity, this balances out, but in industries without increases in productivity, higher wages leads to higher costs. These two features exemplify Baumol's cost disease: static productivity coupled with a rise in real wages driven by the rest of the economy.

Under the Baumol hypothesis, productivity (student-to-staff ratios) should not change in higher education, and real wages in this domain should increase only when real wages increase in the rest of the economy.

However, productivity in higher education did not remain constant from 1987 to 2008. Indeed, based on student-to-staff ratios, productivity declined dramatically. Further, even though real median household income was stagnant for the past three decades, real wages in higher education rose steadily. This is counter to what we would expect to see with Baumol's cost disease, meaning the theory cannot explain all the increases we see in higher education costs.

Bowen's Rule

Bowen's rule theorizes that colleges and universities raise all the money they can and spend all the money they raise on projects that might conceivably improve quality. The economics behind Bowen's rule follow from the combined effects of nonprofit status, competition over experience goods, and unresolved agency problems.

Nonprofit status. The purpose of a nonprofit institution is to provide more services to people who are underserved by the for-profit sector. These institutions are given tax exempt status and asked to provide as much service as possible. As nonprofit organizations, they must follow a balanced budget financial model; hence, service output is capped by available revenue. When the revenue cap is lifted, service output and costs rise.[5] This sets in motion what Bowen calls the *revenue-to-cost spiral*.

Experience goods. An experience good is any good or service whose quality is unknown before it is purchased; consumers must "experience" the service before they can determine its quality. Thus, quality uncertainty is a common characteristic of experience good markets. This is problematic, because each producer has a financial incentive to provide a low-quality product at the high-quality price. Left unchecked, the low-quality products will drive the high-quality products out of the market (a secular decline in quality). This is a classic information-based market failure.

When confronted with issues like this, the market evolves solutions that may or may not always be successful; in this case, the evolved mechanism is reputation competition. When consumers are uncertain about quality, a new provider must establish a reputation for high quality by providing high quality at the low-quality price (exceed expectations). The losses incurred building a reputation are the provider's capital investment in a high-quality reputation. The reputation mechanism will be efficient if (1) consumers purchase the product frequently, (2) consumers can evaluate quality immediately after purchase, (3) consumers quickly abandon those who cheat, and (4) there are only two parties to the transaction. None of these conditions is satisfied in higher education. This is a classic information-based market failure, one that must be addressed by regulatory intervention.[6] Alternatively, when consumers have enough information to separate high-quality providers from low-quality providers, price accurately reflects quality.[7]

Two characteristics of experience goods complicate the higher education market. First, consumers associate higher cost with higher quality. Since customers cannot observe quality before the service is purchased, they use price as a proxy for quality. In higher education, this is known as the *Chivas Regal effect*, based on an expensive scotch whiskey that built its exclusive brand name on high prices.

The association of price with quality leads to a particularly perverse incentive: the more a college or university spends per student, the more consumers associate that institution with higher quality. Recall: Bowen's rule holds that colleges and universities raise all the money they can and spend all the money they raise on projects that seemingly enhance quality. The Chivas Regal effect, which encourages firms to raise prices as a signal of value added, is the perfect enabler of Bowen's rule. Indeed, under the Chivas Regal effect, any attempt by a single competitor to *lower cost* will be interpreted as an attempt to *lower quality*. Since institutions will not attempt to lower cost on their own, disentangling cost reduction from quality reduction requires intervention.

The second feature of experience goods markets is that costs are higher than they would be if consumers were certain about product quality. The more uncertain consumers are, the higher the cost premium. In higher education, students may not know the quality of their purchase until decades after graduation. Notice also that if higher education institutions bundle entertainment with education, they make it more difficult for students to separate the two benefits.

This uncertainty is exacerbated by the absence of vigorous competition between institutions based on documented value added. If undergraduate value added is the first priority among parents and taxpayers (those who pay for higher education), why do we not observe value-added competition? In efficient markets, consumers must purchase frequently and be able to quickly evaluate quality after purchase. When consumers quickly recognize the value added, the provider gets a quick return from quality improvement. In higher education, it takes generations of steadily producing high-quality graduates before the institution gets a reputation for high quality.

The planning horizon for real quality improvement in higher education spans the tenure of multiple presidents and board memberships. An individual president or board member receives little credit or recognition for being one in a series of presidents or boards that patiently sees a program into fruition. On the other hand, the individual president or board membership can invest heavily in fundraising, public relations activities, sports, or physical plants where their personal career benefits are immediate.

The nature of experience goods explains why, in higher education, reputations are important and why transparency is an issue. Unfortunately, it also explains why the elite institutions with high-quality reputations do not take the lead in higher education reform: they have nothing to gain from such an undertaking and considerable benefit to lose by the task—namely, their reputation. With all of higher education looking to the elite institutions for guidance and what may be termed "best practices," they have no incentive to be transparent. In failing to take advantage of their position, they do little to encourage transformative reform. These adverse effects are rooted in uncertainty about value added; make value added more transparent, and many problems will disappear.

Agency problems. The third component of Bowen's rule is unresolved agency problems. In economics, we call the pursuit of self-interest by insiders an "agency problem." The agent (manager, politician, doctor) is someone who is hired by a principal (stockholder, voter, patient) to make decisions for the principal. If the agent's interests are not properly aligned with the principal's interests, the agent may make decisions in her own interest and at the principal's expense.[8] Stockholders have an agency problem when they hire managers to run companies, voters have an agency problem when they "hire" politicians to represent them, and patients have an agency problem whenever they leave medical decisions to their doctors.

Agency problems exist everywhere and nonprofit institutions are no exception, as is frequently demonstrated by scandals at charities and religious organizations. In traditional for-profit industries, agency abuse always results in higher costs, and higher costs always reduce profits. In higher education, the manifestation of agency abuse is more complicated: productivity and performance metrics are poorly specified and often compromised by the nature of experience goods competition. The natural productivity metric would be cost per student, but experience good competition flips that metric upside down. Similar to for-profit industries, agency abuse in higher education increases costs, but consumers associate higher cost with higher quality. There is no mechanism to encourage higher education providers to maintain lower costs. Reputations dominate in experience goods competition, and efficient resource allocation leads to controversy. Controversies damage reputations, which incentivizes governing boards to studiously avoid controversies. Governing boards know that controlling costs will be controversial.

There are three common mechanisms used to control agency abuse: natural constraints, third parties with a personal interest in monitoring agents, and government regulation.

First, the presence of natural/institutional constraints on agency abuse can limit agency abuse. For example, the well-organized market for corporate control constrains agency abuse in corporations. Similarly, elections constrain agency abuse among politicians. There are no comparable constraints on agency abuse in higher education; control of higher education institutions is not contestable in any meaningful sense, and governing boards are not subject to general election.

Second, among publicly held for-profit firms, private investors, money managers, banks, security analysts, and private equity firms have a financial incentive to monitor each firm. Opposition political parties have a strong incentive to monitor the behavior of politicians. But third parties have little incentive to monitor higher education institutions. The news media has a well-developed taste for agency stories in business and politics, but little interest in higher education agency stories.

Third, government regulation also limits agency abuse, particularly in for-profit business ventures. Numerous agencies are tasked with for-profit oversight responsibilities: examples include the Securities and Exchange Commission (SEC), the Federal Trade Commission (FTC), the Occupational Safety and Health Administration (OSHA), the Environmental Protection Agency (EPA), the Food and Drug Administration (FDA), the Internal Revenue Service (IRS), and the Federal Reserve System. Only the Department of Education—and to a lesser extent the IRS—has oversight responsibilities in higher education. The difference between the full disclosure requirements imposed on for-profit firms by government agencies and the absence of disclosure requirements on colleges and universities when they sell students an increasingly expensive education is a stark contrast indeed.

Under ideal conditions, higher education's "shared governance" tradition could be a natural constraint on agency abuse. Under this ideal model, faculty, administrators, and board members would monitor the other groups' behavior. Unfortunately, administrators have undone the model by simultaneously convincing boards that faculty will not tolerate intrusion into academic policy, and faculty that boards will not tolerate faculty meddling in their jurisdiction. As it stands now, shared governance is fragmented governance. Further, board members view direct communication with faculty as a breach of the "chain of command," effectively shutting off any possibility of joint faculty/board monitoring of administrator agency abuse. This gives administrators a free hand.

Similarly, the accreditation process was initially created as an institutional constraint on agency abuse, where institutions would keep tabs on one another. The relationship between accreditors and institutions should be at arm's length. But, in reality, the members of each accreditation team come from other institutions, and they know that they will also be subject to accreditation review. The accreditation team considers their own interests as aligned with the interests of those they are expected to regulate, making them "captured regulators" instead of accreditors. This is a structure that seems purpose-driven not to be effective.

Internal and External Cost Drivers: Which Group Is the Culprit?

Of the four cost theories, two arise from outside higher education and two come from decisions made by education insiders. Government mandates and Baumol's cost disease reflect forces outside higher education that cause costs to rise inside higher education. A moment's reflection reveals why this must be true: higher education is embedded in the macro-economy, and it would be impossible for that macro-economy not to have an impact on cost.

Alternatively, Bowen's rule and bundling activities come from decisions made by higher education insiders. Since the external cost theories tend to absolve higher education of responsibility for rising costs, there is a tendency for higher education to insist that these external cost theories are the real culprits in this story. Since all four theories have sound economic foundations, the issue is in fact an empirical question. What proportion of the total change in costs per student over a defined interval can be attributed to external versus internal effects? My own work on this question suggests Bowen effects are larger than Baumol effects: for every dollar in cost attributable to Baumol effects, over two dollars can be attributed to Bowen effects.[9]

TWO INFORMATION PROBLEMS

The aforementioned cost theories reveal two generic information problems in higher education: uncertainty about value added and insufficient information to control agency abuse. Cost can be lowered and quality improved with more information about value added and by devising more precise performance metrics to control agency abuse. From the nature of experience goods markets, we know that institutions have no incentive to provide this information and every incentive to oppose the resolution of these information problems. Hence, they complain continuously about releasing information that may improve transparency: rankings reports, measures of teaching productivity, or attempts to make operations more transparent.

But addressing these information problems would go a long ways toward greater cost containment.

The Value-Added Information Problem

The consequences of this particular market failure are enormous. Since they do not gain higher income or recognition from exceptional teaching, professors spend too much effort on research. When this happens, value added unravels. "Mission creep" constantly leads to the duplication of graduate programs, few of which emphasize teacher training rather than research. This in turn adversely affects the self-selection process into academia. The inevitable result is a wasteful explosion of dubious research output with little attention to high-quality teaching.[10]

It is worth noting how contrary this is to what those who pay for higher education would prefer. If asked, representative parents and taxpayers would say they want higher education's first priority to be maximizing value added. Increased research output might not find its way into their top five priorities. If they fully understood the explosion of published research in areas that reflect faculty consumption activities rather than social investments in knowledge, they would be appalled by the waste.[11] If you want teachers to maximize value added, you must give them a clear career track that leads to recognition and reward of quality teaching.

Finding metrics to measure the human-capital value added by both individual teachers and institutions is the key that unlocks the governance problem. A single metric will not do; it has to be a system of metrics.[12] Further, it will take experimentation to get it right. Experimentation will have to be imposed on higher education institutions since they have no incentive to undertake the effort on their own. This is an area where technology could be very useful.

The National Survey of Student Engagement (NSSE) would be a good place to start. Through comprehensive student surveys at individual institutions, NSSE quantifies critical education outcomes like student study time per week, the number of writing assignments in each course, availability of faculty outside of class, whether faculty maintain their office hours, and opportunities to work as teams. Today, cooperation with NSSE is voluntary, and those who cooperate with NSSE hold most of the information close and release only that which places them in a favorable light. Notably, it is the elite institutions and the institutions in the lowest-quality tier that refuse to allow NSSE on their campuses. The reason is obvious: neither group has anything to gain from this information. In order to mitigate the information deficit, participation in NSSE should be mandatory for every institution and all the information should be released.

Agency Abuse and Information

The second major information deficit relates to economic performance. The primary deficit here is a financial metric that plays the same role as does profit in identifying agency abuse in publicly held corporations. Economic theory reveals that college affordability declines when the change in the net price of attendance exceeds the change in household income.[13] College affordability improves when the change in net price of attendance is less than the change in household income. If institutions are rewarded on the basis of this metric—or other financial performance metrics directly linked to the public interest—they have an incentive to control cost.

Since simple economic theory is not enough to ensure college affordability, financial reporting reforms are necessary. As it currently stands, falsely reporting financial results to either the National Center for Education Statistics (NCES) or the IRS results in few adverse consequences. We know from numerous scandals regarding data reported to college rankings that institutions are not above gaming the system.[14] Consider the consequences visited upon a publicly held corporation if it falsely reports its financial results in order to game financial markets.

Finally, detailed staffing data is indispensable in any effort to keep financial reporting honest among nonprofit institutions. Accounting definitions can be manipulated, and expenditures made in one category can be charged to another category, but it is much harder to mislead if the monitor has detailed staffing counts by function along with the history of salaries paid in each function. As it stands now, we have detailed data on faculty staffing and salaries, but there is very little data on administrator staffing and salaries. This asymmetric treatment played a significant role in the bloating of overhead between 1987 and 2008.[15]

ANOMALOUS CONSEQUENCES OF THE EXISTING INCENTIVE STRUCTURE

The current incentive structure leads to a series of unexpected consequences, consequences that are contrary to what conventional wisdom implies and which have a negative effect on cost containment. I explore these cautionary implications in the following subsections.

The Adverse Incentive Effect in Student Subsidies

The purpose of need-based financial aid is to increase access to higher education. Theoretically, if the government lowers the net price of attendance to low-income students through a direct subsidy, more students will attend college and access will improve. The critical assumption here is that the price of attendance is independent of the subsidy, and therefore colleges won't adjust their tuition prices in response to subsidy increases.[16] One might reasonably assume this if the subsidized good was a commodity such as soybeans or oil, both of which operate in a global market with pricing set by more traditional supply-and-demand forces. However, the assumption is unlikely to be valid if the providers have pricing power—the ability to set prices rather than have the price set for them by competition in the marketplace. A provider with pricing power knows the subsidized consumer has increased ability to pay and can adjust his price to capture all or part of that increased ability to pay. If the provider captures all of the increased ability to pay, the purpose of the subsidy is defeated. In the case of higher education, the university knows a student with a subsidy can pay more than before, so the university raises tuition; college access among low-income households will likely not improve.

This issue is known as the *Bennett hypothesis*. William Bennett, the former U.S. secretary of education, argued this point in a *New York Times* article entitled "Our Greedy Colleges."[17] Attempts to test the hypothesis led to mixed results: some found little or no evidence, while others found evidence to support the hypothesis.[18] In each case, researchers looked for evidence that a subsidy increase in one year leads to an increase in price in the following year. If you adopt a longer time perspective, the results are clear: between 1987 and 2008, all of the real increases in student subsidies were recaptured by higher tuition/fees and room/board charges net of subsidies.[19]

Need-based aid and merit-based aid increased during this period, and as attendance prices increased more need-based aid was concentrated in the hands of lower-income households. During the same period, the competition for the best students intensified, resulting in increasing merit-based aid flowing to exceptional students. In addition, many states adopted new merit-based aid programs that were not means-tested. Since student achievement is strongly correlated with household income, merit-based aid became more regressive as average household income increased over time. As a consequence, student financial aid tended to be concentrated in the lowest-income quintile and the higher-income quintiles, leaving middle-income families—who have stagnated real incomes—to deal with rising attendance prices. This has serious consequences for economic mobility since households have to pass through middle-income status on their way to higher incomes.

Under the current incentive system, increasing subsidies in the form of either direct subsidies or increased access to debt financing lifts the cap on revenues available to higher education, and by Bowen's rule this means costs will rise as the cap is lifted. The dramatic increase in student debt is the natural consequence, as is the frustration of government policy.[20]

Public/Private Institutions and Cost Control

Some may expect private institutions to have better cost control and be more attentive to their clientele than comparably situated public institutions. But while my experience leads me to conclude that the expectation is true, my studies reveal that in fact public institutions do a better job of controlling costs than do private institutions.

Consider Carnegie I and II private and public research universities. These are the elite research universities that educate almost 4 million students each year. The academic cost per student, the overhead cost per student, and the total cost per student are over twice as high at private research universities as they are at public research universities. Further, between 1987 and 2008, real total cost per student increased by $32,061 at private universities and $13,806 at public universities. Note that in each case we are talking about cost per student, not the price of attendance.[21]

The primary reason for the cost differences is that public institutions are subject to better arm's-length cost monitoring than are private institutions. First, substantial parts of the public institutions' budgets are in direct competition with other demands on state resources, such as prisons, Medicaid, and pensions. The budgets for private institutions do not compete directly with other uses except through household budgets, and many of the private universities have substantial endowments. Second, there is more direct financial oversight from state governments than from private boards. On balance, the monitoring of agency behavior is greater at public than at private institutions.

The differences in total cost per student and the differences in the increases in those costs suggest that all government effects in higher education are not adverse effects, as one might argue based on the government mandates cost theory. There are important roles for government to play in higher education, although the government's current efforts are organized around providing subsidies, promoting college attendance, and advocating for higher education. In contrast with what the SEC, FTC, Justice Department, and the FDA do to insure corporate economic performance, the government does very little to promote improved higher education economic performance.

Bureaucratic Entropy and Staffing Patterns

The term *bureaucratic entropy* was first applied to the tendency of municipal employment to grow faster than the city's population.[22] In this example, the

cost of city services per citizen increases, even if real public service wages/
benefits remain constant. If public service wages/benefits also increase, the
increase in cost per citizen rises even faster. The anomalous part of bureaucratic entropy is that the ratio of employees to population ought to go down
as the population grows (what economists call *increasing returns to scale*).
Further, in the long term the real cost per citizen should decline as technology improves (new technologies will be implemented only if they lower cost
or improve quality).

Bureaucratic entropy is resisted in for-profit firms since the most senior
governing groups (management and the board) have a strong personal
stake in minimizing costs (profits cannot be maximized unless costs are
minimized). The personal stake in cost minimization does not exist in government or the world of nonprofits; those who manage costs have no incentive to minimize costs. Bureaucratic entropy, then, is an agency problem.

Not surprisingly, real wages/benefits per staff member in higher education increased steadily from 1987 to 2008; indeed, they rose faster than
median household incomes. The data reveals that staffing/student ratios
increased in each staff category except one, and they increased significantly
and consistently in some categories. In other words, higher education labor
productivity *declined* from 1987 to 2008, as both cost per staffer and the
total number of staffers increased. This is definitely not the picture painted
by Baumol's cost disease, but it is what one would expect from bureaucratic
entropy and Bowen's rule.

Table 2.1 contains changes in constant dollar total cost per student and
staffing ratios for private liberal arts colleges, public master's program universities, private research universities, and public research universities from
1987 to 2008. Changes in total cost per student at private institutions are
more than twice the change in cost per student at comparable public institutions, which spend less per student and keep their cost increases lower
than do private institutions. The proportion of the total change in cost
accounted for by changes in overhead varies from a low of 47 percent at private universities to a high of 68 percent at public master's program universities. The private research universities more than doubled the size of their
graduate programs during this period, which is the reason overhead costs
were less than 50 percent of the total cost increase at those universities.

The changes in staffing patterns are most revealing. All staffing ratios
were calculated as the number of staff members per one hundred full-
time equivalent (FTE) students. From 1987 to 2008, each type of institution experienced an increase in enrollment between 20 and 30 percent. If
the colleges and universities had maintained the same level of productivity they achieved in 1987, the percent changes in staffing ratios reported in

TABLE 2.1   **Changes in higher education cost and staffing, 1987–2008**

	Private colleges	Public master's[b]	Private universities[c]	Public universities[c]
Total cost[a]	$9,267	$3,456	$32,061	$13,806
Overhead share %	57.0	67.9	47.1	62.0
Academic % change				
FTE faculty	8.5	–3.0	34.8	16.5
Tenure track	3.7	–18.0	32.4	3.2
Contract faculty	58.2	94.3	24.9	38.4
Part-time faculty	–12.8		84.2	61.2
Overhead % change				
FTE executive	26.8	–6.3	52.0	10.3
FTE professional	85.5	59.4	57.2	58.1
FTE nonprofessional	–21.9	–26.4	–22.8	–28.0
Ratio of tenure track/admin % change	–42.8	–45.8	–26.7	–30.2
Number of institutions	227	269	60	146

Source: IPEDS Web site, custom tables, by group, for 1987, 2008, and various intervening years
[a] Constant 2008 dollars
[b] Carnegie master's program universities
[c] Carnegie I and II research universities

table 2.1 would all be zero, implying that staff growth was equivalent to student enrollment growth. If they improved productivity, all the changes would be negative. With the exception of nonprofessional employees, most of the staffing ratios increased. The most consistent increase is in nonacademic professional employees, which increased anywhere from 57 percent to 86 percent at the four types of institutions. Except for public master's program universities, the executive staffing ratio increased between 10 and

52 percent. As a whole, each type of institution dramatically increased the number of administrators per student.

The changes in academic staffing patterns are also revealing. The increases in contract teaching faculty ratios varied from 25 to 94 percent; each type of institution expanded its use of full-time, non-tenure-track faculty over this period. The research universities made a similar commitment to part-time teachers. The largest increase in the tenure-track faculty staffing ratio was at private research universities and most probably represents the more than doubling in the size of their graduate programs. The other institutions made modest increases in their tenure-track faculty staffing ratios. The public master's program universities significantly reduced their tenure-track faculty staffing ratios.

In general, all sectors economized on the use of tenure-track faculty by using contract and part-time faculty more intensively. Further, they raised the productivity of nonprofessional staff by reducing those staffing ratios. The nonprofessional staff category includes clerical/secretarial, skilled crafts, technical staff, and service/maintenance staff. The decline was uniform and persistent over all four nonprofessional categories. Administrators and governing boards made conscious decisions to improve productivity in the nonprofessional staff categories from 1987 to 2008 at the same time they were lowering productivity in administrator overhead.

Unlike the high labor costs of instruction, administrative functions needn't increase proportionally to enrollment; instead, they benefit from increasing returns to scale. Other things equal, the administrative staffing ratios should have declined as enrollment increased by over 20 percent. Even so, a puzzling revolution in overhead cost reduction among for-profit firms occurred during the period from 1987 to 2008.[23] While the rest of the economy was shrinking overhead, higher education was investing heavily in more overhead. This seems inconsistent with growing public concern about value added. The staffing results are consistent with Bowen's rule but not consistent with Baumol's cost disease, further explaining why Bowen's rule is more important than Baumol's cost disease as an explanation for the rise of higher education costs.

The Center Mass of the Agency Problem

Any agent who has control over expenditures is a potential source of trouble. The center mass of the problem must reside in the hands of those with the most control over resources. One would not expect to find a serious agency problem among nonprofessional staff members, simply because they have little control over expenditures. Contract faculty and part-time faculty are employed at will, and the conditions under which part-time faculty struggle reveal that they have little influence over campus policies.[24] So, that leaves three groups of agents: tenure-track faculty, administrators, and governing boards.

The tenure-track staffing data in table 2.1 reveals that only one type of institution—the public master's program universities—actually used contract faculty and/or part-time faculty to replace tenure-track faculty when they added faculty in response to enrollment growth; all the rest increased their tenure-track staffing ratios, although mostly by modest amounts. This reveals that tenure-track faculties have some influence on resource decisions. However, the modest changes in tenure-track staffing relative to administrator staffing strongly suggests that the faculty's priorities are not decisive.

Consider the ratio of tenure-track faculty members to administration members (executives plus professional staff). In 1987, the ratio was greater than or equal to 1 for private colleges, public master's program universities, and public research universities. At private research universities in 1987, the ratio was well below 1, and administrators already outnumbered tenure-track faculty by a considerable margin. By 2008, all of the tenure track/administrator ratios were less than 1.[25] At both public and private research universities in 2008, the ratio of administrators to tenure-track faculty was over 2 to 1. The political weight of tenure-track faculty priorities declined during the period of accelerating costs.

Legal control of expenditures resides in the hands of administrators and governing boards.[26] They hire/fire employees and set contract terms. Therefore, changing higher education governance in order to improve economic performance should start where the problem resides: among administrators and governing boards. Why did governing boards allow an explosion in overhead at the same time many board members energetically reduced overhead in their own businesses?

I do not minimize the agency problems created by tenure-track faculty members. Those problems are real, and they cause costs to rise and quality to decline. The mutual nonaggression pact between students and faculty over grades and teaching evaluations is an example of serious agency problems. Grade inflation has a particularly corrosive effect on value added, since low grading standards drive out high standards. Other faculty agency problems are idiosyncratic abuse of the core curriculum, the campus calendar, teaching loads, and class sizes. Administrations and boards have the legal authority and fiduciary responsibility to resist these trends, but they do not because resistance is an admission that the institution has a problem. Any institution that admits problems damages its reputation relative to all the other institutions that refuse to recognize their own problems. This is the heart of reputation competition in experience good markets—one cannot admit there are problems.

SUGGESTED SOLUTIONS

At the heart of the college cost/quality problem are two information failures: teaching value added, and the information/institutions required to control agency abuse. The value-added problem can be resolved by a metric system sufficient to establish a market for senior or master teachers. The system should be modeled on the productivity metrics that make the market for senior scholars possible. The solution to the agency problem is disclosure requirements similar to those imposed on for-profit firms. Further, the disclosure standards will need to have teeth.

The first priority should be improving the monitoring of value added by institution and by instructor. Measuring value added by institution is a simpler task. I would start by requiring every institution (private and public) to participate and reveal the results from the annual NSSE survey. The second step requires introducing third-party (i.e., other than the institutions or the teacher) metrics to evaluate individual teacher value added. The *Princeton Review*'s 300 Best Professors is an interesting start. Web-based teaching competitions by subject area are a promising prospect, as are peer-reviewed class offerings. Digital technology makes all of this more cost-effective. The metrics should be patterned after those used to evaluate scholars and should be constructed with what is needed to establish a market for master university teachers in mind.

A required parallel development is a system of economic performance metrics: truth in financial disclosure, detailed staffing and salary/benefits disclosure, historical data on total cost and net price of attendance with respect to household incomes, and the adoption of incentive contracting that is consistent with the public interest.

Finally, the agency problem will not be resolved until a new campus charter is in place. That charter must place more emphasis on cost control, less emphasis on raising money, make board members more responsible for controlling cost, make board compositions more contestable, set professional standards for all staff, and clearly define faculty, administrator, and board roles in governance. This new governance charter must make it easier to dismiss any employee who is underperforming and make the reallocation of existing resources a seamless process. Until this happens, any reforms are likely just pulling the strands of the Gordian knot, unlikely to make any real progress.

3

Applying Cost-Effectiveness
Analysis to Higher Education

A Framework for Improving Productivity

Douglas N. Harris

Higher education productivity, as measured by academic degrees granted by American colleges and universities, is declining.[1] Since the early 1990s, real expenditures on higher education have grown by more than 25 percent, now amounting to 2.9 percent of the gross domestic product—greater than the percentage of GDP spent on higher education in almost any of the other developed countries.[2] But while the proportion of high school graduates going on to college has risen dramatically, the percent of entering college students *finishing* a bachelor's degree has at best increased only slightly, or at worst has declined.[3]

Figure 3.1 shows the trend in productivity from 1970 to 2006 expressed in terms of the ratio of degrees granted to total sector expenditures.[4] The downward slope is steepest among universities, where current productivity is less than half what it was forty years ago. Even when adjusted for the growth in overall labor costs in the economy (see figure 3.1's dashed lines), the decline in bachelor's degree production is nearly 20 percent. If these declines continue, maintaining the current rate of bachelor's degree production will cost an additional $42 billion per year forty years from now.[5] This means that even if state support for public higher education did not continue to decline, tuition would have to increase by an average of $6,885 per full-time equivalent (FTE) student in public universities in order to maintain current degree production, almost doubling today's tuition.[6]

FIGURE 3.1   **The productivity decline, 1970–2006**

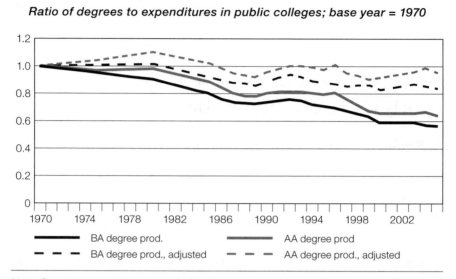

Ratio of degrees to expenditures in public colleges; base year = 1970

	BA degree prod.		AA degree prod
	BA degree prod., adjusted		AA degree prod., adjusted

Note: Calculations are based on the National Center for Education Statistics (NCES) Digest of Education Statistics. Expenditure data was not available beyond 2001; therefore, revenue data was used in its place. Expenditure data is in real (inflation-adjusted) 2006 dollars. Data is available only every five years during the 1970s; the intervening years are interpolated. Data on private colleges is available only sporadically and therefore excluded.

What accounts for declining higher education productivity? Prior research provides an array of potential explanations.[7] Most analysts point to the role of rising costs, while others focus on declining degree attainment.[8] Collectively, these explanations reinforce a widespread perception among both higher education administrators and many scholars that productivity is impossible to control. According to economists Robert B. Archibald and David H. Feldman, "The problem in higher education is that productivity growth often is synonymous with lower quality. Adding more students to each class can diminish the benefit for each student, leading to diminished outcomes and lower graduation rates. Increasing the number of courses a professor teaches would reduce research or community service."[9] Similarly, in a study of college presidents' attitudes, a two-year president said, "I don't think there are any more efficiencies left to be squeezed out of public universities across the nation . . . There are no more efficiencies to be had."[10] So, at least some institutional leaders feel helpless when it comes to improving productivity without sacrificing quality.[11] Even when costs are considered, institutions tend to focus on enrolling more students rather than helping them graduate.[12]

In this chapter, I show that policy makers and college leaders do in fact have some control over productivity, but that they generally lack the information necessary to take the appropriate steps toward improvement. Specifically, decision makers have little information about which programs, policies, and resource decisions are most cost-effective. Relative to other areas of public policy, cost-effectiveness analysis is rarely applied to specific education policies and programs.[13] Even research that looks at the higher education system as a whole rarely considers the relationship between the costs and output (i.e., productivity).[14]

A basic principle of decision making is that we have to compare the costs and benefits of all feasible options, but this rarely happens in analyses of higher education. Even those few studies that do consider cost-effectiveness do not attempt to compare across programs. This is hard to justify since there is little question that—as the later analysis shows—some programs are much more cost-effective than others. In addition, cost-effectiveness analyses often ignore the practical constraints of decision makers, such as the availability of state or federal matching grants and pressures to boost college rankings. This chapter tries to avoid that problem by addressing the distinctive features of higher education and laying out key questions policy makers need to ask themselves when interpreting the results of cost-effectiveness analyses.

After outlining a method for applying cost-effectiveness analysis to higher education, I apply the approach to a range of well-known programs, ranging from financial aid to student services and alternative modes of instruction. While the estimates that come out of this analysis may be useful by themselves, the main aim of the chapter is to highlight a different way of thinking about the decisions policy makers and college leaders face and provide a concrete way forward that can help to reverse declining productivity. Cost-effectiveness analysis cannot and should not replace the judgment of educational leaders, but the information that comes from it can provide useful guidance and perhaps improve the way those decisions are made.

BASIC ELEMENTS OF COST-EFFECTIVENESS ANALYSIS FOR HIGHER EDUCATION

Cost-effectiveness analysis may sound like a complicated academic concept, but the truth is that we use this type of thinking in our daily lives. When buying a car, many people look at ratings in *Consumer Reports*, for example, to find information about the "best values." This is just another way of saying the cars are good, given what you have to pay—that is, they are cost-effective and have a large "bang for the buck." This is not to say that the approach is simple. Not everyone would agree on which cars represent the best value because different people prefer different types of cars and have different driving needs. But it is a useful way to think about and make choices. Given how common this mode of thinking is, it is striking that cost-effectiveness analysis is often absent in higher education. As leaders face increasing pressure to maintain or improve student outcomes in times of tight budgets, they are likely to find this kind of analysis not only useful, but necessary.

Calculating and Standardizing Effectiveness-Cost and Benefit-Cost Ratios

The primary metric for understanding the relationship between program costs and their effects is the *effectiveness-cost ratio* (ECR). The first component of the ratio is the *cost* of a given policy or program, measured by the "market price" of the various components, such as the salary and benefits of staff involved in the program and the cost of maintaining or expanding facilities necessary to implement it.[15]

Unfortunately, data on higher education costs is notoriously incomplete, and remarkably few studies of particular higher education interventions report the resources or "ingredients" involved, or the prices that have to be paid for them. For this reason, in my analysis of well-known college programs, I often had to estimate them myself by making informed assumptions. For example, most publicly available descriptions of programs provide a general sense of the number and type of staff involved in programs. To estimate total costs in the following analysis, I start with this information and then use nationally representative data on the salaries of workers in similar occupations and professions. Going forward, policy makers and institutional leaders should insist on and collect granular measurements of cost to assess cost-effectiveness.

Decision makers also need to know whether the programs they are spending money on are *effective*. But effective in what sense? Policy and research have traditionally focused on providing access to higher education, though the new "completion agenda" has drawn attention to measures of student success: retention, credit accumulation, and degree completion. I focus my analysis on degree completion because this outcome aligns with goals of students, policy makers, and, increasingly, of institutional leaders. It is important to recognize, however, that focusing on a single outcome like degrees may reinforce a trend toward narrowing the functions of education only to those that we measure. The practical implication is that, in using this evidence to make policy decisions, we must account for potential trade-offs among multiple outcomes—degree completion, degree quality, and so on—in a more qualitative manner, with more rigorous evidence for some outcomes than others.

A second issue is that it can be very difficult to know whether a given program really generates effects. Higher education research often relies on simple correlations (e.g., students enrolled in this program were more likely to graduate than the average or apparently similar students). But correlation is not causation. For example, does anyone really think that Harvard has a high graduation rate because its programs cause students to do better? Of course not. Those students graduate because they had exceptional abilities, motivation, and so on, before they got to Harvard. Conversely, colleges and programs should not be punished because they serve students who are less likely to graduate—if anything, they should be rewarded and praised for it. For this reason, educational leaders should try to identify studies that use more rigorous methods, such as randomized trials and "natural experiments" where outcomes are compared before and after some program or policy started. (College leaders can even conduct some of this research themselves using their own faculties and well-trained institutional researchers—more on this later.)

Once we have credible estimates of costs and effects, we can combine them to calculate the effectiveness-cost ratio, or "bang" divided by "buck." A standard metric in economic analysis, larger ECRs generally imply greater productivity.[16] With an outcome such as graduation rate, it is intuitive to standardize program costs for an entering cohort of one hundred students. This means that the costs also have to be calculated for the whole group. For example, consider a program that costs $500 per student, or $50,000 for a group of one hundred students. If the same program increases the graduate rate by one person (per one hundred), then the ECR is 1/50=0.02. (The denominator of 50 represents the $50,000 in costs expressed in thousands of dollars so as to avoid extremely small numbers like 0.00002.)

A key strength of ECRs is that they express outcomes in easily digestible terms. Degrees and costs are ideas that educational leaders can easily grasp.[17] When calculated in comparable ways, ECRs can also be used to make comparisons across programs, so we can say whether one program is more cost-effective than another. With a fixed pot of money, this is a helpful way to allocate resources in ways that generate the best results for students.

Economists often take this type of analysis a step further by calculating the monetary value of effects. In higher education, the most prominent example is the earnings of graduates. The economic return to a degree, measured by increased earnings, is approximately $387,000 for a four-year degree ($282,000 for a two-year degree), excluding other social benefits.[18] This means that, so long as these benefit estimates exceed the discounted costs of producing a degree, then the program passes a cost-benefit test and is said to be "profitable" from a societal standpoint. The advantage of this approach is that it not only allows comparisons among programs but also more absolute judgments—whether there is a positive pay-off. This is especially important when policy makers are considering adding resources to the system. The disadvantage is that the narrow focus on degrees is compounded by the additional focus on earnings. Understandably, educators are often leery of trying to place a dollar value on learning. For this reason, and to focus attention on the potential power of cost-effectiveness, I focus only on ECRs. A more extensive and technical version of this analysis, which includes the cost-benefit approach, is also available.[19]

Placing ECRs on a Level Playing Field

The goal is to create effectiveness-cost ratios that can be reasonably compared across programs. A key challenge is that, even among those relatively few studies using rigorous methods, different studies focus on different outcomes, requiring some type of conversion to a common metric. In higher education research, it is common to report effects on college entry and persistence only, rather than the primary outcome of interest here—graduation. To place the estimates on a level playing field, I have to translate estimates of persistence effects into graduation effects using data and other research on the relationship between entry, persistence, and graduation. Since entry and persistence are prerequisites to graduation, a plausible range of estimates can be made this way.[20]

The same goes for costs. Some programs last only one year, while others go for many years. Some of the longer-term programs have high attrition, so that fewer students are served in later years and this affects the cost per student. Therefore, while I start by reporting costs in annual terms, the final calculations account for the number of years the average student participates in the program.

There are obviously a lot of steps involved in this, with many assumptions made along the way. I have to make some educated guesses about costs using public information and general market prices. I have to translate effects on entry and persistence into graduation, and in some cases estimate how long the average student stays in a program. To provide some sense of the potential ranges for the ratios, I therefore report lower and upper bounds that account for some of the uncertainty.

But the fact that these bounds are necessary presents another argument for college leaders to engage in their own rigorous experimentation. They have the data to track *their own* student outcomes, including degrees. They could also collect detailed cost data with a little more effort. And they could carry out their own experiments and pilot studies to determine what seems most cost-effective in their own institutions with their specific students and their possibly distinctive needs. These more local efforts can complement the more expensive and rigorous studies funded by the federal government, which are becoming somewhat more common but remain rare. There is no reason for college leaders to wait for a miracle "cure" to arise from some national study when they have needs and resources of their own to work with.

Comparing ECRs: Challenges and Practical Questions

Even if there were no uncertainty in these calculations, policy makers would still have to be cautious about blindly adopting the programs with the largest ECRs. Specifically, higher education decision makers should ask themselves the following questions:

- What outcomes did the study measure and therefore how confident are we that the results translate to increased graduation?
- How might the program affect quality?
- Are we likely to see the same results if we implement the program in this state or institution?

The answers to these questions establish the degree to which a given cost-effectiveness analysis is even relevant for a given decision. For example, a study that suggests large effects on the number of graduates is not very helpful if there is also evidence of substantial reductions in academic rigor. This might be a problem, for example, with a program that allows students to finish degrees more quickly. Or a study might examine effects on GPA, but it is unclear how GPA translates to the outcome you are really interested in, such as graduation.

Even if the answers to these basic questions suggest that a study is relevant to a given decision, there are other questions about the local context that have to be considered. The answers to the following questions will affect the likelihood that the outcomes of the study will translate to a particular college or state:

- Given the various funding streams and political constraints, what are my truly viable options?

- Are certain elements of these alternatives likely to be especially costly in my situation? For example, programs that require physical infrastructure might be more costly in urban campuses.
- Are there secondary effects of the programs that are not reflected in the calculations? State policy makers might worry, for instance, that financial aid generates both budgetary costs and induces colleges to raise tuition further. Conversely, many think of financial aid as part of a larger social contract, making cost-effectiveness a smaller consideration.
- Also, might it be possible to obtain third-party funding for some of the alternatives but not others? Institutions may sometimes be able to find matching funds to reduce costs below what the cost-effectiveness analysis assumes. Likewise, state governments can seek funds from the federal government. More generally, while cost-effectiveness analysis treats all dollars the same, all dollars are not created equally among policy makers.

Finally, some leaders I have spoken with about the cost-effectiveness approach wonder about the usefulness of comparing different types of programs. Specifically, there are three different types of comparisons: (1) comparisons across strategies (e.g., instructional improvement versus financial aid), (2) comparisons across programs within strategies (e.g., improving instruction through smaller classes versus instructional technology), and (3) comparisons within strategies but across student populations. I argue that the first two comparisons are important for improving productivity, while the third raises equity concerns that I discuss in greater detail next.

Addressing Efficiency and Equity

The usual aim of cost-effectiveness analysis is to improve productivity and efficiency. But one of the central aims of education is to level the playing field in society so that everyone has a chance in life. This is one of the central arguments behind, for example, affirmative action programs in higher education.

Fortunately, cost-effectiveness analysis can be adapted to incorporate a broader notion of social welfare that includes equity. The first, which I call the *subjective* approach, involves separately analyzing programs and policies aimed at different groups and then making qualitative judgments about the best balance of outcomes for all groups. The advantage of this approach is that it explicitly addresses equity, while recognizing that *equity* can mean different things to different people. Some educational leaders might be more concerned with the equity of outcomes, while others worry that all students have the same opportunities available.

Alternatively, the *quantitative* approach to equity gives numerical weight to the outcomes of groups whose success is of greatest concern. For example, I could multiply outcomes of disadvantaged student groups by a factor of two prior to summing across individuals. While this quantification imposes a strict definition of equity, it also reduces the likelihood that equity will be ignored in the final analysis. Numeric results are often taken at face value in policy deliberations, so handling equity subjectively can mean essentially ignoring the issue. As I discuss later, I use this simple mathematical approach in part of the following analysis.

APPLYING THE FRAMEWORK: THE COST-EFFECTIVENESS OF WELL-KNOWN PROGRAMS

To highlight the potential of the cost-effectiveness approach, I focus most of the remainder of the chapter on applying it to a variety of higher education programs. This is not meant to be a comprehensive review, but rather an illustration of the different ways that ECRs can be calculated and the issues that arise in the comparisons. I also sought a wide range of programs that varied based on strategy employed (financial, instructional, student service), quality of cost and impact information available, level of required resources, institutional context (two-year versus four-year colleges), and student population (targeted to disadvantaged students or broadly available). I define "disadvantaged" students broadly to refer to those whose families have below-average income, though the precise income cut-offs for program eligibility vary somewhat across programs placed in this category.

Educators are often skeptical of economic reasoning in making program and resource decisions, raising concerns about "bean counters" who do not understand education and whose main goal is to do things cheaply. Therefore, it is important to emphasize again that cost-effectiveness analysis identifies programs and policies that are not inexpensive per se, but inexpensive *given the additional learning they produce*. It requires more than just counting costs and effects, but good answers to the questions posed earlier and deep knowledge of the institutional context, students served, and pedagogy.

Common Hallmarks of Higher Education Quality: Student-Faculty Ratios and Full-Time Faculty

I begin with two resource-allocation decisions that have important effects on budgets and are widely seen as key indicators of quality: student-faculty ratios and full-time faculty. While much of the debate about higher education has moved beyond these resources, they still comprise 13 percent of

U.S. News and World Report undergraduate rankings.[21] Here, I consider the costs of each, briefly summarize available evidence on impacts, and report ECRs using the previously explained methodology.

Student-faculty ratio and class size. For a given faculty teaching load, a small student-faculty ratio means small class sizes. Faculty-student interaction outside the classroom may also be facilitated this way. Daniel Jacoby reports full-time faculty salaries of $74,443 ($58,041) and part-time faculty salaries of $16,156 ($12,174).[22] (For brevity throughout the paper, when reporting data simultaneously for four- and two-year colleges, I report the two-year figure in parentheses immediately after the four-year figure, as in the previous sentence.)

The current student/faculty ratio (FTE basis) is 14.8 (19.2) for public institutions.[23] Four-year (two-year) colleges have two-thirds (one-third) of their courses taught by full-time faculty.[24] Based on these ratios and salaries (weighted appropriately by sector for the proportion of faculty who are part-time and full-time, and adding in fringe benefits), reducing the student-faculty ratio from fifteen to fourteen (from nineteen to eighteen) would therefore cost $32,561 ($9,477) per year for one hundred students, excluding capital costs and fringe benefits.[25]

On the effect side of the equation, I found several studies of class size and achievement, and these tend to suggest that smaller classes do yield more learning.[26] Because achievement effects cannot be readily translated into graduation rates, I rely on the recent work of economists John Bound, Michael Lovenheim, and Sarah Turner.[27] They find that reducing the student-faculty ratio by one increases degree completion by 1.11 (0.03) percentage points. The large differences between four-year and two-year results here are noteworthy. While these results are based on fairly simple regression analyses, I report the results because this is such an important component of college costs. The adjusted ECR is 0.0083 (0.0015).

Full-time faculty and adjuncts. One way colleges have attempted to reduce costs in recent decades is through hiring adjuncts or part-time faculty. I calculate the costs of this change based on data on percent part-time faculty and faculty salaries, as well as the precise number of courses taught by part-time/full-time faculty.[28] The cost of switching from the aforementioned actual proportions to all full-time faculty would be $205,742 ($257,674).

Ronald Ehrenberg and Liang Zhang estimate the effects of full-time faculty by comparing graduation rates and percent full-time faculty across time within colleges.[29] Using this approach, their results imply that reducing the percent part-time by 1 percentage point would increase the graduation rate by 0.14 percentage points. Multiplying this by 33 (the actual percent part-time) implies that eliminating part-time faculty would increase the graduation rate by 4.6 percentage points. They do not report results for two-year colleges, but Jacoby does in his regression analysis: increasing the full-time faculty by 1 percentage point is associated with a rise in the graduation rate of 0.15 percentage points.[30] To move from 33 percent to 100 percent full-time would therefore increase graduation rates by 10 percentage points.[31] The adjusted ECRs are 0.0055 (0.0181). The figure is much higher in the two-year sector because the effects appear larger and the costs smaller, compared with the four-year sector.

College Access Programs

Policy makers have focused for decades on increasing access to higher education by targeting disadvantaged middle and high school students. Some of the oldest and most researched access programs are Upward Bound and Talent Search.

Upward Bound. One of the original federal TRIO programs, aimed at increasing college access among low-income first-generation students, Upward Bound provides tutoring, SAT and ACT test preparation, summer and afterschool sessions aimed at improving language arts and math skills, as well as campus visits. These regular interactions with students make Upward Bound more costly. Cohort cost estimates range from $480,000 to $516,000–$677,000.[32] The former and lower figure is based on federal budgetary contributions, while the higher figure is based on opportunity costs in some specific sites, and this reflects the general observation that budgetary costs understate total resources.

A randomized study of Upward Bound has yielded conflicting findings. One analysis by the organization that ran the experiment found no detectable effect on any college outcome, except for a 5 percentage point increase in vocational certificates and licenses.[33] However, more recent analyses of the same data that Alan Nathan and I have conducted suggest that the estimated effects are very sensitive to the specific statistical techniques used and that the effects were likely positive for other high school and college outcomes.[34] Given the controversy over the estimates, and the fact that the one area where the two analyses agree—effects on certificates and licenses—are considered less valuable than bachelor's degrees, I use 2 percentage points as the baseline impact for average low-income students.[35] This yields an adjusted ECR for average students of 0.0015.

Talent Search. The second of the original federal TRIO programs—and the largest in terms of the number of students served—Talent Search provides a combination of academic support, career development activities, and financial aid assistance to high school students.[36] Specific services include test-taking preparation, development of study skills, academic advising, course selection, college orientation, college campus visitation, referrals, general and financial aid counseling, and workshops. Federal contributions amounted to $392 per participant in 2009, which is considerably lower than other TRIO programs. The implied cohort cost is $39,200. With each of these college access programs, I assume that the average student participates for one and a half years.

Studies of similar programs have used less rigorous *propensity score matching* (PSM) methods and found much larger effects. Jill M. Constantine et al. find that Talent Search improves college enrollment by 6–18 percentage points (3–12 in two-year colleges and 3–7 percentage points in four-year colleges).[37] Likewise, Thurston Domina finds that these types of college outreach programs improve college enrollment by about 6 percentage points (though have essentially no impact on high school educational performance).[38] Because of limitations in the methodology, I use the lower end of this range for the Talent Search impact estimates (ECR: 0.0383).

Financial Aid Programs

Tuition is the heavily subsidized price of college paid by students. The cost of these subsidies (in public institutions), as well as grants to students, is essentially the face value of the subsidy or grant. Some grants and scholarships have "merit" requirements based on courses and grades. The situation is more complicated with loans. Susan Dynarski estimates that the government subsidy for Stafford loans, in which all interest is paid by the government while the student is in school and interest rates are subsidized after students leave college, "is about a third of its face value."[39] However, this figure is apparently based on what students with high credit ratings would obtain, and this probably overstates the credit situation of the average student. I estimate that the more typical subsidy is probably closer to 57 percent of face value.[40] I therefore assume the cost to the federal government for a $1,000 loan is $600. This highlights how the cost of a $1 loan is less than the cost of a $1 grant.

With several colleagues, I carried out the Wisconsin Scholars Longitudinal Study (WSLS), which randomly assigned first-time-in-college, low-income students to receive up to $3,500 for each of ten semesters in four-year colleges.[41] We point out that, due to federal rules, aid officers are required to reduce certain forms of aid, especially loans, when students receive grants and scholarships. For this reason, to calculate the cost of the WSLS, I added the net change in grant aid and subtracted the subsidy portion of the reduced loans.[42] Based on some new results from this study, with data covering the first three years, the cumulative average cost per treatment student is $1,785 per year. This is, to our knowledge, the only randomized trial of a need-based aid program.

The grants had small positive effects on GPA and credits, but no sustained impact on persistence.[43] One reason is that much of the aid was supplanted; federal rules required aid officers to reduce other forms of aid and students chose to reduce their loans as a result of the new grant. Some of the analyses suggest that students who *received* the largest increases in their total aid saw positive effects on persistence to the second year of college, but other parts of the analysis suggest that the aid effects fade out in the third and fourth years. We therefore use a minimum of 0 and a maximum of a 2 percentage point increase in persistence.[44] Combining this with the costs, this translates to an ECR of up to 0.0065.[45]

MDRC's Opening Doors. Some financial aid programs are bundled with other student services. MDRC's Opening Doors project included an experiment that combined advising, counseling, and performance-based financial aid. Based on data from two community colleges, MDRC's Lashawn Richburg-Hayes et al. report that average total scholarship payment per student over two semesters was $1,246.[46] Based on the number of counselors employed and the national average salaries of these workers, I estimate the costs of the counselors to be $340 per student so that the total average cohort cost is $1,246 + $340 = $1,586 (per year for two years).

MDRC's study also included an experiment that combined services with performance-based aid. The organization has released a series of reports suggesting that performance-based financial aid increases credit accumulation and enrollment in classes between the first and second semesters.[47] More recently, the researchers summarized new findings that the program increased persistence from roughly 31 percent to 37.5 percent over four semesters, for an effect of 6.5 percentage points. This suggests that the adjusted ECR is 0.0171.

Canada STAR. While I generally focus on U.S.-based results, I make one exception with the Canada STAR study. This is the only randomized trial of a performance-based aid program that occurred at a university, although another is ongoing. Like MDRC's Opening Doors, the STAR study featured both financial aid and student services. In addition to the control group, there were multiple treatments: (a) services only, such as facilitated study groups, (b) scholarship money only, and (c) a combination of a and b. The costs for these options are reported as $302, $366, and $739, respectively.[48]

Joshua Angrist, Daniel Lang, and Philip Oreopoulos report a point estimate for the effect of the funding-only treatment on first-to-second year persistence of 3 percentage points.[49] This figure was not statistically significant, but a much larger impact (more than 6 percentage points) was significant for males. This is important partly because the program ended after the first year, so any effect on second-year enrollment would have been based on residual benefits from the first year rather than the expectation of continued funding. This implies a 3 percentage point impact of aid only and an adjusted ECR of 0.0200. The ECR for the combined financial aid and service is roughly half that size (0.0099) because the services almost doubled the costs and the impact size remained roughly the same.

Other studies of financial aid. I reviewed a long list of studies and consulted the literature review by David Deming and Susan Dynarski regarding the impacts from a large number of quasi-experimental studies.[50] It is common in the literature to report aid effects as increased rates of attendance per $1,000 in aid. However, these calculations typically refer only to a single year of aid from a given program, omitting costs from subsequent years if students remain in college and continue meeting the program requirements. For this reason, as well as the cohort basis of our approach, the ECRs cannot be compared with the usual impact per $1,000 of aid. There is much less evidence on the impact of loans, though the two quasi-experimental studies I know of both find positive impacts.[51] The adjusted ECRs are 0.0064 for loans and 0.0063 for grants, nearly identical to the estimate for the WSLS.[52]

Student Services and Other Programs

Other strategies for increasing the number of college graduates include student counseling, other services, and improved instruction, especially for students who are far behind when they enter college.

Student counseling. As part of the MDRC Opening Doors initiative, low-income students who were just starting college, and who had histories of academic difficulties, were provided additional counseling and given a small stipend of $300 per semester when they used those services in two Ohio community colleges. The average stipend was $210. Counselors had a much smaller than usual caseload (one hundred nineteen versus one thousand in the control group) because of the expectation that they would be spending more time with each student. Students also were given a designated contact in the financial aid office. Researchers found that students did use counseling and financial aid services at greater rates than control group students (who also had access to standard campus services). Based on the number of counselors involved and Bureau of Labor Statistics (BLS) data on average counselor salaries, I estimate counselor costs of $340 per year per student. Adding the time of counselors to the student stipends, the unadjusted cohort cost is $54,898.

MDRC studied the Opening Doors initiative with a randomized trial. Impacts were statistically significant during the year the services were provided, though most of the initial effects diminished over time. The treatment increased persistence by 7 percentage points in the first semester by the end of the first year after which the program ended. Follow-up analysis suggests that the post-program impact was cut in half (to 3.7) the first full semester after the program stopped and declined further thereafter. It is unclear what would have happened had the program continued. The impacts might have diminished even if the program had continued. More plausibly, the total impact of the program might be reflected in the impact estimated at the time the program ended: increasing the graduation rate by 3.7 percentage points. As an upper bound, consider that the impacts could have continued to accumulate if the program continued—that is, the program might have impacted the persistence rate and the initial benefits might have compounded. I take 3.7 percentage points as a middle-ground estimate of the impact on graduation. The adjusted ECR is 0.0281.

Miscellaneous student services. Douglas Webber and Ronald Ehrenberg point out that spending on noninstructional student services such as student organizations, intramurals, student health services (including psychological counseling), supplemental instruction (e.g., tutoring), and admissions and registrar offices has grown more rapidly in recent years than instructional expenditures.[53] They use institution-level data, from the Integrated Postsecondary Education Data System (IPEDS), to study the potential impacts of different categories of student services as well as other typical categories of college spending.[54] They find that spending on student services tends to increase student persistence, especially at colleges where students have low college-entrance-exam scores and lower family incomes. Instructional spending is also positively associated with graduation. Specifically, they find that a $500 per student increase in student services spending would increase the college graduation rate by 0.7 percentage points. This yields an adjusted ECR of 0.0034.

The adjusted ECR for the Opening Doors program (0.0281) is six times larger than that suggested by Webber and Ehrenberg (0.0034). What explains this divergence? While the general spending on student services that Webber and Ehrenberg study reflects somewhat different types of services than in the MDRC experiment, and notwithstanding Webber and Ehrenberg's careful analysis, the large differences in ECRs may suggest that the regression-based estimates are biased downward. Also, Webber and Ehrenberg focused on four-year students, while Opening Doors focused on two-year students.

InsideTrack. The company InsideTrack provides coaching services to nontraditional college students (average age of thirty-one years). According to Eric Bettinger and Rachel Baker, "The coaches call their students regularly and in some cases have access to course syllabi, transcripts, and additional information on students' performance and participation in specific courses. InsideTrack uses this additional information in a set of predictive algorithms that assess each student's status for the purpose of reaching out to them on the right issues at the right times."[55] The company charges a fee of $1,000 per year per student.[56] As the service is provided by a for-profit company, this price is likely to be a reasonable estimate of costs, though it is unclear whether colleges themselves incur other costs. I use the reported price.

The InsideTrack coaching program has been studied with a large multisite randomized trial and is one of the most convincing studies available. Bettinger and Baker report effects on both persistence and graduation.[57] Even though the services are provided for only one year, effects on university graduation were 4 percentage points. This yields an ECR of 0.0400.

Remediation. So far, I have considered programs that attempt to influence students indirectly—by changing the general faculty resources available (student-faculty ratios and adjuncts), providing various forms of services (e.g., counseling and mentoring), and offering financial aid. But this means I have ignored what is arguably the core activity of colleges: instruction. While few if any studies link instructional practices to persistence and graduation, there has been considerable attention paid to remediation in recent years.

A growing concern is that students who enter college are not adequately prepared for college-level work. While this is partly seen as a flaw of high school preparation, many colleges try to address the issue through remediation programs. Placement in remediation is often based on scores on standardized tests. Texas spends $172 million per year on remediation programs that educated 162,597 (mostly four-year) students in 2006.[58] This translates to $1,057 per student, or $105,700 per cohort. Francisco Martorell and Isaac McFarlin find that remediation in Texas had no influence on student outcomes.[59]

Some have expressed concern, however, that the quality of the typical remediation program is relatively low and that more extensive, high-quality programs would have a positive impact. Alicia Dowd and Laura Ventimiglia estimate the total costs of a high-quality remediation program, Pathways (which includes a combination of math and language arts), at $1,700 per student session.[60] This yields an unadjusted cohort cost of $170,000 per year that, as expected, is somewhat higher than the cost of standard remediation previously reported.

While some studies have identified positive short-term impacts of remediation on early persistence, two rigorous studies find no impact on degree completion.[61] However, a quasi-experiment by Eric Bettinger and Bridget Long finds that remediation increases the probability of a student receiving a degree by 10 percentage points.[62] This leads to a bit of a conundrum. If we accept the Martorell and McFarlin results, then the ECR is 0, but if we accept Bettinger and Long, the ECR is 0.0588.[63] This, along with Upward Bound, is among the few cases where there are multiple rigorous studies, allowing such conflicts to emerge.

INTERPRETING THE RESULTS

The results of the cost calculations are summarized in the lefthand column of table 3.1. Costs for a cohort of one hundred students clearly vary widely, from as low as $20,281 for reducing the student-faculty ratio slightly in two-year colleges to more than $1 million—fifty times as much—for Upward Bound. From a productivity standpoint, this means that reduced faculty-student ratios could produce tiny impacts and still be worthwhile. Likewise, expensive programs may be cost-effective, but only if they generate very large impacts on student outcomes.

The second column reports the estimated effect on graduation. Finally, the last column divides the effects by the costs—the ECRs discussed throughout this section.

The results vary widely, from an ECR of 0.0015 for Upward Bound and two-year faculty-student ratios to 0.0588 for remediation. No single strategy stands out as particularly cost-effective. The results vary most within the instructional category, while financial aid seems to generate more consistent, but low, cost-effectiveness ratios. While the purpose here is not to draw conclusions about specific policies, these observations highlight the potential value of this approach.

The majority of the ECRs are related to four-year degrees, but we should not forget the distinction between those and two-year degrees. We also see evidence that programs, such as student services, that appear to

TABLE 3.1 **Cost-effectiveness of higher education programs**

Program	Adjusted cohort cost (real $)	Estimated effect on graduation	Effectiveness-cost ratio (ECR)
College access (disadvantaged)			
Talent Search	58,800	2.25	0.0383
Upward Bound	1,015,500	1.50	0.0015
Financial aid			
Grants	355,000	2.25	0.0063
WSLS-min	633,675	0.00	0.0000
WSLS-max	308,140	2.00	0.0065
Loans	233,700	1.50	0.0064
Merit aid (GA/AR)	410,000	3.00	0.0073
Merit aid (Canada STAR)	150,060	3.00	0.0200
Financial aid with services			
Canada STAR	302,990	3.00	0.0099
Opening Doors (2y; disadvantaged)	304,512	5.20	0.0171
Instruction			
Student/faculty ratio (4y)	133,500	1.11	0.0083
Student/faculty ratio (2y)	20,281	0.03	0.0015
Full-time faculty (4y)	843,542	4.60	0.0055
Full-time faculty (2y)	551,422	10.00	0.0181
Remediation (Bettinger/Long) (disadvantaged)	170,000	10.00	0.0588
Student services			
Student services (Webber/Ehrenberg)	205,000	0.70	0.0034
Student counseling (2y; disadvantaged)	105,404	2.96	0.0281
InsideTrack (4y)	100,000	4.00	0.0400

Note: Adjusted costs are the annual costs reported in the text multiplied by the average years of participation in the program. The effects on graduation sometimes reflect effects reported in studies where the researchers studied graduation, and in other cases reflect an effect on college entry or persistence that is adjusted so that it reflects the expected effect on graduation.

be effective in one sector (MDRC Opening Doors study of two-year colleges) seem ineffective in another sector (the Canada STAR study of a four-year college).

Of course, all of this assumes that we take the ratios at face value—that is, if we can ignore the questions posed at the beginning of this chapter. I also report the same point estimates from table 3.1 in figure 3.2 (the darker bars), but add bands to reflect the reasonable ranges. Some of the point estimates have no ranges because the estimates were based on actual graduation rather than assumptions about the multipliers to convert the estimates on entry and persistence. Of course, all the estimates contain unknown degrees of sampling error that are not reflected here.

The lighter bars for each program in figure 3.2 reflect equity-adjusted ECRs, under the assumption that the outcomes of economically disadvantaged groups are twice as important as for the average student. If you agree with the equity adjustment, then you can focus only on the top bars. Using this approach, targeted student counseling, Opening Doors, and WSLS (maximum estimate) all see their ECRs leap-frog at least one program not targeted to disadvantaged students. Remediation could be added to the list because, while family income is not an explicit consideration in assignment to remediation, disadvantaged students are more likely to have the lower level of academic skills and test scores that trigger remediation participation. In this respect, a well-executed remediation may be the most cost-effective option for this group.

I recognize that some might have alternative definitions of *disadvantaged*, and some might value the outcomes of these groups in different ways. Also, precise impact estimates of the proportion of students deserving any disadvantaged designation are not available. Again, the advantage of including these equity-adjusted results is that they reduce the likelihood that the importance of equity will be lost in policy deliberations.

Recall that economists also sometimes carry out cost-benefit analyses that focus on the increased earnings of college graduates. Benefit-cost ratios for most of the programs are available upon request, but note that 72 percent of the programs discussed in table 3.1 pass a cost-benefit test. Among those that barely pass the cost-benefit test are grants, loans, and merit aid, though each of these also has many more cost-effective programs ranked above it. This highlights the fact that programs can "look good" when we view them individually and consider only whether they pass a cost-benefit test, but the same programs look worse when we compare them to the alternatives.

FIGURE 3.2 **Equity-adjusted and bounded cost-effectiveness ratios**

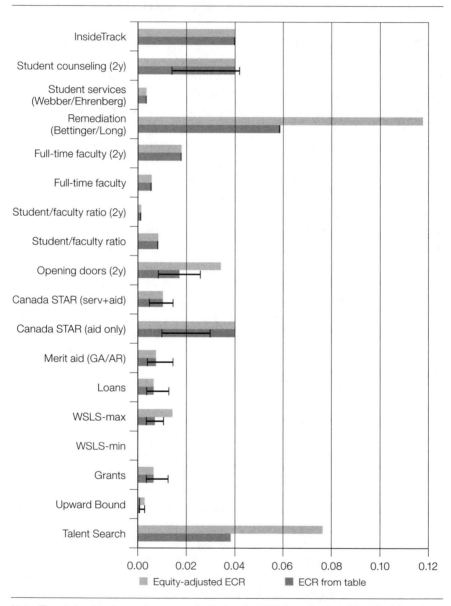

Note: The darker bar for each program indicates the ECR from the text. The black bands within some of those lower bars indicate bounds for estimates where program evidence is available only for college entry or persistence and therefore a range of impact multipliers are used. The equity-adjusted ECRs are based on the assumption that the outcomes of disadvantaged groups count twice as much as the average. The bands also apply to the equity-adjusted ECRs but are omitted so that the x-axis spans a narrower range, allowing for greater clarity of the small ECR levels.

CONCLUSION

The combination of growing demand for college credentials and declining degree productivity is a serious problem. It will be very difficult to reach the lofty education goals that policy makers are setting—or even avoid continued decline in tight fiscal times—without improving productivity. I argue, in contrast to the "cost disease" and the larger debate on higher education, that some productivity improvements are possible. Some programs are extremely expensive with little evidence to justify those high costs. Moreover, the differences in measured cost-effectiveness are so large that it is hard to ignore them. Among those programs with positive effects, the largest ECR is thirty-nine times larger than the smallest ECR.

While the number and nature of the assumptions in this analysis should clearly give us some pause when using research to inform policy, their main function is to prompt policy makers, researchers, and analysts alike to pose the questions necessary for reasonable interpretations of the evidence. My goal with this analysis is to add some useful structure to those decisions, not to encourage decisions based on mindless and mechanistic applications of ECR rankings. There is a risk that the assumptions and caveats I have laid out here might be ignored in the decision-making process, and that would partly undermine the objective, though that might be at least as likely if, as in most studies, these assumptions are never outlined. Of particular concern is that we have almost no evidence on the impacts of programs on degree *quality*. As with most tools, I think this one can be helpful if used well and possibly damaging otherwise. Given the significance of the cost and productivity problem, and the apparently vast differences in cost-effectiveness observed here, I believe this approach is worth considering.

I do not claim that colleges could get back to productivity rates from decades past. The cost disease and other pressures driving costs up and degrees down are real, powerful, and to a certain extent unavoidable. But that should not excuse the dearth of rigorous evidence, and the failure to integrate costs and effectiveness in policy decision making. The absence of the type of information that is needed to improve productivity—a hole that I hope this study begins to fill—is perhaps the strongest evidence that we are falling short of our productivity potential.

Going forward, new research will no doubt aid in filling some of the empirical gaps that hamper this analysis. Data to study higher education is increasingly available from research purposes through, for example, the National Student Clearinghouse and developing state administrative data systems. Moreover, adding analysis of costs has long been possible but rarely carried out. I have provided a framework on which future cost-effectiveness research can be based, but this should not be left to just the occasional review article. Every study of impacts should at least briefly discuss program costs, or else it tells only half the story. College leaders should consider filling these research holes on their own since cost-effectiveness often varies depending on the campus context.

The larger point is that colleges are not completely helpless in addressing productivity as some appear to assume. These results suggest a need to break out of this mind-set, to actively search for new and better ways to help students, and to study program costs and effects more carefully so that policy makers and college leaders can make more informed decisions about how to allocate scarce resources.

ACKNOWLEDGMENTS

I gratefully acknowledge financial support of the Lumina Foundation. For their useful advice, I wish to thank Charles Clotfelter, Colin Chellman, Matthew Chingos, Kristin Conklin, Sara Goldrick-Rab, Andrew Kelly, Michael McPherson, Susanna Loeb, David Mundel, Michael Olneck, Noel Radomski, David Weimer, John Wiley, and participants in symposia organized by the City University of New York, the Lumina Foundation: Making Opportunity Affordable initiative, the Wisconsin Center for the Advancement of Postsecondary Education (WISCAPE), and the Association for Education Finance and Policy. For research assistance, I thank Gregory Kienzl, Regina Brown, Alan Nathan, Byoung-Ik Jeoung, and So Jung Park. All errors are my own.

4

A Strategic Approach to Student Services

Five Ways to Enhance Outcomes and Reduce Costs

Ari Blum and Dave Jarrat

S ince the end of the Second World War, the United States has made tremendous progress in improving college access. In just ten years, between 1999 and 2009, enrollment in degree-granting postsecondary institutions increased by 38 percent, from 14.8 million to 20.4 million.[1] This trend, however, has not driven a commensurate increase in graduation rates, which have consistently hovered around 56 percent.[2] The number of dropouts in the United States has increased at roughly the same rate as the increase in the number of college graduates. Policy makers, researchers, and practitioners are beginning to take notice. During the past three years, the focus in higher education has shifted markedly from simply improving college access to improving access with success—a trend that has been coined the *completion agenda.*

This agenda comes at a time of equally pervasive attention to the cost of higher education. The great recession of 2010, the "Occupy" movement of 2011, and the passage of new federal regulations to hold many colleges and universities more accountable for loan repayment have all driven the national conversation toward institutional cost containment and passing those cost savings on to students in the form of lower tuition.

On both sides of this conversation, there are some who argue that these two agendas are mutually exclusive. How can colleges improve retention and graduation rates while simultaneously reducing costs? Though these two agendas collide at times, especially at first glance, they do not have to. In fact, by focusing resources on proven solutions to drive student retention and graduation rates, institutions can reduce costs to themselves, their students, and society at large.

In this chapter we argue that student support services—if properly configured, effectively targeted, and delivered early in the student life cycle—generate savings for institutions, students, and society overall. For the purposes of this discussion, *student services* refers to various forms of assistance provided to students outside the context of formal instruction in order to increase their likelihood of success. These services typically include academic advising and tutoring, financial aid counseling, and nonacademic coaching and mentoring. By lowering student acquisition costs, increasing retention and graduation rates, reducing time to completion, and decreasing expenditures on remedial education, student service investments can address many of the primary cost drivers in higher education. And, in addition to lowering costs, effective student services can also increase revenues for universities by maximizing the lifetime value of each student, improving operational efficiency and increasing the overall throughput of students.

Throughout this chapter, we draw on our own experience working for a third-party service provider in the student services landscape, InsideTrack.[3] We start with a very brief overview of rising costs and the new completion agenda in higher education. We then discuss five strategies that universities should keep in mind to maximize the impact of student service investments. Finally, we close with remarks on obstacles and best practices.

COSTS AND THE COMPLETION AGENDA

Domestic and international pressures for higher educational attainment have created a sense of urgency about improving college completion rates. To regain America's position as a leader on this metric, President Obama has charged the nation with obtaining the highest proportion of college graduates in the world by 2020, which would mean adding 8 million graduates to our population.[4]

Student attrition not only hampers our nation's ability to fulfill this completion agenda, it also drives up the cost for everyone involved. According to a study by Mark Schneider of the American Institutes for Research (AIR), of the 1.1 million full-time students who entered college in 2002, the 500,000 who failed to graduate within six years cost a combined $4.5 billion in foregone income and federal and state income taxes. Schneider concluded, "This is just the tip of the iceberg. While this report focuses on only one cohort of students, losses of this magnitude are incurred annually by each and every graduating class."[5]

Colleges and universities also bear the cost of students who fail to graduate. Student attrition drives up the cost of each completed degree and puts the institution at a competitive disadvantage. The cost to engage, recruit, and orient new students often makes them substantially more expensive to serve than returning students. This differential is pronounced in the rapidly growing online learning market and among nontraditional student populations, especially as new federal regulations hold institutions more accountable for student success. For many providers, the stakes of student success have never been higher.

Finally, the most evident and principal casualties are the would-be graduates, who frequently face the daunting prospect of repaying hefty loans without the increased earnings that a degree typically delivers.

STUDENT SERVICES CAN DRIVE COSTS DOWN BY IMPROVING OUTCOMES

There is no doubt that providing impactful student services can ensure that more students make it to graduation. The question is whether or not the direct cost of these services is offset by a reduction in other institutional costs, allowing for a lower average cost per completion. We argue that, while requiring some up-front investment, student services that are properly configured, effectively targeted, and delivered early in the student life cycle create long-term, direct cost savings for institutions and learners. Successful student service programs result in increased student engagement, satisfaction, and retention; reduced time to completion; and decreased need for remedial education, all of which can directly reduce institutional expenditures and individual student tuition and opportunity costs. Institutions also benefit financially through lower student acquisition costs, higher lifetime revenue per student, increased student throughput, and reduced regulatory risk.

The return to society at large is also substantial. According to the latest analysis by Complete College America (CCA), states alone spend $3 billion each year on remedial courses, an average of more than $1,764 per student served, with very poor results.[6] Spending a fraction of that money to provide additional support to the same students placed directly into credit-bearing courses could save billions of dollars and accelerate increases in national labor pool productivity, tax revenues, and overall global competiveness. The CCA analysis highlights several institutions that have applied this concept with positive results. Austin Peay State University in Tennessee eliminated remedial math courses, instead placing students in credit-bearing courses and offering specialized math workshops. As a result, twice as many "remedial students" are passing their initial college-level math courses. The University of Maryland at College Park similarly replaced its remedial math courses with corequisite math courses where remedial students receive additional support for the first five weeks of the fifteen-week duration. Completion rates for these students are now the same as for nonremedial students.

STRATEGIES FOR USING STUDENT SERVICES TO REDUCE COSTS

There is a long and rich literature on the potential for student support services to drive improvements in student outcomes.[7] And yet, while the effectiveness of support services in promoting student success is widely recognized, research has paid less attention to the cost-effectiveness of investments in student services. Thus, it is less evident how institutional leaders can make investments in support services that ultimately drive down costs for institutions, students, and society. From our experience working with support structures at universities across all segments of the higher education landscape, we believe universities can maximize the impact of student service investments on short- and long-term costs by adhering to five key strategies. Combined, these five strategies focus attention and resources where they are needed most and maximize long-term return on investment.

Strategy #1: Focus on Reducing the Cost per Degree Earned

Facing unparalleled pressure to contain costs, colleges and universities often decide to cut student service spending across the board. We argue that this impulse actually drives up costs in the long run, and that institutions should instead look for ways to better invest their student support dollars to drive stronger outcomes, generate new revenue streams, and create cost savings for themselves and their students. Shifting to a focus on the cost per degree completed will drive institutional leaders to find cost-effective ways to promote student success. Jane Wellman, executive director of the National Association of System Heads (NASH) and former head of the Delta Cost Project, summarized the dilemma by saying, "Focusing on the cost per student perpetuates the dysfunction in how funding in higher education is allocated. In contrast, focusing on cost per outcome shifts the emphasis to investing to realize the greatest impact."[8]

Universities are not alone in taking a blunt-force approach to cost containment. Leading strategic consulting firm Booz & Company asserts that for most organizations, cost cutting translates into across-the-board slashing that "spreads the pain." Although intuitively attractive and often politically expedient, this approach can weaken the organization. Instead, organizations should treat cost reduction as an opportunity to identify and reinforce their key capabilities, while divesting themselves of those activities that do not truly reflect their strengths and long-term goals.[9]

In higher education, the equivalent strategy is to focus student support spending on those activities that are most impactful and cost-effective in promoting academic progress and success. By investing in services that can improve completion rates and accelerate time to completion, institutions create financial benefits both for themselves and for their students. A virtuous cycle develops when students are more successful. Their success elevates the school's brand reputation and competitiveness, while also making it more likely that the student will refer a friend or colleague to the institution. The result for the university is lower average student acquisition costs and an increase in the total throughput of students—both of which reduce overall costs.

The financial markets have noticed the importance of these investments: financial analysts who cover for-profit education providers now offer higher stock-price-valuation multiples for publicly traded universities that have developed initiatives to drive improved student outcomes.[10]

Retain students to minimize the cost of attrition. For decades, the focus in higher education was on increasing access, and incentives favored enrollment over retention. Evidence included stock prices of for-profit universities driven by their growth in new students, state funding mechanisms for public universities based on head count, and accreditation and regulatory regimes based exclusively on educational institution inputs.

Over the last several years, a number of forces have converged to alter the cost-benefit equation in higher education. Increasingly, investors, regulators, accreditors, taxpayers, and students are focused on outcomes. Consider examples such as performance-based funding of state universities, stock price valuations based on retention and graduation rates, and federal regulations based on student loan defaults.

Successful outcomes are now at the center of the cost-containment equation, as they address three key drivers of institutional spending: recruitment costs, lost tuition, and capacity underutilization. The cost of recruiting a single undergraduate is growing substantially. According to the National Association for College Admissions Counseling (NACAC) Annual State of College Admission report, the average cost to recruit and enroll a new student at public and private nonprofit universities increased from $1,684 in 2004 to $2,408 in 2010—a compounded annual growth rate of 6.1 percent.[11] According to BMO Capital Markets, during the same period, the median cost per start for seven of the largest for-profit providers increased from $1,925 to $2,560.[12] Spending on recruitment, along with the cost of orientation, setup, and helping students through the challenges of their first year, is fully leveraged only if the student persists through completion. As Neal A. Raisman, author of *The Power of Retention*, succinctly puts it:

> The churn and burn of continually bringing new students through the front door, and then just watching them go out the back door, is killing college enrollments and individual and institutional futures.[13]

Raisman developed a Customer Service Factor 1 (CSF1) equation for estimating the cost of student churn to an institution:

$$CSF1 = [(P \times A = SL) \times T]$$

In this equation, P represents the total school population, A is the annual attrition rate of all students, SL is students lost annually from total population and revenue production, and T equals annual tuition at the school.

For example, at a school with a population of five hundred students, an annualized attrition rate of 39.6 percent (or 198 lost students), and annual tuition of $13,000, the equation shows an annual tuition revenue loss of over $2.5 million from student attrition:

$$SCF1 = [(500 \times 39.6\% = 198) \times \$13,000]$$
$$= \text{annual revenue loss of } \$2,574,000$$

Many institutions offset the annual tuition lost on students who fail to persist by increasing tuition prices on new and continuing students. The bottom line is that the students who stay end up paying for the students who drop out. At public institutions, taxpayers foot much of the bill.

The Raisman formula also shows the power of decreasing attrition by 5 percentage points, thereby adding the equivalent of twenty-five new students who, at $13,000 per year, each generate additional annual revenue of $325,000:

$$CSF1 = [(500 \times 5\% = 25) \times 13,000] = \$325,000 \text{ more revenue}[14]$$

In addition to the increased tuition revenues generated by reducing attrition, improving retention also directly reduces costs for the institution itself—especially in online environments and in those institutions serving "posttraditional" students. The specialized services needed to recruit students, process their enrollments, and orient them to their program all generate costs. If those resources are spent on students who later drop out, the investments are wasted. However, if an institution—especially one leveraging online learning—can move a greater percentage of its student body through to subsequent semesters, it will realize the savings in the following year.

To better understand this, consider a nonprofit, private online program where capacity is not bound by major fixed-cost investments in buildings, dorms, facilities, and so on, and where first-year and later-stage courses have similar student-to-teacher ratios. In this model, because student-teacher ratios are roughly constant across first-year and later-stage students, the additional costs of recruiting, orienting, and supporting first-year students is the primary cost driver.

According to the NACAC, the average cost to recruit and enroll a new student at a private nonprofit university in 2010 was $3,000.[15] Data from BMO Capital Markets and the Delta Cost Project put the instructional cost of serving a single student at a nonprofit, nonresearch institution in 2009 at approximately $8,000.[16] It is easy to see in figure 4.1 how the proportion of the overall student population consisting of first-year students impacts the cost structure of the university.

In this example, it costs $9.2 million to serve a one-thousand-person student body made up of 40 percent first-year and 60 percent returning students, and $9.8 million to serve a one-thousand-person student body made up of 60 percent first-year and 40 percent returning students. This $600,000, or 6.5 percent, cost differential can be offset in some traditional settings where large lecture courses in freshman year give way to smaller, more expensive seminars in later stages of the student life cycle. However,

FIGURE 4.1 **The total cost to serve one thousand students, by first-year student proportion**

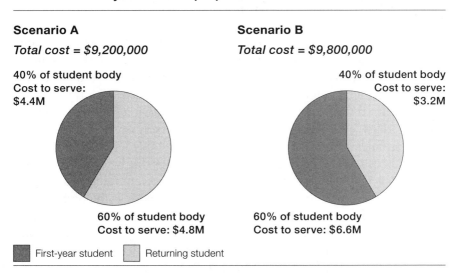

Scenario A
Total cost = $9,200,000

40% of student body
Cost to serve:
$4.4M

60% of student body
Cost to serve: $4.8M

Scenario B
Total cost = $9,800,000

40% of student body
Cost to serve:
$3.2M

60% of student body
Cost to serve: $6.6M

■ First-year student   □ Returning student

as the postsecondary landscape increasingly moves toward serving adult students in online and other nontraditional settings (e.g., occupational training), the more pronounced this effect becomes.

Fundamentally, then, universities face the same situation as many other businesses, particularly as federal student aid becomes more scarce and regulatory compliance more expensive: it is more economical to retain an existing student than to recruit a new one. This makes wise investments in student services, especially those that can reduce student acquisition costs while improving outcomes, ever more critical.

Strategy #2: Focus Resources with Data-Driven Decisions

While effective student support services can reduce long-term costs by reducing attrition, not every student support initiative is impactful, and many are not cost-effective. In the current environment, institutions must increasingly make strategic decisions about how to allocate their resources. Data-driven decisions can reduce spending on ineffective programs, creating immediate cost savings that can be passed on to the student in the form of lower tuition.

To ascertain whether investments are achieving the goal of reducing long-term costs by improving student outcomes, colleges and universities need to measure what is working and what is not, create cultures of accountability, and ensure that decision making is based on data-driven evidence. University leaders rate their institutions poorly on these attributes. In a 2011–2012 survey conducted by *Inside Higher Ed*, less than one-third of chief academic officers rated their institutions as very effective in using data to aid and inform campus decision making (see table 4.1).[17]

Obstacles to data-driven decisions in student services. Most senior university administrators would agree that data-driven decision making is critical. Nonetheless, when it comes to evaluating different student service options, emotional and operational issues often interfere with the process. Some administrators take issue with providing services to some students and not others, even if it is for the purposes of assessing their effectiveness through a randomized controlled experiment. There is also a general reluctance to focus services on the students who are most likely to be affected by them, rather than the students who are most at risk of failing. It is important to provide support to all students, especially those at the highest risk. However, an exclusive focus on the lowest performing students can undermine the allocation of scarce resources to the students who, on the surface, appear to have a higher likelihood of success but who will miss the mark without an increment of additional support. Though there may be considerable

TABLE 4.1   **CAOs versus presidents on their institutions' use of data-driven decision making**

Percentage of CAOs and presidents reporting 6/7; scale 1 = not effective, 7 = very effective

	Provosts/ CAOs	Presidents
Providing a quality undergraduate education	66.3	69.7
Preparing students for future employment	50.0	56.5
Recruiting/retaining talented faculty	48.7	45.4
Offering support services for undergraduates (advising, etc.)	43.4	40.8
Ensuring the professional development of junior faculty	32.2	24.3
Using data to aid and inform campus decision making	30.9	35.9

Source: Kenneth C. Green, Scott Jaschik, and Doug Lederman, *The 2011–12 Inside Higher Ed Survey of College and University Chief Academic Officers* (Washington, DC: Inside Higher Ed, 2012).

overlap between the most at-risk students and those most likely to benefit from increased services, leaders charged with getting the most "bang for their buck" must base allocation decisions on data rather than anecdotes.

Even in cases where administrators are comfortable allocating resources based on impact and cost-effectiveness, they also face obstacles in designing effective controlled studies. Common flaws include small sample sizes, selection bias, and inconsistent measurement. While these issues are well documented and often avoided in academic research, institutional leaders are typically unaware or unable to incorporate best practices into their assessment and decision-making processes, particularly when it comes to personalized student services.

Despite these hurdles, it is possible to carry out rigorous evaluations of new approaches to student services. For instance, Chapman University, a prominent private liberal arts institution in southern California, conducted a well-defined, multiyear controlled trial to examine the effectiveness of InsideTrack's executive-style coaching program. In this study, the college and InsideTrack divided the entire freshman class into two statistically balanced groups of students. Administrators flipped a coin to randomly assign students to treatment and control groups; the treatment group received weekly coaching sessions provided by InsideTrack in addition to the university's standard services, while the control group received only the standard services. Measurements taken at the end of the year, based on metrics agreed to in advance by both parties, showed that the treatment group had a higher retention rate than the control group. In addition, the results suggested that coaching also had a measurable impact on a number of other student engagement and success metrics, including student grade point averages. After two more years of similarly positive results from controlled testing, the university decided to provide the coaching to all incoming freshmen. For more than a decade, InsideTrack has conducted similar controlled studies with all of its clients, including studies regarding the impact of coaching on specific student populations, such as out-of-state, Latino, international, and military students.

In addition to conducting randomized controlled studies, which are difficult and time-consuming, institutions can utilize a number of innovative methods to generate data and help administrators discover the services that students value and need most. For example, mapping the student experience, from inquiry to graduation, will reveal how student services currently fit into the student life cycle and pinpoint areas for improved coordination and delivery. Another useful exploratory technique is enrolling individuals to "secret shop" their own and peer institutions. This practice provides a valuable firsthand assessment of the student experience.

Strategy #3: Invest in Efficiency Through Technology and Economies of Scale

While effective student services reduce long-term costs by improving student outcomes, reducing the costs of the service functions themselves produces direct, short-term savings. Delivering student services cost-effectively at scale not only reduces costs and frees up resources for universities to invest elsewhere, but it can also save students time and money. From our experience working with institutions, we see three key strategies that produce the core of the cost savings:

- Increasing coordination across functions
- Integrating technology systems and providing student support professionals with access to these systems
- Aligning people, processes, and technology to function seamlessly

Coordination across functions. Ask typical students what's not working at their university, and a key frustration will emerge: the lack of a clear point of contact to obtain information and/or fix problems. Often, students bounce around between departments and staff members, not knowing whether their problems registering for the next term are an issue for the registrar, their academic adviser, or their financial aid counselor. In light of concerns about how poor coordination causes students to fall through the cracks and leads to wasted expenditures on duplicated adviser efforts, a number of institutions we have worked with are actively integrating and streamlining student support functions—for example, merging financial aid, academic advising, and other support services into one-stop student support centers. This integration results in lower costs through (a) elimination of duplicative roles, (b) improvement in negotiating power with vendors, and (c) more efficient processes, all of which reduce administrative effort.

The first step in coordinating student support functions is to assess the student experience vis-à-vis the institution. The institution must map the student experience from application to graduation to understand how student services currently fit into the life cycle. With this map, the institution can identify areas needing improved coordination or streamlining. Possible improvements often include better integration of admission and retention functions, assigning responsibility for initial student retention to admissions staff (typically through the first six months, or until students complete core classes and begin taking classes in their major), and refining the timing, frequency, and content of communications with students.

Other innovations we have seen include the creation of "grad teams" composed of staff from admissions, academic/student services, and financial aid who work together on a student-by-student basis. These teams work to ensure seamless transfers between departments, by transmitting student-specific knowledge and creating rapport in order to ensure that students don't fall through the cracks. Many of the recent software innovations for postsecondary institutions allow for the sharing of detailed data across advisers and instructors, allowing them to work as a team when addressing student performance and retention issues.[18]

Coordination across departments also makes it easier to find the root causes of major problems. For example, a leading art and design university found that it was losing students immediately after a particular first-year class. Through cross-functional analysis, administrators discovered a simple disconnect between the institution's financial aid and academic calendars—students couldn't obtain the funds they needed to buy books and supplies prior to the first day of class. Once this disconnect was addressed, retention improved dramatically. In another example, DeVry University put in place consolidated one-stop-shop service centers that house all student-facing functions, saving students time and producing cost savings by enabling the sharing of administrative resources, office equipment, and supplies across departments.

Finally, coordinating procurement and other behind-the-scenes functions can also create savings. Institutions that coordinate planning and purchasing activities can prevent duplication of efforts, secure volume discounts, and avoid the costs associated with incompatibility. For example, many institutions use joint contracting between the admissions office and student services to fund process consulting, outsourced services, and IT projects.

Regardless of the ultimate solution, the first step is to understand the student life cycle and look for the inevitable bottlenecks and duplicative efforts that, when eliminated, will certainly drive down the cost of service staffing and improve leverage across and outside the university.

Integrating technology. Coordinating activity across functions is even more difficult when technology gets in the way. In an ideal world, an adviser working with a student would call up a single dashboard, offering a complete view of the student's status. In the real world, however, most universities today rely on multiple disconnected information systems to track and serve students—such as online application software, customer relationship management (CRM) systems, student information systems (SIS), learning management systems (LMS), financial aid systems, and early alert systems. Each system typically operates separately, creating "information silos" that are accessed one by one. Thus, advisers, who may serve hundreds of students and track dozens of open action items at a time, must move from one student information system to another—and after doing so, may even find that they lack access to the very system they need. Switching between systems is not only inefficient, but it also creates disconnects in which the continuity of service breaks down.

In some cases, staff can rely on regularly scheduled "batch imports" of data from the disconnected systems, but this approach can lead to problems if the data element is time-sensitive and gets stale quickly. For example, staff may have no way of knowing if a key intervention, such as a call from a financial aid adviser, has taken place. Thus, the staff cannot track the intervention's effectiveness.

While challenging, creating a single integrated platform for managing the entire student life cycle is a goal worth pursuing. Several universities (particularly in the for-profit sector) have fully integrated their course registration, academic (LMS and early alert), and student services (CRM or case management) systems, affording support staff a more holistic view of student data. When an issue comes up, an adviser generates an "issue ticket," which triggers notification of the right people for follow-up and remains open until the issue is resolved. This integrated system helps the adviser clear the queue in a timely and efficient fashion, while providing students the prompt, tailored service that may mean the difference between staying in school and dropping out. Some of these same institutions are now working to integrate marketing, admissions, financial aid, and alumni outreach systems, as well as technology-enabled services, such as student mentoring and tutoring.

By investing up front in system integration, institutions reduce administrative overhead and enable staff members to manage more students more effectively. These strategies directly reduce the costs of student support services.

Integrating people, processes, and technology. While technology systems create an opportunity to reduce costs by eliminating duplicative roles and inefficient work, they can also increase costs if not paired with the right training and methodologies for the people who use the systems. For example, many institutions have some form of early alert system to "flag" students who are at risk of failure. Yet, very few have strategies in place to address the various flags once they are raised.

Imagine a simple, software-based alert system set to generate a flag when a student misses a class. Responding to that flag requires advisers to assess the root cause of the absence and develop a sensible remedy. The alert is helpful only inasmuch as the adviser is prepared to respond appropriately. Without a clear process, the flagging system can actually drive more work without generating positive results.

Contrast this with an approach that not only generates a flag, but also prompts the adviser to take a specific action, which he has been effectively trained to perform. Take it a step further by allowing the adviser to go against the recommended action based on his professional judgment. Now, capture the recommended action, the actual action, and the end result in a system that can evaluate the adviser's judgment in different situations. Finally, use the resulting analysis to demonstrate to the adviser when he should follow the prompts, and when to adjust the prompts if they prove less successful than the adviser's judgment. This is the approach InsideTrack uses to continuously improve its coaching services, and it has proven incredibly valuable in supporting a culture of measurement and accountability.

Strategy #4: Account for the Posttraditional Student

In order for student services to deliver the long-term cost savings that result from improved outcomes, institutions must design services to accommodate different parts of the student market. Today, many student service operations are designed around yesterday's typical student. In the last decade, the traditional college student—a recent high school graduate supported emotionally and financially by his or her parents—has become increasingly outnumbered by students who are older, more likely to attend part-time, and more likely to be working and/or raising a family during school. According to a 2011 report by the Center for Postsecondary and Economic Success, today's typical college student is no longer an eighteen-year-old recent high school graduate who enrolls full-time and has limited work and family obligations. Instead, nearly 47 percent of college students are financially independent, 46 percent are enrolled part-time, 36 percent are over the age of twenty-five, and 32 percent are employed full-time.[19] Though this posttraditional student now represents the largest subset of students nationwide, many colleges still make decisions based on the profile and needs of the traditional student. As stated in the Advisory Committee on Student Financial Assistance's 2012 *Pathways to Success* report to Congress on improving student success rates:

> Despite their prominence in the student population, nontraditional students are still not adequately served in the higher education community. For example, too often institutions offer classes at times that are inconvenient for the nontraditional student, or do not make available adequate financial aid for these students, or the students themselves do not find campuses easy to navigate.[20]

The additional demands and academic needs that this group faces can drive up costs for institutions that fail to account for posttraditional students in designing their student support functions. For example, many universities find themselves expanding remedial or developmental education programs in an attempt to address adult students' deficiencies in basic math and English skills. However, there is some debate as to whether this traditional approach to remediation is well suited to posttraditional students, with groups like Complete College America arguing that placing students directly into credit-bearing courses while providing them with enhanced support could both save money and improve outcomes.[21]

Because the success of higher education will be more and more closely linked to the success of the growing population of posttraditional students, serving these students well is increasingly critical to achieving any long-term cost savings from improved student outcomes. In fact, the long-term survival of many universities may depend on their ability to cost-effectively meet the needs of posttraditional students. Spending in traditional areas—new buildings, sports programs, and residential services—may need to give way to investments in online courses, prior learning assessments, and flexible, accelerated programs designed with career outcomes in mind.

Services for the posttraditional student. Beyond aligning programs and schedules to the needs of busy, career-minded students, there are a number of service interventions that can promote success in a cost-effective manner. Investments in financial aid geared to part-time, year-round learners, and mentoring aimed at effectively balancing work, family, and school demands are two prime examples.

A number of institutions provide useful templates for effective posttraditional student services. DeVry University, a leading for-profit institution, uses a one-stop-shop advising model, named Student Central, that provides students with combined financial consulting and academic advising through one central location.[22] Brandman University, a leading private, nonprofit university focused on serving adult learners, offers personalized, professional academic advising to every student and encourages faculty and staff to help students access resources and services.[23]

Both of these institutions also offer one-on-one success coaching provided by InsideTrack. In its latest Academic Annual Report, DeVry noted that this increased level of support is translating into an improvement in persistence of more than 12 percent, leading it to expand the program.[24] Other institutions have had success with strategies such as offering enhanced tutoring, adjusting course sequencing and pace based on entrance exams, and providing recorded lectures, video chat, and other supplements to live instruction.

Strategy #5: Leverage Partnerships

Maximizing the impact and cost-effectiveness of any initiative requires bringing the best possible team together. While many of the strategies discussed in this chapter are well within the scope of an existing student services function, institutions already carrying out a multitude of complex tasks may find that they are better served by partnering with outside providers who have already created a cost-effective approach to solving a problem.

On the plus side, outside service providers offer numerous advantages. First, they are experts in their fields and bring a breadth and depth of experience unlikely to exist within an individual university. Because they can amortize investments across a large client base, they can invest more heavily in specialized people, processes, and technology. Specialized service providers can also draw on their experience to develop best practices to improve impact and cost-effectiveness. Perhaps most importantly, partnering in one or multiple service areas can free colleges and universities to focus on the areas that they define as their core competencies.

On the minus side, outside providers create more touch-points for the student and require a strong coordination of effort to ensure that roles are clearly defined in order to avoid outreach confusion. Third-party providers must also be culturally consistent with the institution's values and able to communicate back to the school key elements of the student experience to drive improvement in processes and systems.

In student services, outside providers are available to support a number of functions, from well-established activities like student mentoring and tutoring, to more experimental offerings, such as online award systems for boosting student motivation and private social networking sites to strengthen community among students and alumni.

The following subsections provide information on a handful of providers that are currently working with universities to improve students' experiences and outcomes.[25]

Student coaching and mentoring: InsideTrack. InsideTrack provides one-on-one executive-style coaching for college students to help promote student success and prepare students for postgraduation careers. InsideTrack coaches help students plan their career path, master life skills such as time management and prioritization, and persist through obstacles that arise while they are in school. The organization works with a broad range of traditional, adult, and online programs at a variety of universities, including Penn State University, University of Dayton, Florida State University, and Columbia University.[26]

InsideTrack's coaching methodology draws on student engagement research by noted authorities, integrated with proprietary research refined over the past decade with more than three hundred fifty thousand students. In a typical meeting, the student and coach work one-on-one on key issues, such as learning to balance work, family commitments, and financial challenges with a demanding academic load, or on skills critical to long-term success, including leadership, time management, critical thinking, and budgeting.

The efficacy of InsideTrack coaching was confirmed in an independent study conducted by Stanford University professor Eric Bettinger. The study, which reviewed the academic records of more than 13,500 students from eight colleges and universities across multiple academic years, found that InsideTrack coaching increased retention and graduation rates by 10 to 15 percent and proved a more cost-effective way to achieve retention gains than many previously studied interventions.[27] This study was recently reviewed by the Department of Education What Works Clearinghouse and found to meet its strict evidence standards.[28] InsideTrack coaching is currently the only college drop-out prevention solution to meet these standards.

Academic tutoring: SMARTHINKING. SMARTHINKING provides online tutoring to help colleges and universities increase student achievement, boost retention, and enhance learning.[29] Students calling into the tutoring center are connected with an expert educator who works with them using a virtual whiteboard.

A study by the Division of Florida Colleges found that students enrolled in developmental education courses or first college-level courses in math or English who used Smarthinking's services received higher grades than those who didn't.[30] In a separate analysis, participants reported that Smarthinking helped them to improve their grades and increase their confidence. Instructors also reported that students' final scores improved after using Smarthinking.[31]

As a result of these and other effective interventions, Smarthinking has gained the respect of college leaders. As Dr. Bill Carver, president of Nash Community College in Rocky Mount, North Carolina, described in a recent press announcement, "Smarthinking has been an extremely valuable service for Nash Community College. As an open admissions institution, we have a diverse student population with various needs. Smarthinking allows us to provide our students with 24/7, on-demand academic support so that they can get help on or off campus, at night or on the weekend, and, most importantly, at the teachable moment."[32]

Motivation programs: uBoost. uBoost is a student motivation program that uses online rewards and recognition to increase the frequency of desired behaviors in students and employees.[33] uBoost has been working with K–12 schools and corporations since 2007, and has recently expanded its focus to include higher education.

According to the company, uBoost can help colleges and universities improve student outcomes by rewarding specific behaviors—such as course registration and attendance—that are correlated with student retention. Services can also prompt students to focus on their goals by tracking and rewarding progress toward degree completion. uBoost can also act as an alert program by monitoring activity within the LMS and automatically sending messages to both the student (directing her to support services) and the academic counselor (for personalized follow up) when needed.

uBoost has also partnered with Kaplan Test Prep to provide positive incentives to students preparing for their SAT/ACT tests, rewarding activities that will lead to higher scores. These incentives include recognition through Facebook news alerts, exclusive digital badges, and points that students can redeem for donations to charities of their choice. According to Kaplan (when announcing the partnership), similar programs designed for students being tutored have greatly accelerated progress.

Private online communities: Inigral. Through its Schools App product, Inigral enables institutions to create a private, branded, Facebook-based community, through which students can get to know their classmates, share news on topics in which they're interested, and become involved in college activities.[34] According to the company, retention rates for students using Inigral's Schools App are 8.6 percent higher for freshmen and 1.9 percent higher for transfers compared to students not using the application.[35]

The product has been applied at institutions of all types, including Harvey Mudd College, the University of Toledo, North Carolina State University, and the University of California-Berkeley, to achieve a variety of goals. Arizona State University (ASU), for example, found that Schools App allowed its students to create bonds across its five campuses. Further, students at Maricopa Community Colleges, who often transfer to four-year colleges, use Schools App to network with ASU students before transferring. According to Kari Barlow, assistant vice president of ASU Online, "With the Schools App, we were able to connect students with one another even before they arrive on campus, and facilitate connections beyond the classroom."[36]

Third-party or in-house? Managing the investment decision. Every institution has a set of core competencies that helps define its culture, its student experience, and its outcomes. By defining these competencies, the institution can focus its efforts on reducing cost and improving outcomes for each of the identified areas. To realize the full, long-term cost benefits of improved outcomes, institutions must find the right balance between focusing on their core competencies and investing in efficiencies therein, and partnering with organizations on tasks that are outside of the institutions' core area of focus and can be delivered more cost-effectively by an outside provider.

ADDRESSING FINANCIAL ISSUES

The steps required to generate long-term cost savings through improved student outcomes can be challenging to implement in the real world. Universities looking to rethink student services must be prepared to address budget constraints and effectively measure return on investment.

Overcoming Budget Challenges

Finding the budget sources to implement student success initiatives can also stall forward progress. While these investments yield financial benefits correlated with improvements in student outcomes over time, they often require up-front capital investment. Developing a financial plan and finding the resources to make the initial investment can prove challenging. Universities must find a source of funding that doesn't deprive students of other necessary services—a problem that is not trivial in today's economic environment for education.

One politically difficult but obvious place to start is to review planned investments in areas unrelated to student outcomes. Such an analysis may show, for instance, that the demand for residential buildings and sports facilities is diminishing as the population of online and commuter students grows, and that the funding earmarked for these operations might be better spent on services that meet the needs of this new type of student. The cost savings from efforts to increase efficiency and eliminate redundancies in student service operations may also be a source of funding, as some of these initiatives have been proven less effective than others.

As data on student outcomes becomes more public and more important to prospective students, the decision to invest in outcomes over marketing and recruiting may become more politically attractive. Federal regulations and state budgets that tie funding to student outcomes are also changing the financial equation at many universities.

In the end, however, the analyses and trade-offs are complex, and decisions about investments and divestments can be painful and meet with resistance from current stakeholders. Keeping the needs of students and the university's values and vision in mind will help all of those concerned stay focused on goals and strategies that can help ensure its long-term health and success in an increasingly competitive higher education market.

Measuring Return on Investment

There are a variety of ways to measure return on investment (ROI), using a mix of quantitative and qualitative metrics. One straightforward method we have used with numerous clients over the years is the Raisman formula to derive net tuition revenue resulting from increased student retention, compared to the expense required to generate that increased retention. This method ignores many of the benefits derived from improved student outcomes, including lower acquisition costs, reduced regulatory risk, greater student satisfaction, and increased brand value and competitive differentiation. Nonetheless, it provides a useful estimate of the incremental dollars available to fund other investments or control tuition increases.

The results from this ROI analysis vary widely across institutions, depending on their baseline retention rates, tuition rates, discounting levels, and other factors.[37] But analyzing these returns is critical to ensuring that institutional spending is helping to achieve institutional goals. For instance, we have found that for most of the institutions with which we work, a dollar spent on student coaching to improve retention and completion rates generates two to four dollars in additional total tuition revenue. This return on investment opens up the possibility of reducing per-student tuition pricing.

LOOKING AHEAD

The demographics and economics of higher education are shifting in ways that potentially put them at odds with one another. The average student is less well prepared for college, more time-constrained, and more likely to be pursuing a degree online and/or through a self-directed program that requires a greater level of commitment and discipline. Meanwhile, market and regulatory pressures have shifted the focus in higher education from student access to student success. Addressing these issues in tandem will require strategic investments in support services that cost-effectively enable students to achieve their goals.

We are just beginning to see the impact of the completion and cost-containment agendas. No one knows what the future holds. But one thing is certain. As long as completing an education provides greater benefits than simply starting one, and the cost of education to individuals and institutions matters, then impactful and economical student support services will remain among the wisest investments we can make.

5

Bain Goes to College

Rethinking the Cost Structure of Higher Education

Jeffrey J. Selingo

When consultants from Bain & Company landed at the University of North Carolina at Chapel Hill in the winter of 2009, Joe Templeton was heading into the final months of his three-year term as chair of the faculty. In his cramped office filled with hundreds of books, Templeton listened intently as three Bain consultants described the work that they were about to start. The global management consulting firm, well known on Wall Street for restructuring Fortune 500 companies, had just been hired by the nation's oldest public university for a somewhat unusual assignment for a higher-education institution: find millions of dollars in savings, and fast. As in other states, lawmakers in North Carolina were confronted with a gaping hole in the state spending plan—$3.4 billion in North Carolina's case—as a result of the sudden downturn in the economy the previous fall.[1] Public universities in the state were bracing for big cuts, up to $60 million for Chapel Hill alone.[2] On campus, where administrators had already begun their work with Bain when the budget crisis hit, tensions were running high among faculty members. The 217-year-old university— with 29,137 students, a $2.49 billion budget, and 11,909 employees—was under the leadership of a new chancellor, Holden Thorp, who had just taken office the previous summer after a stint as dean of the university's College of Arts and Sciences.[3] Just forty-four at the time, Thorp was by far the youngest president among the prestigious group of research universities in the Association of American Universities, and he remained untested in a crisis. The work with Bain would come to define the early years of his presidency, for good or bad, and would make the Chapel Hill campus a forerunner in using consultants like Bain to restructure operations to better compete for limited financial resources in the future.

But first Thorp had to sell his faculty on the idea. While the chancellor remained unproven, Templeton was a fixture on campus, a thirty-five-year veteran professor of the chemistry department. Unlike on most campuses, where the top faculty representative is elected by a small group of professors, at Chapel Hill the entire faculty voted for the chair. With his important connection to the faculty, Templeton's advice and support would be key to the ultimate success of the Bain project. That first meeting in Templeton's office, however, would illustrate the difficult road ahead in bridging the divide between a change-averse academic culture and a data-driven business culture. The Bain consultants arrived in suits with a stack of PowerPoint slides. Their consultant-speak was like a foreign language to Templeton, an Iowa native who had spent his life on a college campus. Templeton knew that such an approach would likely not sit well with the seventy-member Faculty Council, the influential faculty group that was scheduled to hear the consultants' presentation near the end of the spring semester. So, over the course of several meetings, Templeton worked with the consultants on their pitch. "I gave them a completely honest assessment about how faculty would respond to the presentation," Templeton recalled. "I told them that faculty care most about their professional activities."[4]

The Bain effort at UNC barely touched any of the expenses associated with the university's academic core. By design, Bain focused only on the university's administrative operations (although the firm also studied the utilization of space on campus and the university's centers and institutes). "As soon as Bain made it clear to the faculty that they weren't going into the classroom or the research lab to tell them how to do their job, I felt it was a huge step forward," Templeton says. The Faculty Council meeting went off without a hitch. When Bain first started its work at UNC, leaders there were hesitant about involving too many people in the process for fear that it could derail the effort. But by the end, the lead Bain consultant on the project, Jeff Denneen, was persuaded that including faculty leaders early on was vital to the success of the project. When Bain later landed work at two other universities, Denneen pushed to have faculty leaders put on key committees.[5]

After Templeton's term ended as chair of the faculty, he took on a new role: leading the university office responsible for putting Bain's recommendations in place. Despite his support for the consulting firm's work, Templeton is certain he would have reacted differently if the academic side of the house had been included in the project. "I would have opposed it," he said bluntly. "There is a pretty fine sieve to get into the Ivory Tower. I'm not eager to have consultants think they are going to improve the educational efficiency of what professors do."

And there remains the major hurdle to hiring management consultants to remake colleges and universities into institutions true to their core business: academic departments and schools are off limits. Faculty members don't want outsiders telling them how much time to spend on research, when to teach, how to run their departments, or virtually anything else about how they spend their time. Faculty members see themselves at the center of the university. They share in its governance, and any critiques from outsiders about how to do their jobs differently impinges on their academic freedom. But putting such limitations on consultants severely curtails the impact they might have in helping college leaders untangle their legacy business model and rethink the cost structure of higher education over the long run. About 62 percent of expenses on a major public research campus such as UNC are tied up in education-related activities, according to the Delta Cost Project.[6] Keep those costs off the table, and presidents and trustees are left trying to stretch their dollars with one hand tied behind their backs. "We're saving them 10 to 15 percent," Denneen told me about the universities that his firm has worked with. "That's real money, but it still pales in comparison to what's left on the table in terms of academics."

CHANGING NEEDS FOR CONSULTANTS IN HIGHER EDUCATION

Consultants are not new to higher education, of course. They have been roaming around college campuses in one capacity or another since the early 1900s.[7] But because they were largely focused on discrete functional areas of the operation—usually on the business side—they often escaped the notice of faculty members, and their hiring rarely resulted in any controversy on a campus. In the early days, colleges and universities brought in outside consultants, including attorneys, accountants, and architects, for their specialized expertise to perform audits or assist with campus planning. By the 1950s, as the growth of higher education led more institutions to raise private dollars, a new breed of consultant emerged to help with fund-raising campaigns. The 1960s and 1970s saw a major explosion in the number and use of consultants, as institutions became more complex and trustees brought their corporate experience with consultants to their service on higher education boards. This is the time period when colleges and universities started to employ marketing firms to help with admissions, search firms to help them recruit top leaders, and other consultants to assist in chasing government or foundation grants and then staying on to help administer those projects and evaluate them. The passage in 1965 of the Higher Education Act, which included various grant programs to strengthen institutions, was "perhaps one of the single largest causes of the boom in the use of consultants in the smaller colleges," maintained former College of St. Scholastica president Daniel H. Pilon, who has studied the history of consulting in higher education.[8] Not only were the consulting engagements in higher education centered on specific departments or needs, but the consultants themselves were mostly one-person operations or small firms made up of former academic leaders. "There was often an assumption that if one knew enough about something or performed a particular role effectively, one could consult about it effectively as well," Pilon wrote in *New Directions for Higher Education.* The fact that the majority of consultants were former college presidents or administrators, often working in retirement, was one reason faculty and staff members seldom raised any concerns. Rather than seeing them as outsiders, they viewed them as former colleagues.

The idea of hiring a broad management consulting firm to review operations across the university was virtually unheard of on most campuses until the fall of 2008, when a global financial crisis paralyzed the American economy. The fallout from the resulting recession triggered a series of events that suggested the financial model in higher education was beginning to shift, perhaps permanently. Endowments took a nosedive. State tax revenues dropped precipitously. And the collapse of the housing market meant that families could no longer tap the value of their homes to help pay for rising college tuition bills. College leaders were suddenly faced with a confluence of problems that were larger and more complex than any one division of an institution could handle. Most of all, solving these problems was probably beyond the capacity of the tiny consulting firms with which colleges and universities had mostly worked in the past. That's when the bigger players in the consulting world—Bain, McKinsey, Accenture, and Huron—increasingly began to appear on college campuses. For years, all of these brand-name consulting firms had advised corporate, government, and nonprofit clients on overhauling their organizations to solve tough business problems. With the exception of Huron, their higher education practices were relatively small. "We never thought we needed help on this scale in the past," Thorp, the Chapel Hill chancellor, told me. "Whenever we got into trouble we always found a new way to generate revenue. But this time was different."[9]

An anonymous donor suggested that UNC hire Bain & Company and agreed to pay its fee, which the university has never disclosed. It remains unclear whether UNC would have paid for Bain's work out of its own funds given the extensive budget cuts the university was weighing at the time. "We never had to answer the question," Thorp said. But his counterparts at other universities did, and Bain's hefty fees certainly played into initial opposition to its work by faculty and staff members at the University of California at Berkeley and Cornell University. Both universities hired Bain in 2009, following its project at UNC. At Berkeley, Bain's work cost a reported $7.5 million. Cornell, as a private university, refused to disclose how much it paid Bain.[10]

Bain is far from the only player in this space, although it seems to generate the most controversy on campuses, in part because its work is so public. Other consultants, including McKinsey, Accenture, and Huron, have been hired by the University of Connecticut, the University of Wisconsin, the University of Miami, and the University of Kansas.

Huron takes a more benign approach to higher education than Bain, largely because many of its consultants previously worked at colleges (unlike Bain). "We start with respect for academics," said John R. Curry, a managing director at Huron. "They are unique scholars, and we try to understand the context of institutions."

To many in the academy, the idea of paying an outside consultant millions of dollars to save millions more was an unfamiliar concept. Faculty and staff members saw money going to consultants that could have been put toward their own research or paychecks. For faculty members, in particular, bringing in management consultants was yet another intrusion of business practices into their insular world, where ideas and mission were supposed to prevail over a singular focus on the bottom line. They worried that the consultants failed to appreciate some of the inherent inefficiencies of the higher education system, key among them tenure and shared governance. They also questioned how people with little or no experience working in higher education would be able to recommend how to restructure it for the better. Some suggested that administrators turn to experts on campus, such as in the business school. "Bain tells you broadly what to do and then leaves," said Ronald G. Ehrenberg, a higher education economist and professor at Cornell (he also was a member of Cornell's board of trustees when Bain was hired). "The university is left to make the decisions on what to do. The pressure of needing to make decisions quickly leads to processes which don't have a lot of faculty input."[11]

At Cornell and Berkeley, Bain focused solely on the business operations of the universities. Separating the business side from the academic side is not always as straightforward as it might seem, however. "The lines are blurred in some cases," Ehrenberg said. "Processing a check is clearly a business function, but faculty, especially in the sciences, feel that choosing supplies for their lab is their job."[12] As a result of Bain's work, Cornell adopted a new procurement system that limited the number of suppliers, which allowed the university to negotiate lower prices. "A preferred vendor might have a cheaper overall price," Ehrenberg said, "but not the one thing you want." This is just one example of the differences that Bain consultants discovered between the workplace cultures of academe and corporate America: faculty members have almost free rein over what to buy and where to buy it, ultimately driving up costs for the university. Most employers give their workers a few choices for a desktop computer, for example, but they don't have unlimited options. Professors, however, don't see themselves as "employees" in the traditional sense and often believe that having a choice in everything from when to teach to which textbooks to use in a course is a right of academic freedom. The critical question is at what point does limiting options impact the core academic experience for the customer—the students? At Cornell, the perception among faculty members is that new financial and purchasing systems designed to lower prices and increase efficiency (by having fewer people involved in the transaction) has added to their administrative workload, leaving them less time for other tasks, including meeting with students. "The new systems we have put in place require behavioral changes, and that has been difficult for some people to accept," said Joanne M. DeStefano, Cornell's vice president for finance and chief financial officer.[13]

Bain is often a convenient scapegoat for critics on the campuses where it worked—even for changes the consultants never recommended—because the firm's approach is such a departure from the way the universities operated in the past. "Our campus has spent two decades hiring people to solve problems or deliver new solutions," said Frank Yeary, a vice chancellor at the University of California at Berkeley. "We threw people at problems, rather than technology."[14] Over the course of thirty-six years, Bain built a $2 billion global consulting practice advising corporate, government, and nonprofit clients.[15] For Bain, universities are no different than other mission-driven nonprofits, and the higher education industry as a whole certainly is not as unique as people inside it make it out to be. Universities buy products. They supervise employees. They use technology. They manage space. But for the most part, the institutions were abysmal at tracking how efficient they were at any of those activities. "In my opinion, we had not a prayer to do this on our own," Yeary said. Like administrators elsewhere, Yeary told me that Bain was able to bring the tools, people, and experience to first find, and then make sense of, the numbers about how the administrative side operated.

While most industries outside of academe are accustomed to working with management consultants by now, Bain consultants said that the initial hesitation they encountered on college campuses was no different than the first time they walked into any company. In any workplace, the fear of the unknown is worrisome for employees. Still, Bain established a much more deliberate and extensive strategy for engaging university employees in the transformation process than it had with similar corporate projects. With business clients the size of UNC, for instance, Bain consultants would typically interview fifty employees. At UNC, they interviewed nearly three hundred; at Berkeley, more than five hundred. The goal was to address two prevailing issues present on many campuses in tough budget times: distrust of the administration and the belief that faculty members should have a significant role in making decisions. The ideal of shared governance is not unique to higher education, but the way it is practiced in academe often leads to inefficiency and redundancy because leaders find it easier to simply delay decisions. As a partner at Bain, Denneen said he helps choose the leaders who make the decisions, but "we are very clear on our decision roles and rights, and what we are allowed to do and what we are not allowed to do as individual partners." In higher education, he told me, "there's not a lot of clarity about roles and rights. Faculty choose to participate in some decisions, and ignore others. It's completely ad hoc and depends on how much they care. The fear of faculty backlash really tamps down on the ability of presidents to change universities."

COMMON DRIVERS OF INEFFICIENCY IN HIGHER EDUCATION

Like any large company, universities have legacy enterprise resource planning (ERP) software systems spread across campus that manage everything from payroll to paying invoices. In higher education, these extensive databases have grown up over time in fits and starts. At research universities, in particular, individual units (departments, schools, and colleges) are mostly autonomous, so they built their own bureaucratic structures through the years to support their operations. On top of that infrastructure, add the organization of the central administration, and you can see how redundancies happened in both people and technology. As a result, some campuses have a patchwork of computer systems that aren't well connected, or the capabilities of the software aren't being fully utilized. Until Bain arrived, it was as if the universities were storing their bills and receipts in shoeboxes. Administrators and professors had plenty of assumptions about where they were wasting money, but few of them had hard evidence. Bain helped provide that evidence.

When you first glance at Bain's final reports from its projects at Berkeley and UNC (Cornell did not release its report), the savings recommended by the consultants probably wouldn't surprise anyone who has worked at least a day in higher education. Perhaps it's the extent of the savings that would be alarming. Bain zeroes in on the biggest cost drivers in an organization. According to Michael Mankins, a partner in Bain's San Francisco office who worked on the Berkeley project, the firm expects to extract savings from a client that are equal to ten to fifteen times its fee.[16] That is why Bain's engagements have been limited so far to big research universities. The firm's philosophy and high fees work only on a large scale (the minimum Bain engagement costs around $2 million).[17] Although Bain ended up recommending different cost-cutting strategies at Berkeley, Cornell, and UNC, it identified common inefficiencies and barriers to change across all three campuses in four broad categories, detailed in the following subsections.[18]

Unneeded Hierarchy and Complexity

Bain's final report for UNC was 107 pages long. On page six, under the headline "UNC-CH has a complex org structure," appears a ten-color organizational chart with 380 little boxes, each representing a department. Over the years as the university grew, and due to efforts to promote long-serving employees to some sort of managerial role, the organization's complexity expanded exponentially. Bain found that some areas of the university were ten layers deep in management. More than half of the supervisors had three or fewer employees reporting to them. Nearly two hundred supervisors had only one employee reporting to them, which resulted in small departments and frontline workers who were too disconnected from decision makers.

The situation at Berkeley was similar. There, the average manager supervised about four employees. Like at UNC, more than half of the supervisors had three or fewer employees reporting to them. To give you an idea of just how deep the organization was at Berkeley, in one level of management that was four steps below the chancellor, there were 525 supervisors earning $57.6 million in salary and benefits. This dense layer of management created significant bureaucracy and often paralyzed the organization by tying up key resources in endless meetings. Denneen dubbed it the "swirl": an almost endless loop of meetings that resulted in more work but no decisions. At UNC and Berkeley, Bain recommended that the universities reduce the number of supervisors and flatten the organization structure by moving closer to industry benchmarks: six to seven employees per supervisor in "expertise-based functions," such as human resources and finance, and eleven to thirteen employees per supervisor in "tasked-based functions," such as custodial and food services.

A vast hierarchy, of course, is a function of a complex institution. Colleges and universities operate like mini-cities: they are inherently complex organizations. In addition to managing undergraduate and graduate programs, the biggest and most complex of universities operate hospitals, hotels, retail outlets (including bookstores), museums, restaurants, athletic facilities, power plants, patent and licensing offices, extension programs, and publishing arms. The problem is that most universities devote too much of their limited management resources and capital to these peripheral operations and could be better served by having these services provided by outside parties. "You have to look at your strategy and then start lining up your activities and budgets and see where you're putting money, but not adding value," Denneen said.[19] Most of these peripheral operations fail to align with the core mission of most universities: service, teaching, and research. Universities fail to recognize their shortcomings because they benchmark themselves against the wrong institutions, he said. They too often judge the efficacy of their operations against their peers in academics or research, not the institutions that are at the top of the pack in terms of efficiency or results.

Bain's work seems to support a series of reports in recent years that attribute part of the cost problem in higher education to "administrative bloat." A 2010 study by the Goldwater Institute found that from 1993 to 2007, the number of administrators per one hundred students grew by almost 40 percent, while the number of employees engaged in teaching, research, or service grew by only 18 percent.[20]

Fragmentation and Redundancy

Complexity breeds redundancy because as a university grows every new entity feels entitled to its own support structure. Take information technology as an example. At UNC, there were seven different e-mail platforms running on campus. By consolidating them into a single platform managed by the central technology office, the university expected to save $1 million a year. At Berkeley, Bain found that the university had more than nine hundred computer servers, spread throughout more than fifty buildings on campus, because every school or department decided it needed its own storage solutions. The result: the average server on campus was only half-filled (leaving plenty of underutilized server capacity), some had limited backup in case of a disaster, and nearly all of them were located in buildings where the cooling systems were not designed for servers, meaning that energy usage was costing the university more than necessary in those facilities.

Not only was technology fragmented and redundant in these individual units (schools and departments), but so were employees, especially in technology, finance, and human resources. At Cornell, there were nearly one thousand department-level administrators who performed multiple functions, including traditional tasks for human resources. At Berkeley, Bain discovered some sixty units that had four or fewer full-time employees in human resources and finance. Another eighty-nine units had four or fewer full-time employees in technology. Because such critical functions are distributed throughout campus, front-line employees, having few colleagues, lack sufficient back-up support and also find it difficult to become experts in any single area. As a result of Bain's recommendations, Berkeley created a shared services center, which combined in one place certain human resources, finance, research administration, and information technology work that had been performed in many different locations across campus.

Lack of Standardization

When the Bain consultants arrived at the University of California at Berkeley, the institution owned nearly eighteen thousand laptop and desktop computers. Of those, no single manufacturer provided a majority of the machines. Dell had the largest share on campus with 40 percent, but the university owned seven different desktop models and six different laptop models from the company. The same was true for other manufacturers: Apple had 20 percent of the market with six different models; HP and IBM, together, provided less than 15 percent of the computers with twenty-two different models combined. And then there were various other brands floating around campus, including Sony, Compaq, and Gateway.

As noted earlier, faculty members thought it was well within their purview to request any computer they wanted. But with Berkeley buying so many different makes and models, the university was unable to negotiate volume discounts with any of the manufacturers. "Essentially every computer cost them more than it should have," said Mankins, who led the Berkeley project for Bain. And it wasn't just computers. "Imagine paper," Mankins explained to me. "Just white printing paper, seven different suppliers, twenty-four types per supplier. Over one hundred different types of printing paper and they don't have a contract with anyone. You could go to the local Kinko's and buy paper if you wanted." As a result, the university was paying anywhere from $28 to $101 for a box of five thousand sheets of paper. All across the campus, Bain consultants found the university was paying radically different prices for the same product, from a dozen ballpoint pens (92 cents to $11.93) to a case of microtube racks for science labs ($74 to $115).

For an individual professor, saving a few bucks on a case of microtube racks might not seem like a big deal, but when combined with higher prices on hundreds of other products and when scaled across the entire university, it meant millions of dollars in potential savings a year. In 2008–2009, for instance, Berkeley used eighteen thousand different vendors. The top 10 percent of vendors accounted for 90 percent of Berkeley's spending. In other words, the university was spending just a little money with thousands of different suppliers, about $32,000 per vendor according to Bain's calculations (well below the industry benchmark of $140,000 per vendor). The same was true at UNC. The Chapel Hill campus had more than twelve thousand vendors it paid in a typical year, but spent less than $2,000 annually with three-quarters of them. Bain suggested that all three universities find opportunities to implement "strategic sourcing agreements," which would limit choices of suppliers for employees, but also dramatically lower prices that the institutions paid for products and services.

Misaligned Incentives

Most of all, administrators on the three campuses say that Bain's approach helped shift their strategies on cost cutting from those that most higher education institutions utilize whenever times get tough. The problem is that these oft-used methods fail to address structural cost issues and hinder a university's ability to improve its overall performance. Among the traditional solutions that Bain identified as problematic:

- *Across-the-board cuts.* Such actions might seem fair because everyone shares in the sacrifice, but they penalize units that operate efficiently, reward those that are inefficient, and encourage everyone to stockpile resources, knowing that one day they will need to give something back.
- *Hiring freezes.* Such actions are typically temporary (so they don't solve long-term budget shortfalls) and are not aligned to overall strategy.
- *Salary actions.* Wage freezes, pay cuts, and furloughs have a negative impact on morale and recruiting.
- *Academic program cuts.* Shutting down programs or reducing budgets impacts the core mission of the university, and when done in the heat of budget cuts, is typically not aligned to long-term strategy.
- *Student service cuts.* Such actions have a negative impact on student morale and admissions, both keys to revenue.

Because they are so often used, these actions offer a time-worn path of little resistance for campus leaders. At universities, there are few incentives to make decisions of any significance. "There's all these penalties for making the wrong decision, but no cost at all for not making a decision,"

Mankins said. "So over time, people choose not to make decisions at all. They are talented debaters. Everybody has some reason for why it doesn't work. So the pace of decision making is slow." This lack of accountability, Mankins said, extends to annual performance reviews of employees. At Berkeley, nonacademic employees were reviewed using a five-point performance ranking system (1–2—below expectations; 3—meets expectations; and 4–5—above expectations). Of the thirteen thousand employees in the system, only *seven* received a 1 or 2 rating. With little differentiation between high performers and low performers, there was no incentive for employees to do better, and there were few consequences for failing to do the job. "For professors, Berkeley has these robust standards to get tenure, but it's a stretch to even say they have standards on the nonacademic side," Mankins said.

THE FUTURE FOR MANAGEMENT CONSULTANTS IN HIGHER EDUCATION

In the corporate world, Bain engagements focused on organizational transformations run upward of eighteen months and cost between $8 to $10 million.[21] Given the concern at universities about the cost of consultants, campus administrators typically look for shortcuts in the process to lower the price. As a result, the overall impact of the work is also sometimes limited. Administrators at Cornell and Berkeley say one mistake that they made was failing to assign more full-time employees to work alongside the Bain consultants, so that when the engagement was over and the consultants left campus, the cost-saving projects that were identified could more quickly and easily get under way.

In the end, the Bain consultants emphasize that they don't control the ultimate outcome—their clients have the right to accept or reject any of the recommendations they make. Indeed, it is extremely rare for any client to realize all the potential savings identified. Generally, clients see about 60 to 80 percent of the suggested savings. Public universities might potentially yield even less given the realities of their missions, politics, and regulations.[22] Berkeley, Cornell, and UNC estimated it would take years after Bain left their campuses to achieve the cost savings identified by the consultants (all three universities operate Web sites outlining their progress to date):

- Berkeley (http://oe.berkeley.edu): After Bain identified $112 million in projected annual savings, a campus steering committee recommended pursuing five areas that could result in $75 million in yearly

savings by fiscal year 2016. For fiscal year 2012, the savings were
expected to be $25.4 million.[23] Yearly, the Berkeley vice chancellor,
said that getting "early wins" after Bain left was particularly important because the campus needed to know it could succeed at undertaking such massive changes. In four months, the university reduced
the number of middle managers by nearly four hundred, a 25 percent reduction.

- Cornell (http://asp.dpb.cornell.edu/): When the university hired Bain
  it was facing a $135 million deficit in subsequent years, even after
  officials had cut $70 million from the budget. Bain was asked to find
  an additional $100 million in annual savings.[24] As a result of sev-
  eral actions taken in the wake of Bain's work, the university expects
  annual savings of $75 to $85 million by fiscal year 2015.[25]
- University of North Carolina (http://carolinacounts.unc.edu/): Bain
  recommended changes to save the university up to $161 million a
  year.[26] By 2012, three years after Bain's engagement had ended, the
  university completed more than 70 of the 139 projects identified by
  the consultants, saving nearly $50 million annually from permanent
  state dollars.[27] Those projects included consolidating the university's
  information technology services and restructuring the procurement
  process for office supplies. Another $30 million in annual savings is
  expected by fiscal year 2014.[28]

While those cost savings are significant, they remain a small fraction of
the multibillion-dollar budgets of those three universities. It took a financial crisis of epic proportions to finally persuade these universities that the
time had come to rethink the bureaucracies that had been haphazardly
constructed over decades thanks to growing revenue from state and federal coffers, endowments, and student tuition. Perhaps more significant for
these campuses, given the insular culture of academe, was that they realized identifying the cost savings and building the case for change would
be almost impossible without independent help from the outside. "Many
staff and faculty members have a very negative or cynical attitude about
pronouncements about big changes from high campus officials," said Tom
Schnetlage, the chairman of the Berkeley Staff Assembly. "There's a long
history of campus task forces producing reports containing long lists with
significant recommendations for change, where nothing ultimately happens."[29] While Bain raised concerns among some faculty and staff on campus, Schnetlage says the idea that university leaders were willing to engage
with a consulting firm like Bain was a clear signal that the recommendations might actually go somewhere this time around.

A focus on streamlining the massive support functions of a university is a good start for leaders looking to stretch their dollars. But stopping there is like a homeowner cleaning out the closet of a cluttered house without touching the rest of the home. If the homeowner doesn't perform a top-to-bottom cleaning, it's easy for the clutter to find its way back into that closet. Higher education has a long history of mission creep, of constantly wanting to do more. As a result of the Bain work, these three universities attempted to put processes in place to prevent the bureaucracies they trimmed from emerging again. But that behavior is difficult to monitor without a culture of deep trust and accountability. UNC, for instance, consolidated the licenses that various schools had held for course-management software and put them under the control of the central information technology department. But a year later, after the central department informed the schools that it was switching to a different product without ever getting their input, the schools took back control, wiping out any savings.[30]

Exposing only the business side of the university to outside examination also feeds a long-held impression among faculty members that the administration is bloated. In some cases, that is what consultants might indeed discover. At UNC, Bain consultants found that administrative support per student grew faster than academic support between 2004 and 2008 (6.6 percent versus 4.8 percent).[31] Even as their administrative operations were being examined by Bain, all three universities were looking for ways to streamline their academic infrastructure. But those efforts were small by comparison and did not involve independent consultants. I asked every administrator I interviewed at Berkeley, Cornell, and UNC if they could ever imagine bringing Bain (or a firm like them) to inspect the academic side. They all expressed doubts. "It would be peculiar for management consultants to look at academic disciplines," Andrew Szeri, dean of the graduate school at Berkeley, told me.[32] Even a few Bain consultants agreed with that assessment. But how about behaviors that add to the institution's costs but are clearly on the line between academics and business? Take space utilization as an example. As on most campuses, Bain found that classroom space at UNC was not being used to its full capacity. In its final report, the firm suggested several potential options: standardize class times, have the registrar centrally schedule more classes, increase the number of classes in off-peak hours, and utilize seminar spaces in residence halls.[33] But the UNC faculty viewed allocation of space as an academic issue, and administrators argued that it wouldn't lead to any immediate savings because the buildings already existed on the campus.

For right now, the work of management consultants is limited to large campuses with big budgets because it is easier to find inefficiencies in $3 billion budgets than $500 million spending plans. But Bain consultants find the financial problems facing higher education to be widespread. An analysis done by the firm in 2012 found that one-third of all U.S. colleges and universities face financial states significantly weaker than before the recession. Another quarter of colleges find themselves at serious risk of joining them. In the paper, Bain laid out steps that colleges of any size can take to put their financial house in order.[34]

Bain's engagements at Cornell, Berkeley, and UNC were clearly an expansion of the traditional uses of consultants in higher education. For the first time, one firm diagnosed problems in multiple units. But Bain's work also exhibited that limits remain, namely the academic culture. Bain consultants told me on several occasions that academe is not as different as faculty members like to think it is. In the corporate world, consultants help a company structure itself to maximize profits. In the nonprofit world, the goal is to structure institutions so that their work is better aligned with their mission. But it is possible that the missions of research universities are not even comparable to other nonprofits. Their research mission is always evolving. Discoveries take time and there is always a desire to do more, to explore new emerging fields. Even as Cornell was addressing its long-term financial health, it was the successful bidder in a high-profile competition to build an applied science campus in New York City. Cornell's president, David Skorton, told me that it was a once-in-a-lifetime opportunity, largely paid for with a $350 million gift to the university.[35] But management consultants might see a new campus as a detour to becoming a more focused university.

As I talked with faculty members about Bain, I was often reminded of just how resistant academic culture can be to ideas from outsiders. There was the silly stuff. One professor complained to me about how he could no longer buy his favorite pens at Staples because of the procurement changes his university implemented as a result of Bain's work. There were also serious concerns. Templeton, the UNC professor and former faculty chair, said he came to greatly appreciate the approach of the Bain consultants. But even he described the cultural divide between those who have lived and worked in higher education and those who haven't. "I'm still not sure they understand that Holden [Thorp] has so many constituencies," Templeton said. He recalled a meeting he had soon after he was appointed to his new position to lead the implementation of the Bain recommendations. "A business person turned to me and said the key to my success would be power, process, and people," Templeton said. "I said this is a university. We'll see how far we get with pushing, persuasion, and pulling."

EPILOGUE

In the spring of 2011, the University of North Texas at Dallas put out a request for proposals to build the university of the future. The eleven-year-old institution, which gained independent status within the University of North Texas system in 2009, had grand ambitions to grow from a tiny two-building campus with two thousand one hundred students to a major urban university with sixteen thousand students by 2030.[36] Its idea was to seek outside help in "creating a national model of best practices for emerging universities."[37]

Mark Gottfredson, a partner in Bain's Dallas office, received the request and thought it would be a "significant opportunity" for the firm's growing interest in higher education.[38] "It's not often that you get the opportunity to build a university from the ground up," Gottfredson told me. But after discussions with North Texas officials, he realized they couldn't afford Bain's fees for such an engagement. Still, he didn't want to lose the chance to develop ideas that could be used on paid projects in the future. So, in September 2011, Bain agreed to provide $1 million in pro bono consulting services. Over the next five months, in conjunction with the university's president, a team of five Bain consultants surveyed twelve hundred high school students in the Dallas area, talked with more than a dozen local employers, and visited colleges elsewhere that were built for the local economies, including Georgia Gwinnett College and California State University at Channel Islands. They developed a framework built on "three pillars"—high quality, low cost to students, and expanded access—and in early 2012, presented their model to UNT–Dallas administrators and the seventeen-member Commission on Building the University of the 21st Century:

- *Year-round track.* The academic calendar consists of three fifteen-week trimesters with classes that are centrally scheduled in multipurpose facilities. Gottfredson said that the typical college classroom is used only 40 percent of the time. Bain projected that 60 percent of the overall cost savings at this new university would come just from better utilization of space.
- *Hybrid.* Bain considered a fully online university, but concluded that a hybrid model would better serve the more traditional eighteen-to-twenty-two-year-old student that the institution was interested in attracting (in addition to adult students). The face-to-face instruction would account for an hour a week, with online meetings for two hours each week.
- *Teaching focus.* Faculty members would focus most of their time on teaching up to twelve courses a year and spend no more than 10

percent of their time on research and publishing. Gottfredson said they settled on this model after talking to faculty members who disliked having to research and publish to get ahead in academe. "The faculty will come on with the knowledge that teaching and student success is important," he said.

- *Academic programs.* Only a few majors are offered, largely tied to the local economy, including business, education, criminal justice, and information systems. Bain suggested that everyone take the same first-year classes to create the idea of a cohort.
- *Cost.* As described, the model would cost $6,000 a year. If students are on schedule to graduate within four years, they will be reimbursed for their final two trimesters. For students who receive Pell Grants and work on campus, the out-of-pocket expense would be about $2,000 annually. Bain projected that by 2020, UNT–Dallas could produce three thousand graduates a year at a cost of $30,000 each, compared to $60,000 for a public university, and $150,000 for a private university.

Ultimately, the Board of Regents of the University of North Texas will consider which of Bain's ideas to adopt. But as the firm's recommendations became public in the spring of 2012, professors on the Dallas campus raised objections, as did a few members of the 21st Century Commission, even the president of the university himself. "We're going to have to tweak some things to have academic integrity," the outgoing president, John Ellis Price, told me.[39] He wants to add more face-to-face meetings in hybrid courses and more research time for faculty members. I pointed out that both ideas would add costs to the bottom line and make the university look more like any other. "It may add a few hundred here and a few hundred there, but we'll still have a lower-priced degree," he said. Maybe so, but the tension between academics and the bottom line obviously exist even at a new university, like North Texas.

Whether the University of North Texas at Dallas emerges as *the* model of higher education for the twenty-first century or not, the ideas that Bain championed as part of its design could be keys to reducing costs in the future. In recent years, Texas has become a focal point in the debate over the public role in higher education, as the governor and state lawmakers have slashed appropriations, questioned the productivity of faculty members, and pushed institutions to think in new ways about controlling costs. The UNT–Dallas plan is an outgrowth of that debate, and higher education leaders elsewhere should expect the same pressures to come to them (if they haven't already) as states and families will have less and less ability to deal with rising college costs. Perhaps Bain's ideas for UNT–Dallas are out-liers for a conservative higher education industry. Maybe the majors are too narrow and train students for a job, rather than educating them broadly. Maybe the teaching load on the faculty is too much. Maybe Bain is assuming too much of the ability of high school graduates in the Dallas area, only 16 percent of whom leave school prepared for college-level work.[40]

The question remains if Bain's work at North Texas or at the three research universities can be applied elsewhere by college leaders who are looking for advice but don't want to pay the big fees that come with consultants. While Bain maintains that it customizes its work depending on the client, many of its broad recommendations can be applied across colleges and universities. That means that Bain's work could have far-reaching consequences in the higher education cost debate without its consultants ever showing up on campus.

6

Unbundling Higher Education

Taking Apart the Components of the College Experience

Michael Staton

T he consensus that the U.S. higher education system is the best in the world has taken a dark turn. Many public figures have brought attention to the state of higher education recently. Mark Cuban, a famed entrepreneur and recipient of lucky money from the first Internet boom, wrote a viral blog post about higher education's unsustainable cost structure. Robert Reich, the proudly liberal former secretary of labor under Bill Clinton, wrote a piece called "The Commencement Address That Won't Be Given," in which the message to graduating seniors was "You're f*cked."[1] America's most august news show, *60 Minutes*, spent half an hour profiling PayPal founder and vocal higher education critic Peter Thiel.[2] Though Thiel can be contrarian in his views, many are starting to repeat his thesis that blind faith in college degrees has led to an irrational market, and this irrationality has encouraged runaway spending on an education system that is providing too little value at far too great a cost.

What's the problem? In *Disrupting College*, Clayton Christensen and his coauthors argue that the escalating cost problems stem from institutions simultaneously operating three fundamentally incompatible types of business models.[3] A university has to be a research facility that collects specialists to diagnose problems and find solutions, serve students and add value to their lives and to their ability in turn to add value to the labor market, and facilitate the network of organizations, athletics programs, faculty, graduate students, and alumni. According to Christensen's years of work on the subject, no business can sustain more than one type of business model in the long run due to administrative overhead and other inefficiencies. Yet American universities are expected to juggle three while trying to simultaneously control costs and increase quality. Christensen judges that no policy or leadership reform could effectively control costs and increase quality at once within the existing model, as the operating complexity of the institutions within the current system is simply too great to manage.

Contradictory demands on our nation's schools have contributed greatly to, if not been the outright cause of, much of our problems. School is simply a destination to get an education—a bundle of services that over time has become increasingly complex and expensive to provide. The consequence is that, instead of competing on educational outcomes, schools compete on the metrics that have defined the most successful schools—student-faculty ratio, endowment size, selectivity, graduate programs, research funding, renowned scholars, and regarded publications. The result has been an arms race in which nearly all institutions have increased their spending to invest in many directions at once. What started out as a relatively simple bundle has become a complex and expensive one, and society has begun to question its value as we reach a point where students no longer need a physical destination to get much of what an education comprises; they can now get at least some major parts on the Internet.

Many industries have embraced innovations that have swept over the economy, boosting productivity, lowering prices, and improving quality; however, most colleges and universities have chosen to batten down the hatches, finance more of the same, raise tuition, and hope for the best. Entrepreneurs now see an opportunity that institutions are willingly leaving open. But institutions and entrepreneurs are not predestined to be at odds. There is a way forward in which nearly everyone can emerge as a winner, but it requires the fast application of the principles of survival for organizations that are being disrupted and disaggregated.

The coming unbundling will not only take apart the three business models that Christensen argues cannot effectively exist within an organization, but emerging efforts will likely go much further, breaking up the student experience into its component parts.

The great unbundling of higher education is not likely to cause the immediate dissolution of college and thus a collapse of our education system. The introduction of competition is, however, likely to create a sense of urgency for finding new models of delivery and management techniques, creating new roles for faculty, and innovating around alternative means of facilitating postsecondary education.

This competitive pressure will not apply equally across all of the value propositions of an education. On the contrary, some are prime targets for insurgent providers with new, low-cost models, while others will be much more difficult to provide online or in any format other than a four-year residential college experience. The goal of this chapter is to identify the various value propositions that colleges and universities currently promise to their students, identify which of those are easier and harder to unbundle, and describe some of the ventures that have emerged to provide a small part of the value of higher education. The point is not to argue that these entrepreneurs will replace the existing system, only that their presence suggests a market opportunity that higher education institutions would be wise to respond to.

WHAT IS COLLEGE? TAKING A LOOK AT THE COMPONENT PARTS

What is college? I define it here as a *packaged bundle of content, services, experiences, and signals* that results in an education with both inherent and transferable value to the learner. The end goal of this educational package is to prepare learners for the job market, as well as to instill the knowledge, procedures, and values that make individuals effective at navigating, succeeding within, and adding value to our society. The bundle is outlined here in figure 6.1, in the order in which each component can be replaced by technology (the darker the box, the more replaceable the component).

Part of the goal of figure 6.1 is to help define a common language around the value propositions of higher education. A favorite question (especially of entrepreneur Burck Smith, author of chapter 10 in this volume) is, "What is a quality education?" I don't know that this is a fair question of such a complex bundle. It is better to ask, "What is quality performance feedback?" Or, "How do we define a quality affiliate network?" Only when we get specific with which value proposition we are discussing will we truly be able to define quality or benchmark and compare prices. (As someone who was trained to teach in the classroom, I spent much time studying and using Bloom's taxonomy.[4] If anyone feels inclined to call this "Staton's taxonomy," do feel free.)

The Content Loop

A large piece of what we refer to as "education" is tied up in what I call the *content loop*: lectures, readings, notes, and studying. The professed goal of the content loop is to move the learner to a minimum standard of understanding. The content loop involves three coherent jobs:

- *Content authoring and production* includes creating lectures, gathering readings, and some aspects of professorial publishing. Anytime an instructor is putting energy into producing materials that need to be read, watched, or otherwise interacted with, they are in a sense recreating content for each class.

FIGURE 6.1 **The component parts of higher education**

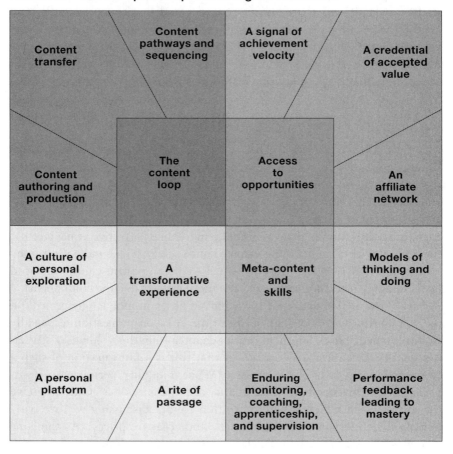

- The traditional format of *content transfer* is a lecture and discussion, assigned readings, and texts. This is an imperfect format for the transfer of information from instructor to pupil. The process of content transfer is starting to move into electronic delivery in myriad forms.
- Content is rarely delivered without a broader context. Rather, it is woven together into a course or series of courses that create a pathway to understanding. Instructional design is an emerging profession that acknowledges that the *content sequencing and pathways*—that is, the packaging of content—needs more deliberate practices than most assume.

Not too many of us would argue that the lecture-and-paper model of learning is the best we can do. The benefits of technology in the content loop are clear: scale, automation, and the personalization of pace, media, and modality are all not only possible but already under way.

Access to Opportunities

The value proposition of education that seems to matter most to the majority of students (and policy makers) is access to opportunities. Our higher education system, in theory, fills the job market with prepared knowledge workers. Postsecondary institutions have three tools at their disposal:

- *The signal of achievement velocity*, representing some combination of aptitude and motivation, is basically interpreted from *U.S. News and World Report* rankings on selectivity. There is an admissions tournament, and the brightest high school students are thus let into a hierarchy of institutions, about which society seems to assume a certain trajectory of achievement and success—for example, those who get into Princeton will, on average, outpace those who get into Texas A&M.
- School is not just about the admissions process: it adds value with the education it provides. *A credential of accepted value* communicates a certain rigor and minimum expectations about graduates' skill sets and knowledge base. So while Texas A&M may not beat out Princeton in the admissions game, its degree holders in engineering may have more value than those who majored in "softer" subjects at Princeton.
- *An affiliate network* enables access to opportunities through a set of institutional relationships as well as the facilitation of the near-complete acceptance and due treatment of its members. Institutions often directly create relationships with alumni and employers who continually find graduates fit for the jobs they have open and frequently access recent graduates.

The conventional wisdom has typically been that higher education and access to opportunity are one and the same. However, tying graduates' future job prospects to institutions that see job preparation as an ancillary purpose seems ill fitting and inefficient. Technology is disrupting this part of the higher education value proposition—finding information about individuals is becoming easier on the Internet, specialized software enables massive processing of candidates, and individuals are increasingly able to signal their own value to the market with alternative signaling methods.

Metacontent

While the content loop is all about information transfer, there's a deep agreement that much of the value of "teaching" is not strictly about the transfer of information. Instructors serve as a major touchpoint from a complex system that intentionally or unintentionally imparts "metacontent" valuable in a democratic society and to our labor market. The transfer of metacontent takes place in three ways:

- *Models of thinking and doing* include how to present ideas, speak in public, engage in individually driven discovery, conduct research, perform analysis, and write effectively.
- Though often inconsistent, indirect, and with prohibitively high faculty-student ratios, institutions create an environment where relationships based upon *mentorship, coaching, apprenticeship, and supervision* are sometimes actively facilitated but often spontaneously develop across age groups.
- Most institutions attempt to provide accountability structures, incentive systems, and other opportunities to give *performance feedback*. For trades, there are exit exams, and advisers often have to sign off on a student's coursework. Upper-level courses often require students to practice some form of work with a greater degree of mastery, under the assumption that most graduates are ready practitioners of, well, *something*.

In the end, while the content loop is important, the qualities we most value in the college-educated are encapsulated in the idea of a supervised "coming of age." It is the metacontent we really value. We want productive workers, active citizens, and members of society fluent in fundamental cultural understandings and practices.

Personal Transformation

At least within the dominant narrative, one of the priceless values of getting a college degree is the inherent personal transformation that takes place as a consequence of being in a residential college for four years. While this traditional trajectory is no longer the typical college experience, it is nonetheless the inspiration for much of the value of college, and is enabled in three ways:

- A *rite of passage* is a relatively unique series of experiences that create a common bond between participants, often regardless of time, and allows individuals aware of the brand to make assumptions about another graduate's experience.
- Most decisions to get a degree are not centered on "learning." For undergraduates, they're often based on the promise of moving from

blue-collar or hourly wage work to white-collar careers with upward trajectory. For graduate degrees, the decision to attend is often a career reinvention. For this, students seek a *personal platform* that serves as an accepted staging ground to move to a different career trajectory.

- In the undergraduate context in particular, the student experience is set up as a community of people who are coming of age and need a *culture of personal exploration*. The iconic "undecided" major is popular for a reason: in the United States we feel that most eighteen-year-olds are not equipped to make decisions about their life's career track. They should be able to test out ideas, disciplines, and communities of practitioners before making up their minds.

While policy may be focused on the concept of access to opportunities, middle- and upper-class families, as well as those in a mid-career rut, are buying a personal transformation.

WHICH OF THESE SERVICES ARE (IR)REPLACEABLE?

For convenience and effect, I now lay out in more detail the services currently provided by a college experience, as I see them, in order of their "replaceability" by fragmented, simplified services on the Internet. In figure 6.1, we move from the darker-colored, easily replaced services to lighter-colored services that would be rather difficult to replace with technology. I will illustrate market entrants that could serve as alternative service providers for the specified services and what traditional higher education institutions should do to prepare, react, survive, and thrive in a world that is challenging their current models. One of the great ironies of the coming disruption is that schools spend most of their time focused on the services that are the most easily replaced. It is likely that their first response to competition would be to retreat into focusing on the less tangible aspects of the college experience.

Many of my examples are defined by my own experience and view into the world, which is wildly tainted by the ecosystem of innovation in Silicon Valley. It is perhaps Silicon Valley's own hubris that leads me to believe that what is true here and in my sector (emerging technology companies) will thus be true for the rest of the world.

THE CONTENT LOOP

1. Content Authoring and Production

Easily replaced, easily embraced. With the rise of inexpensive and accessible content production tools (particularly video and interactive presentation), the winds of technological change are blowing in favor of the individual expert as a content producer. Almost anyone can make his own Web site, textbook, or video series. Many a teacher and professor has spent endless hours "reinventing the wheel," creating her own content. However, moving forward, nonexperts will be curators of content rather than producers.

As a baseline, the first area to really shake up the ecosystem may be interactive textbook providers, as they are on the verge of reinventing content as we know it. In perhaps the biggest example, Apple announced a content production software package for interactive textbooks, as well as a special place in iTunes for these interactive textbooks called the iBookstore. Three of the country's biggest textbook producers—Pearson, McGraw-Hill, and Houghton Mifflin Harcourt—have agreed to partner with Apple on iBooks 2.[5]

It's not just the textbooks that are being delivered through technology, however; it's the entire course package. Apple has also sponsored iTunes U, a section of iTunes dedicated to lectures, since 2007. Udacity and Coursera were both born out of Stanford courses that managed to attract one hundred thirty thousand learners worldwide at no additional cost to Stanford, a phenomenon now known as *massive open online courses* (MOOCs).[6] Coursera just took the early lead by announcing partnerships with twelve additional campuses, including Caltech, Duke, and Johns Hopkins, offering nearly one hundred courses that have enrolled six hundred eighty thousand students internationally; it also just raised $22 million from the world's most elite venture capital firm, Kleiner Perkins Caufield & Beyers.[7] This confirms that the leading experts at the leading institutions will get into the content loop game, not leaving it to publishers.

Increasingly, learners are also consuming content produced by other students. OpenStudy is a network of learners discussing problems and helping one another. Users can earn special distinction for answering questions quickly or with great frequency, and students can also "follow" their favorite contributors.[8] Quizlet now has 17 million learners creating study materials for one another. Memrise, founded by world memory champion Ed Cooke, of *Moonwalking with Einstein* fame, just released an iPhone app.[9] For every company mentioned here, there are many more providing similar services. There is nearly a mass movement of companies that are trying to make learning content a peer-to-peer phenomenon. While some of these will die off for lack of revenue, and others will be acquired and bundled into some other set of services, the idea of crowd-sourcing content creation directly to and among students is here to stay.

Perhaps the biggest societal impact thus far has come from the Khan Academy, a nonprofit with over $6 million in funding, including a contribution from the Bill & Melinda Gates Foundation. The video series, created by Salman Khan, has allowed practitioners to experience what many call the *flipped classroom*, the idea that lecture and content delivery can now be done outside the classroom, and the classroom can now be devoted to higher-order activities. While Khan's work has typically focused on K–12 education, he has been critical of higher education quality, particularly the coupling of content delivery and assessment that predominates at colleges.[10] And Khan is just a pioneer; a company called Educreations just raised a significant first round of investment to allow "every teacher to have their own Khan Academy."

The idea that professors will need to create, select, curate, or author their own course content is coming to a close. The low-cost delivery of remedial, introductory, and general education courses is already being enabled through technology, as embodied by companies like StraighterLine, which provides access to coursework and assessment on a subscription basis for $99 a month. Even hard-to-find courses like rare languages and occupational training courses are also delivered through the Internet with near ubiquity. At some point, our postsecondary system will realize that unbundling content production will allow valuable instructor time to be shifted to working on higher-order tasks with students.

2. Content Transfer: Delivery, Monitoring, Assessment, and Remediation

Easily replaced, easily embraced. Much of what we think of as school involves a content transfer—for example, students taking notes from lectures and completing the assigned reading. Given advances in technology and changing student preferences, the lecture-based classroom with simple readings can no longer be the student's primary experience. Content transfer will be accomplished through rich media—video, games, text, and interactive graphics, diagrams, and illustrations. This opens up two distinct possibilities: adaptive learning and the flipped classroom.

More important than rich media are sophisticated programs that can efficiently move students through content and ensure that all students are meeting a minimum standard of knowledge and comprehension. Content will have various programs running behind it, enabling instructors and others to monitor progression through content and assess competency. It will also include automated monitoring (the injection of small questions to ensure that learners are progressing with the content), assessment (quizzes that ensure a minimum level of retention and understanding), and remediation (the additional content assigned to learners to make up for any shortcomings in that understanding and retention). Thus, we can move to a self-paced and competency-based system of education. This type of system, especially when owned by one piece of software, is referred to as an *adaptive learning platform.*

There is also the possibility of an unbundled adaptive learning platform. On the assessment side, services like ProctorCam, a startup out of Boston, have found ways to verify the identity, focus, and integrity of the assessment according to data captured from simple cameras included in computers currently sold. Services like these get around the need for human proctors in online assessments. Western Governors University now uses Web cams to proctor exams remotely, providing the hardware to students when they matriculate.[11] These kinds of technologies will eventually become "plug and play," allowing more and more schools and individuals to create their own adaptive learning platforms that guide learners through a content loop.

Higher education should embrace this movement by allowing students to learn basic content and go through their general education courses online, freeing up instructors to focus on more advanced courses and focus classroom time on higher-order comprehension, analysis, synthesis, and forms of project-based learning.

3. Content Sequencing and Pathways

Hard to do well without significant authority. Difficult to individualize without personalized data sets. Currently unchallenged. Should stay core through course design and degree requirements, but needs dramatic improvement through technology. In theory, school offers coursework in pathways—roads that lead to an end result—that takes the learner through a sequence that builds understanding and mastery in the face of increasing complexity and breadth. Again, this is based on the assumption that those defining curriculum pathways were the leading accessible authorities, but this is no longer true. Many instructors will thrive as a curator of content loops and building blocks; others will relegate this to the apps that will provide adaptive sequencing and pathways.

Students will have easy access to curriculum packages that are more constructivist, provide scaffolding, and have a tighter alignment to either the standards of the system or the job market. Like in Plato Learning and Rosetta Stone, the sequencing and pathways will often be embedded in an entirely bundled content loop provider. Other times, the pathways themselves will be a service of aggregating and making sense of all of the content.

In the realm of traditional degree granting, Austin Peay State University (APSU) built and launched Degree Compass, a course recommendation engine that attempts to make course selection like getting books on Amazon or movies on Netflix. "We've got a pretty strong assurance that we're able to steer students toward courses they will be successful in," says

Tristan Denley, the Provost of APSU, "better than they're able to steer themselves."[12] Private companies are also in the "course selection" game. Services like MyEDU are working on similar capabilities.

Higher education should invest in more thoughtful sequencing and pathways in two ways: (1) show closer links to advancing competency and mastery over interdisciplinary domains, and (2) more closely align programs to the needs of the job market. Utilizing technology platforms to achieve this, perhaps even allowing the technology to own it, is likely.

ACCESS TO OPPORTUNITIES

4. A Signal of Achievement Motivation and Velocity

Easily replaceable. Web services should be complemented with individual coaching and even become a core part of the curriculum. More often than not, graduates are finding work in fields where they are expected to learn on the job, and their academic programs had little to do with the skills and knowledge they need in their career. In this instance, a degree is a signal to the job market that corresponds more closely to motivation, socialization, and learning capability than to previous competency.

"20 Under 20," a program developed by Peter Thiel and Founders Fund, an investment firm in San Francisco, gives $100,000 to recipients to "stop out," or opt out, of college to pursue ambitious projects that may lead to significant advances across different industries. The Thiel Foundation actively markets the program as being only for the world's most precocious minds—under twenty years of age—in STEM (*science, technology, engineering, and mathematics*) areas. It receives hundreds of applicants, making its filtering process equivalent to that of a highly selective university. Even more impressive, nearly all of the applicants are trying to leave the most selective universities to pursue the fellowship, making it the world's most selective filter *on top of* the world's most selective filter, like the Rhodes or Marshall scholar programs.

While 20 Under 20 is not an online service, what makes alternative signals potent in an online world is the speed at which you can look up other signals and dissect what they mean. Elite memberships, application programs, test scores, and more are all just a click away and verifiable to boot. As the narrative of success regarding college dropouts increases, and stories about unemployable college graduates continue to echo, people may start to see how easy-to-access signals of achievement velocity can provide much of the value of a college degree.

Higher education will ultimately need to embrace these emerging online signals of achievement velocity, perhaps including the art of online signaling, as part of their programming. In the end, students graduating with a degree should be more capable of assembling an online portfolio of signals than those not pursuing a degree.

5. A Credential of Accepted Value: Fundamental Understandings and Estimated Competency

Challenging to replace in certain circumstances, but easily replaced in others where visualizing skill sets or normalized assessments are common. Also should be complemented with individual coaching and even become a core part of the curriculum. Despite the importance of signaling achievement velocity, the postsecondary degree is still based on the notion that the credential represents some estimated level of competency that employers can use to determine expectations about what individual students know and their corresponding capabilities. Given the variation in content and quality across the education system, people are starting to acknowledge that a diploma sometimes does not correlate tightly enough to demanded skill sets. An executive at the startup Minerva University calls the current accreditation bodies a "guild system designed to limit supply."[13] Given the difficulty of becoming a degree-granting institution, the expense of accessing a degree-granting institution, and the ease of creating signals, portfolios, and profiles online, the credential of accepted value is finding other forms.

Many potential employers seeking specific skill sets already require additional signals such as a portfolio of work, or the completion of exercises during the recruiting period. Students already spend significant time preparing for the recruitment process in fields such as engineering, architecture, biotech, graphic design, and animation. As people develop their identity across the Web, the need for an abstract piece of paper as a credential of accepted value is rapidly diminishing. Given that much of what students are willing to pay for is access to opportunities, it's no wonder that investors are very interested in how to disaggregate the credential from the rest of the college experience.

The Internet is introducing alternative signals that demonstrate skills and proficiency in specific domains of interest. Whether it be assembling prior work, answering challenging questions for others, or gaining a reputation among networks of users, these online signals have already become core to finding employment opportunities in domains like software engineering. For example, both StackOverflow and GitHub have individual profiles where you can see work samples and other bits of valuable information when assessing someone's qualifications. Similarly, designers can now be evaluated by a quick view of their online portfolio. One of the most popular, Dribbble, is home to thousands of designers. Designers can follow one another, and their work can be "loved" by the community of users. Many employers, including myself, use Dribbble as a way to filter and scout design talent, rendering attendance of design school relatively moot. Entelo, a company started by Jon Bischke, aggregates these online profiles and allows potential employers to efficiently search through potential candidates, enabling them to explore what Bischke calls the "reputation graph" across many different sites that have online profiles.

Degreed is a site where students can enter their coursework, irrespective of the school or accreditation, and the service will compute a score of estimated competency. Similar to a Klout score, it can supplement a résumé or job application. Employers can look up anyone. Degreed was one of the winners of the Open Badges competition, and is made up of esteemed and notable names in the education space, including the founders of Zinch and Flat World Knowledge. In the words of its founder, David Blake, Degreed is out to "jailbreak the degree."[14]

It is easy to imagine a future where employers can identify prospective recruits or screen applicants through an easy-to-use assessment system. LearnUp.me is just such a system. Funded by notable venture capital firm Greylock, LearnUp provides assessments sponsored by large employers looking for basic employees. If reported performance on these assessments becomes a credential of accepted value, then it may contribute to additional questions about the value of an expensive degree.

Similar to the prior signaling discussion, higher education needs to reformulate existing coursework into projects of authenticity and significance, ensuring that the students amassing skill sets have the opportunity to demonstrate those skills in real-world settings and in ways that are captured and communicated to employers more clearly.

6. An Affiliate Network and Community

Easily competed against at low cost. Remains immense opportunity for higher education, though needs a renewed focus. Leveraging emerging affinity networks will be important. Many colleges and universities, as well as private primary and secondary schools, include membership in their affiliate network as part of their value proposition. Ideally, students create deep and lasting relationships with a network of outstanding peers and active alumni who are resources later in life. Building a network no longer requires a shared geographic location. Peer learning networks that are tightly integrated with a learner's interests and career path can be found through social networks with a distinct culture of finding and sharing. Learners can easily gain access to peers and peer mentors through the Internet.

In an interconnected world where signaling is easier than ever before, organizations are building exclusive affiliate networks simply off of organizational culture. Sandbox is just such an example. Sandbox has only six hundred fifty members worldwide. It has strict criteria for entrance: members must be referred and under thirty. Simply put, it is trying to be the affiliate network for the most ambitious and clever young minds on the planet. One of the founders, Nico Luchsinger, has even claimed that the company is building a model of education for the future: "We didn't think we were building something in education. But the more it develops, the more we realize we are. I'm sure there will always be a role for some types of schools, but we can already feel a lot of the value of programs like an MBA being irrelevant." The price of Sandbox, by the way, is free.

Tech incubators also have the properties of affiliate networks. Y Combinator, the most well known of the incubators, is famous for the ways in which it engages its "alumni." The incubators' ability to recreate an affiliate network (as well as many other value propositions discussed in this chapter) has led them to be called "the new graduate school."[15]

The question becomes, then, how can the value proposition of an affiliate network hold for universities in the face of such stiff competition? If they do choose to compete, they will need to do a much better job of priming their entrants on the cultural norms of the affiliate network, and they will need to instill within each individual the norms of the network. There also must be ongoing consequences for not holding true to those norms. More appropriately, postsecondary institutions should try to take advantage of, and place their students into, the rise of these varied affiliate networks.

Higher education should focus heavily on ensuring that their affinity networks with the advantage of location are as active as possible. In-person networks could, if organized and supported well, provide more value than those with no physical location or assets. To maintain this advantage, institutions should focus heavily on student culture, peer-to-peer learning, and challenging projects that bring students together in ways unlikely to occur through the Internet.

METACONTENT AND SKILLS

7. Models of Thinking and Doing

Hard to do well. Currently unchallenged. Should stay core but needs dramatic improvement and true focus. Content delivery is more than "stuff to learn" that will ultimately be assessed by a test. Those with greater understanding of pedagogy are quick to point out that buried within boring lectures are models of thinking and doing that are transferred from the instructor to the student. Derek Bok notes that faculty nearly unanimously agree that "teaching students to think critically is the principal aim of undergraduate education."[16]

The most common of these models is making logical arguments with data and examples. If a class is modeled well, students learn through exercises, problem sets, and individual and collaborative projects. As students move into near-graduate-level work, they begin to understand the rules and formats of knowledge exploration, creation, and sharing, and how to navigate complex bodies of knowledge to gain insights, solve problems, and even lead people. Instructors, especially at higher levels, are primarily focused on illustrating and giving students feedback on their comprehension of these models of thinking and doing.

While retention and comprehension can be easily measured through computer-based assessment, it is more difficult to measure application, analysis, synthesis, and evaluation (from Bloom's taxonomy, a standard text for teachers and instructional designers). Dissecting assumptions, defining motivations, and analyzing context are all processes that can be modeled and taught, both directly and experientially. While trained and clever assessment writers can carefully craft multiple-choice questions that approach these higher-order processes, it's likely that learners need to actively discuss and write, as well as apply knowledge to creative tasks and projects that further hone these procedural skills.

Yet, "critical thinking" and other models of thinking and doing are not mysterious schemas that can be transferred only in the context of the classroom. First, students can learn metacontent from collaboration with and feedback from their peers. They can also access the world's best thinkers and doers through video. Organizations like TED and the Aspen Institute are some of the first "viral content" on the Internet among the educated. New "startup schools" like Altius Education, Fidelis College, and University Now all are approaching metacontent through various rubrics and evaluation techniques, and—like most startups—are trying to identify ways to do so in scalable ways with technology and workflow innovation. However, assessing and providing qualitative feedback on such models of thinking and doing will remain difficult for the foreseeable future.

Higher education should quickly embrace this trend by using examples of work by the world's best experts, allowing the Internet to have a larger voice in providing demonstrations of thinking and doing. Instructors can then move to focus on the direct relationship with the student, becoming coaches through more thoughtful quantitative and qualitative feedback and using rubrics and evaluations that lead to student mastery.

8. Mentorship, Coaching, Apprenticeship, and Supervision

Despite some efforts, difficult to replace. Should be an area of focus and expected defensibility. If everyone can learn from the Internet for free, why not just do that? As it turns out, it's hard and it's boring. While the Internet has proven useful at both helping people stay connected with those they already know and connecting them with opportunities (applicants to employers, single people to potential matches, etc.), the authentic asymmetrical relationships (mentorships, apprenticeships) created among peers, faculty, staff, and alumni will likely prove more difficult to recreate. While those striving to move up in the world have a strong motivation to find mentors, in general potential mentors have no drive or time to find and filter new young people to mentor. While not impossible, disintermediating mentorship may prove to be a substantial design challenge.

The idea of mentorship in higher education also usually connotes some kind of expertise transfer from a subject matter expert. Yet now there are services like Cramster and Quora where you can pay additional money or credits to ask a subject matter expert to answer specific questions. This kind of one-on-one subject matter help is even being unbundled by bundled providers. Southern New Hampshire University unbundles the role of faculty for its competency-based online program through a subject matter expert who can intervene or help out on request. There's a "learning guide" that helps to set up pathways through content and coach on motivations and strategy. University Now and Altius Education separate the grader from the instructor. InsideTrack provides "success coaching" to students going to school and has demonstrated retention outcomes.

Because the mentorship function of higher education will be difficult to disrupt, traditional higher education should focus on this as a source of comparative advantage and invest more heavily in facilitating and providing mentorships, coaching, and apprenticeships with existing faculty and staff, as well as community members and alumni. Moreover, students need to be coached in how to extract value from these mentorships. Within the shared environment of academia, the "pay it forward" value of helping, coaching, and advising needs to stay front and center, but with a focus on outcomes for students.

9. Performance Feedback Leading to Mastery

Basic knowledge comprehension easily replaced; complex skill assessments nearly impossible. Extreme opportunity for institutions to refocus and own. Despite the worst habits of lecture-based courses, students gain from much coursework the enormous value of getting extensive qualitative feedback on their performance of complex skills. Part of the mythology of getting an undergraduate degree is a strenuous senior seminar or capstone project. In graduate school, there's the dissertation board. An ideal college experience is imagined as being pushed and evaluated against impossibly high standards by sages in robes.

While feedback on simple math or code problems is relatively easy to do at scale, feedback on speech, presentation, writing, and communication is markedly difficult to automate or scale. Again, it does not mean it cannot be done; recently, Tom Vander Ark, formerly of the Gates Foundation but now a partner at Learn Capital, opened a competition to create an essay-grading algorithm that would outperform the average professional grader. The winning design outperformed all but one.[17] While it's easy to imagine assistive algorithms that increase the speed and output of grading, I believe it will prove more difficult to give complex performance feedback that provides insights into improving writing past a basic essay structure. But that's just writing—there are infinite forms of media and output that learners may be asked to tackle. The more complex and human the task, the more qualitative the feedback needs to be, and the more important interpersonal communication becomes as part of the feedback cycle to approach mastery.

The rise of incubators in the entrepreneurial community is largely based on the metacontent and skills bundle, and they provide very rigorous performance feedback leading to mastery. They have consistent check-ins where mentors apply high standards and give detailed verbal feedback about the state of their business plan, product, progress to date, and all the other myriad concerns of starting a company. This is why even though the entrepreneurs give up around 5 percent of their new venture for almost no money, they find the exchange incredibly valuable and more than worth it.

Like mentorship, providing feedback on higher-order skills is an area of comparative advantage for traditional higher education. Institutions should embrace the fact that technology is getting better at delivering and assessing simpler content and skills and focus more of their attention on the feedback leading to mastery.

A TRANSFORMATIVE EXPERIENCE

10. A Rite of Passage

The Internet cannot replace, but other services may provide alternatives. Extreme opportunity for institutions to refocus and own. While many students think of a residential college experience as a newfound freedom, part of the value proposition to parents is providing their children with a supervised coming of age. An unbundled education lacks much of the cultural and social experience surrounding the education itself and has no mechanism to trigger the increasing responsibilities and gradual maturity that are central to the college experience. Embedded in this supervised coming of age is a rite of passage.

Short of reviving *Second Life*, I have trouble understanding how the Internet replaces this. Currently, there are various internship sites, and it may be possible that through a series of well-designed travel experiences someone can compete with this aspect of the university.

Outward Bound serves as a rite of passage for many young adults. In cultures where military experience is near-mandatory, participation in military training and service also serves as a rite of passage. Low-budget travel can often create bonds within participants. If you've been hosteling in Spain, you're likely to immediately feel a connection with someone that's done the same. DevBootcamp has managed to be so rigorous that alumni feel bonded in special ways; Shereef Bishay, its founder, even claims that "everyone cries at least once" because the experience "pushes everyone to their limit."[18]

Higher education should focus on its core strength here. What helps students come of age? Events and curriculum that build character, provide opportunities for leadership, and force student to interact with different cultures and ideas.

11. A Personal Platform: Career, Character, and Impact

The Internet cannot replace, but other services may provide alternatives. Extreme opportunity for institutions to refocus and own. When people want to get an education, particularly postgraduate professional degrees, they are looking to jump-start a career, change career paths, or accelerate an existing career path and redefine the existing career ceiling to a higher one. This value proposition seems necessarily tied to some period of time to use as a personal platform. Society and the job market seem to understand and accept going to school as an appropriate time to retreat from the job market to focus on oneself and redefine a career trajectory.

It is difficult to imagine unstructured and unbranded blocks of time (in formal programs or not) legitimately replacing the personal platform value of higher education. The main barrier here, though, is the strength of the signal and credential. If entrants in the signaling or credentialing space, such as Degreed or Entelo, were to demonstrate improved signals to the job market, the idea of using travel, retreats, or unstructured educational programs to spend the time block necessary to replicate a personal platform seems more possible.

The rise of "hacker academies" has formed alternative personal platforms for aspiring software engineers. DevBootcamp is one of several, and those wanting to reinvent themselves as Web developers can apply, enroll, and shoot out ten weeks later with a job in a whole different profession. For those trying to change roles or programming languages, it's a legitimate way to spend ten weeks and get placed in one of dozens of cool Bay Area tech companies. Hacker academies beg the question: if the personal platform needs to be an in-person experience, perhaps it can be condensed, dropped in price, and more aligned to a career outcome?

A personal platform is difficult to define and was nearly omitted in favor of the component parts already explored. It certainly contains prior value propositions of an affiliate network, a signal of achievement motivation and velocity, and a credential of estimated competency. However, any analysis of the marketing of degree-granting programs and the motivations cannot omit that there are a few additional services and experiences related to their career direction and trajectory that people are buying when they choose to pursue an educational program.

12. A Culture of Personal Exploration

The Internet cannot replace, but other services may provide alternatives. Extreme opportunity for institutions to refocus and own. An implicit value of higher education is the interaction with people from different cultures and subcultures. It is assumed that going through this experience with a diverse set of people who all work together to share their progress toward personal transformation creates a positive feedback loop. The externalities of people sharing their ideas, values, experiences, desires, motives, ambition, and trajectory creates a culture of personal transformation. Where else but college can you get information about different passions, hobbies, and career paths from the fliers on one elevator wall?

Things like study abroad, cultural events, student activities, and even partying are all laid out as a series of transformative experiences. This social and internal transformation may be impossible to achieve on the Internet, but it may be possible through alternative in-person programs. Unschool Adventures—a company founded by Blake Boles, author of *Better Than College*—runs travel programs targeted at those not going to college so they can use travel as the mode of personal exploration.[19] The cultural acceptance of a "gap year" similarly emphasizes travel as a mode of facilitating a personal transformation.

A more adult, mid-career version is Singularity University, which is not a university at all. It is a kind of camp held at NASA Ames in Silicon Valley that selectively admits accomplished professionals who want to change the world. The University has an introduction to the world's hardest problems, sets forth grand challenges, and lets students choose a challenge surrounded by peers and mentored by some of the most accomplished people anywhere. These students then work together to propose a project that has the potential to make an impact on more than a billion people within a decade. It offers no credential and costs a decent sum, yet has twenty-two hundred applicants for only eighty slots.

Higher education should focus on its core strength here. What give students a personal transformation? Events and curriculum that build character, provide opportunities for leadership, and force students to interact with different cultures and ideas.

CLOSING COMMENTS

The taxonomy I lay forward is meant to establish a conversational framework for institutions, entrepreneurs, and investors. What value will you provide? Which value propositions should be bundled? Which ones are best provided through technology? Which are valuable to consumers, students, parents, employees, and employers, and who should be paying how much for what?

While everyone in higher education should feel the stiff new competition, they have time to learn to compete. Online services do not put everyone out of business. While pundits and thinkers have long suggested that the Internet will "disintermediate" retailers, this has not been the end of retail as some have hypothesized; indeed, most of the famous retailers we knew of fifteen years ago are still performing alongside, or even within, a mature online retail industry. Physical retail stores have competed and held market share by moving toward unified consumer experiences and an intense commitment to quality regarding fit, look, returns, and brand identity and loyalty. Similarly, in-person education will adapt and find its positioning in the focused but total experience it provides learners.

Yet, unbundled services on the Internet promise to put downward pressure on costs. First, if a consumer can assemble the entire value at a reduced cost, this creates a price ceiling of competition for the whole industry. While this will turn out to hold true, how and when it will play out is unknown. Second, and more importantly, if institutions that currently manage the entire bundle can start allowing technology to work its magic and see themselves as providers atop whatever can be conveniently and cheaply accessed online, they will be able to focus on the quality of those services best left to in-person environments at lower cost. Whether they pass that lower cost on to students is another issue entirely.

7

Classes for the Masses

Three Institutions' Efforts to Create High-Quality,
Large-Scale, Low-Cost Online Courses

Ben Wildavsky

In the years he spent as a professor of political philosophy, Greg von Lehmen's interests centered on such questions as how careful readers should understand the concept of *phronesis*, a Greek word often translated as "practical wisdom." This academic pedigree might at first glance seem incongruous for a senior leader of the University of Maryland University College (UMUC). After all, UMUC is among the world's largest open access universities, delivering most of its classes online to nontraditional students, many of them members of the U.S. Armed Forces. A profile like this might not seem to augur well for an institution's quality and intellectual seriousness. Von Lehmen, who spent several years as provost before recently being named head of external relations and initiatives, admits that he was a little dubious himself. Despite his leadership position at the university, he wondered whether an asynchronous online course could really be, he says, "as rich as a face-to-face class."[1]

Von Lehmen decided that the best way to answer the question to his satisfaction was to personally teach an online class. And after teaching Introduction to Political Science, he was persuaded. To be sure, he doesn't dispute that online courses sometimes lack the energy of the best discussions in the best brick-and-mortar classrooms. But he is convinced that student learning doesn't have to suffer: "My conclusion is that I think you can teach a demanding online course that produces learning outcomes that are as good as you could have for a face-to-face class."

At a university where students badly want to acquire the kind of practical wisdom that von Lehmen studied in his own scholarly work, his assessment of the quality possible in online classes is encouraging. But what does it really mean to develop a high-quality online course, particularly one that can be delivered at scale and at modest cost?

The question is important for both pedagogical and practical reasons; it underlies much of today's discussion about improving productivity in postsecondary education. Traditional models of developing and delivering courses—each stage of which typically runs through an individual professor—are expensive, requiring faculty time, physical space, and a fixed daily and yearly schedule in which classes can be offered. Colleges recoup those costs by charging a relatively modest number of students—those who are physically enrolled—relatively high tuition (extremely high in the case of many private institutions) to attend and receive credit.

This slow-to-change cost structure represents an enormous opportunity for UMUC and other technology-driven providers during an era of growing demand for affordable access to postsecondary degree programs. Placing instruction, content, and assessment online gives colleges the potential to realize significant economies of scale by attracting tens of thousands, or even hundreds of thousands, of students. Such numbers permit providers to recover the cost of course development and infrastructure while driving down the cost of delivery—and potentially the price to students.

There is, of course, no single model of online course delivery. Course design and methods of instruction can vary considerably. So does the context in which online classes are offered, as well as the cost model on which edu-entrepreneurs build their efforts. At the same time, thoughtful online educators seem to have several things in common in their efforts to harness technology in the service of effective pedagogy: they pick the curriculum carefully and are comfortable with a high degree of standardization, they pay close attention to methods of keeping large numbers of students engaged, they train instructors thoroughly, and they use data systematically to track student learning and to monitor student participation. This chapter profiles three online course providers: UMUC, the University of California's "UC Online" initiative, and the much-discussed Silicon Valley startup Udacity. Drawing largely on site visits and interviews with academic leaders and administrators at those institutions, it aims to shed light at a micro level on several noteworthy efforts to provide high-quality, low-cost classes without regard to barriers of time and space.

UNIVERSITY OF MARYLAND UNIVERSITY COLLEGE

While much is made of the brand-new institutions that populate the landscape of online higher education, UMUC has a relatively lengthy pedigree. It grew out of the University of Maryland's night school for adults in the

1920s and was formally established in 1947 as an independent institution called the College of Special and Continuation Studies. It became University College in 1959, then UMUC in 1970. Along the way, it was a major provider of classroom education to U.S. military personnel in Europe, then in Asia, and eventually in Iraq and Afghanistan. As of the late 1990s, when the university first began offering online courses such as Accounting 220, a large majority of its enrollment continued to be overseas. But the balance has now shifted to the United States, where about fifty-nine thousand of the institution's ninety-two thousand students are enrolled. Along the way, the Internet revolution transformed the core teaching activities of UMUC. While there are still some brick-and-mortar classes, particularly overseas, 75 percent of enrollments are now online. Little wonder, then, that a visitor to one of the university's central administration buildings encounters no students. Instead, the polished office complex just inside the Washington Beltway—a few minutes from FedEx Field, home of the Washington Redskins—is filled with deans, assistant deans, academic advisers, librarians, curriculum designers, technology specialists, student services staff, student recruiters, and more. Any university's back office and governance operations might be found in such a structure, but this businesslike edifice is also where much of the academic substance of UMUC's 120 academic programs gets hammered out.

Given its relative longevity, UMUC could be viewed as the Establishment of American public online education, akin to Great Britain's hugely influential Open University. It boasts a large online enrollment, and it has proven staying power (the mysterious resignation of its president in the spring of 2012 notwithstanding). It enthusiastically embraces its mission of providing access to underserved students. Von Lehmen boasts that UMUC awards nearly as many bachelor's degrees to African Americans each year as all of Maryland's historically black colleges and universities combined. It has thrived by pioneering models that remain too rare in traditional American higher education but have become increasingly common in fast-growing online institutions, both public and for-profit.

Designing the Program Systematically

Compared to most universities, UMUC takes an unusually systematic and centralized approach to what is taught and how it should be taught. The process is lengthy. For a just-completed curriculum redesign, the university worked with an employer and alumni advisory group to decide what program outcomes were needed. Next, it reverse-engineered to meet these goals: it mapped ideal programs, developed program and course "outcome guides," and then designed courses and created teaching guides for each class. Worksheet-like program and outcomes guides provide a concrete way to track what students know and can do. They ask what core concepts and skills learners need to acquire to demonstrate proficiency in program and course outcomes, what key assessments will be used to provide evidence of student proficiency, and what students should be able to do as a result of each course and program.

Cynthia Davis, longtime head of academic affairs for UMUC and now acting dean of the undergraduate school, says this kind of practical, systematic mapping of content, assessment, and outcomes is particularly helpful for nontraditional students. Members of the military, for example, often proceed slowly through degree programs because of deployments and other responsibilities. This means that a predictable sequence of courses with standardized content is crucial. "We want a student who takes a course in Heidelberg to have essentially the same course as one in the United States, because it may be a prerequisite for a course they take here," Davis says.

Using Technology More Effectively

Once curriculum has been designed, how should it be taught? As an early adopter of online teaching, UMUC quickly learned what is now conventional wisdom—that simply videotaping classroom lectures is ineffective. The challenge was to harness technology as a tool for more effective pedagogy. Thus, from the beginning of its online efforts, UMUC needed to find a balance between academic experts and instructional designers. (Instructional design is a subspecialty in online higher education that has grown so popular that one can earn a master's degree in the subject.) On the academic side, subject matter experts include the course creator, peer reviewers, and curriculum specialists. They work closely with a team, led by an instructional designer, that includes an editor, a Web specialist, a graphics expert, and often a programmer. It was this combination that contributed to the explosion of online course offerings in UMUC's early days, says Sharon Biederman, who heads the university's Office of Instructional Support Services. "What distinguished UMUC was our understanding that while we had faculty who were experts in their subject matter, they were not necessarily experts in converting that from a lecture to something that was not only full of content, but something that was interactive."

Ensuring Active Faculty and Student Participation

This quest for interaction—for engaging students in their online classes—is a preoccupation among UMUC faculty and administrators. They aim to ensure that students become engaged in three principal ways—by interacting with course content, with faculty members, and with one another.

Typically, course designers try to engage students in course content through a process known as *scaffolding*. A student first reads class material; next observes a chart, table, or video (often called a *learning object*); then interacts with the course content in some way; and finally is quizzed on the material either through a self-assessment exercise or a graded assessment. In a criminal justice class, for instance, a forensics lab unit begins with students viewing a slide show depicting examples of different powders, both licit and illicit. To help students understand how a narcotics task force tests substances for drug content, they are next shown a variety of objects, including a scale, lab instruments, and powder in plastic baggies. Using virtual tools, they are able to drag each bag of powder onto the scale, clip off its top using scissors, dump the contents into a bowl, and weigh the sample. Students then watch a video showing a lab technician applying different chemicals to each sample in order to see the chemical reaction that occurs and determine what the substance is.

When students' exposure to academic content comes in the form of watching taped lectures, UMUC course designers endeavor to keep learners connected by breaking up those lectures into bite-size chunks. "The faculty always say, 'Let's put this thirty-minute video in,' and the instructional designer will say, 'No, we have about a ten-minute attention span here, and maybe even five minutes,'" observes Biederman. "If you just have a talking head, there's a limit to how much people can stand it." Instead, a thirty- or forty-five-minute lecture might be broken into segments of three to five minutes, with questions from the professor interspersed for students to keep in mind as they watch. Students then move to the "conference" section of the course—an asynchronous discussion forum that is accessed through the learning management system (LMS). The professor might throw out a question that brings together some of the video clips the students have watched, then moderate the discussion with students. UMUC class sizes are relatively small—the maximum number of students is around thirty-two—and the university makes clear to instructors that they are expected to interact about academic content with students on a weekly basis, and to respond to any student questions within twenty-four hours.

This isn't always easy to accomplish, according to Richard Schumaker, UMUC's director of Faculty Professional Development and Training: "Often instructors who are from more traditional environments where they lecture . . . may be used to coming in and doing office hours, but they may not be so comfortable [with such regular, direct interaction]." The role of an online instructor is really about facilitating rather than teaching in a traditional sense, he adds. To ensure that instructors are meeting their obligation to maintain a regular classroom presence, UMUC keeps tabs on how often faculty are participating in class discussions. The LMS tracks instructors' interactions and sends a report automatically to program directors each week. "There may be legitimate reasons [for extended classroom absences], but it's sort of a tripwire for us," says Alan Carswell, who runs a popular, two-year-old master's program in cybersecurity as chair of the Department of Cybersecurity and Information Assurance at UMUC's Graduate School of Management and Technology.

The requirement for active participants extends to students as well—indeed, at UMUC and other online providers, the role of student-to-student learning is significant. This makes pedagogical sense, course designers say. "If you think of a face-to-face classroom, you're not only learning from the faculty member—you're learning from the person next to you," says Emily Medina, an instructional designer in UMUC's course development unit. Just as instructors are required to interact regularly with students, students are required to respond to comments by other students several times a week, and their interactions are expected to be more than perfunctory. Instructors use a grading rubric that grades students on whether their comments advance the discussion in a useful way. Placing a priority on students' interactions with one another is an important learning tool, Biederman notes: "There's lots of research showing that students retain information better if they get it from another student than if they read it."

Tracking Data and Activity

A frequent theme in conversations with UMUC administrators is the importance of tracking data on student engagement, academic success, and degree attainment. The university knows, for example, that students who have completed a college writing class before enrolling at UMUC are much more likely to persist in their studies. It knows that regular attendance in the online classroom—just as in its brick-and-mortar counterpart—correlates with higher grades. It also knows that if a student isn't actively involved in the online classroom within the first week, von Lehmen says, "that's a real danger sign."

But academic leaders would like more sophisticated capabilities that would allow them to track students' online activity even more closely. UMUC is in the midst of choosing a new LMS that will allow it to do simple but important things like e-mail a student if he hasn't signed on for the first few days of class. More significantly, an improved LMS should allow the university to make use of "learner analytics" to see how often students look at individual assignments, what they do in response to each assignment, and how much they learn as a result of these actions. UMUC is also work-ing on a predictive analytics project, funded by the Gates Foundation, that will use data mining to try to understand which factors are most closely associated with success in college. In addition, it is working with Carnegie Mellon University's Open Learning Initiative to develop adaptive learning techniques. These generate immediate data on students' progress and tailor lessons to their particular strengths and weaknesses in subjects like biol-ogy, statistics, and computer literacy.

Providing Intensive Faculty Training

For those interested in teaching at UMUC, faculty training is elaborate, beginning with a mandatory monthlong orientation program, which cov-ers both theory and practice of digital learning. New instructors have to set up a class of their own, with guidance from seasoned facilitators, and also observe a couple of other classes to see the kinds of exercises and techniques other faculty members use to engage students. Once they begin teaching, all undergraduate instructors have faculty mentors who are charged with observing their classes, providing support and guidance, answering ques-tions, and so forth. Those who struggle are assigned coaches.

During their training, they're taught about the importance of bringing themselves to life in the online classroom. "If you don't do that, your class-room is flat," says Kim Stott, executive director of UMUC's Center for Teaching and Learning. Concrete steps for an instructor to establish a per-sonalized identity might include not just posting a photo and capsule biog-raphy, but also communicating to students exactly why she is drawn to the subject of the class. When these kinds of efforts are paired with regularly engaging students about coursework, instructors can achieve a pleasant paradox of the online classroom: greater personal attention than is some-times possible in a regular course. "The bright spot is that a face-to-face class can be dominated by someone and the shy people can hide in the back. Online I can make everybody talk," Davis says.

She and others also note that online students—particularly the nontra-ditional students who predominate at institutions like UMUC—respond particularly well to being given a roadmap telling them exactly what they need to do to learn material and then demonstrate mastery. This can mean avoiding free-form class discussion. In the case of Davis's Modern Brit-ish Literature classes, she finds that she has to moderate discussions care-fully. "You have to be much more explicit with students. You can't just say, 'What do you think about this poem?' You have to give them more directive questions . . . [but] you can get them to the same places."

Weighing Cost Versus Scale

To those who believe that online delivery will yield quick and easy cost savings, Greg von Lehmen is quick to offer a number of contrary observations. For one thing, UMUC faces the significant expense of building and maintaining an information technology infrastructure good enough to create a rich online experience. There is the need to maintain, in online form, many of the student services found on a conventional campus—advising, a library, a helpdesk—not to mention the usual spending on data warehousing and administrative overhead. Training and ongoing support to online instructors is also considerable: the university's Center for Teaching and Learning trains over six hundred adjunct faculty each year. In addition, the university must factor in future uncertainty over how many active-duty troops will be serving in Europe and Asia, where it operates under contract with the U.S. Department of Defense to offer degree programs on military installation. Its classes operate on approximately a break-even basis, and would be difficult to downsize immediately.

All this said, von Lehmen is convinced that the online model is compelling financially for the reason usually cited: scale. UMUC was able to expand by seven thousand students over the past five years with an increase in operating costs of just $92 million, plus some modest capital investment. This is "remarkable," von Lehmen observed at a February 2012 meeting at the American Enterprise Institute.[2] He noted that the enrollment growth is the equivalent of creating a reasonably sized traditional campus—but at much lower cost. Buying computer servers and hiring additional staff costs a lot less than erecting new buildings, he points out. What's more, the adjunct instructors who are often hired by large online providers—particularly when they are expanding quickly—cost much less than traditional faculty. "While online education is not inexpensive," von Lehmen says, "it's less expensive than brick-and-mortar education—the costs at the margins are lower."

Von Lehmen notes that although UMUC receives very little support from the state, it is able to charge tuition that is highly competitive with that of other Maryland institutions (each of which sets its own tuition). At $250 per credit hour, UMUC's tuition, with fees, is the second lowest in the Maryland system, after Coppin State University. "Our cost structure is such that we are able to operate at scale and at a lower comparable tuition rate," he says. "More people should be doing what we're doing because there are lower costs per margin. There's no near-term end to this fiscal exigency for higher education in the United States—the model's got to change."

Offering a Different College Experience

The advent of massive open online courses (MOOCs)—for which students typically pay little or nothing and receive no course credit—may increase this pressure to change. For now, UMUC is exploring how MOOCs might be used as part of a competency-based degree program, in which students are tested on and given credit for prior learning. This is a very different model from most online programs, including MOOCs, and UMUC is just beginning to think about how a full MOOC-driven, competency-based degree program could be created. UMUC has shown itself to be open to other kinds of cost-saving partnerships: in September 2012 it announced that it will award transfer credit for certain classes given by StraighterLine, a for-profit that offers online general education courses for $99 a month.

Heading to the elevator after concluding a series of interviews, von Lehmen returns to the question of how well the online classroom can match the experience of face-to-face teaching and learning. Wearing his political philosopher's hat, he muses about Aristotle's view that the soul and the physical body cannot be separated. The implication is that there are inevitably limits to the kind of learning experience students can have via the Internet. "There's something about the college experience of being together, at least for some part of the experience, that is really valuable."

But he reiterates his view that a different qualitative experience need not mean different learning outcomes. And online classes don't need to replace traditional courses in all cases to be used more widely in blended instruction classes. This will happen, von Lehmen is confident, not only because of the need for cost cutting in an era of budget austerity, but because technology is improving fast enough to offer compelling ways to meet the demands of new generations of digital natives.

UC ONLINE

If UMUC's history, size, and financial success make it an incumbent in the online education marketplace, the University of California's online initiative, UC Online, is working hard to gain a toehold just within its own ten-campus, two hundred twenty-thousand-student system. Launched with ambitious declarations in 2010, the online project has encountered numerous challenges in a system renowned for its quality but not necessarily hospitable to change.

The online program was given a high-visibility public introduction in a 2010 op-ed by Christopher Edley Jr., dean of the Boalt School of Law at the University of California, Berkeley. "Online education could become central to the University of California," wrote Edley, a former Clinton administration official, in the *San Francisco Chronicle*.[3] The university's brick-and-mortar model is inadequate to UC's future needs, he declared, citing the dire budget problems that then, as now, threatened the university's excellence. Even if the budget gap could be eliminated, the university would remain unable to accommodate growing numbers of qualified students seeking educational opportunity.

Edley's solution: an innovative pilot project creating twenty-five to forty online courses. Ensuring quality as good as that of on-campus classes would be imperative, he stressed, noting that the quality of the more than one thousand online classes already offered by UC's extension schools is mixed. Under the new program, the on-campus experience would be unaffected, while a whole new crop of tuition-paying UC-eligible students would have the opportunity for an academic experience from which they would otherwise be shut out, he contended. If the pilot succeeded, some might ultimately have the chance to earn a transferable associate's degree. "Fully online undergraduate programs in selective institutions will happen," Edley concluded. "The question is when, and led by whom. The leadership should come from the world's premier public university—which belongs to California."

Facing Early Challenges

Two years later, UC Online is indeed moving ahead, but not exactly at a speed that suggests it will meet Edley's goal of leading the nation anytime soon. A number of factors have slowed progress. Faculty resistance, particularly professors' anxiety about the quality of online classes that yield UC credit, has probably been the biggest stumbling block. A key personnel change didn't help: the initiative's champion at the university's headquarters, Daniel Greenstein—vice provost for academic planning, programs, and coordination—recently left UC for a job running the Gates Foundation's postsecondary success strategy.

Budget obstacles have been significant, too; leaders of the initiative initially promised to raise private funds to get the plan off the ground. When those funds didn't materialize, they turned to plan B—a $6.9 million interest-free loan from UC's Office of the President. The loan, which is supposed to be repaid over seven years, comes "from a program that encourages system-wide efficiencies," according to a university fact sheet.[4] The publication goes on to note—as if to preempt criticism—that the university dollars being loaned to the online initiative could not otherwise be used for faculty salaries, student services, or ordinary academic programs. To bring in the dollars needed to service its loan, UC

Online is resting its hopes on a plan to enroll not only UC students but also nonmatriculated students. The former will be charged nothing beyond their standard tuition and fees for online classes, but the latter will pay fees of $1,400 to $2,100 per four-unit class (each of which will bear academic credit). Any revenues beyond what is needed to cover instructional costs will be used both to support the ongoing online program and to create a new revenue stream for participating academic departments. The extra funds can be used by departments pretty much as they wish, which has huge appeal given California's budget meltdown.

With its initial plan established, in the spring of 2012 UC Online offered six inaugural classes to students already enrolled at the university. They covered a range of subjects and campuses, from Preparatory Calculus at UC Merced to Global Climate at UC Davis. By the summer, the program began adding another nineteen classes, with still more courses in the development stages. According to Keith Williams, the new interim director of UC Online, the average cost for developing each course is in the mid-$50,000 range, with variation across subjects. However, these numbers do not include what are presumably significant costs for personnel, ranging from instructional designers and administrators to builders of technology infrastructures.

Working Toward Cross-Campus Enrollment

Thus far, UC Online has devoted a good deal of attention to offering high-enrollment "gateway" courses—the kind that appeal both to nonmatriculating students as well as undergraduates already at the cash-strapped university, where students may have to wait a quarter or even a year to enroll in these popular courses. "That's where we're having trouble having enough slots—getting students in and not slowing their progress through the university," says Williams, a veteran UC Davis lecturer who specializes in biomechanics.

But these worthwhile objectives have quickly run up against the vagaries of cross-campus enrollment and transfer. While non-UC students can take online courses offered at any of the system's campuses, the same has not yet been true of regularly enrolled UC students. All of the nearly five hundred undergraduates who took the first six classes in 2012 were studying with instructors who teach at their home campuses. In other words, the initiative hasn't been able to take advantage of one of the core characteristics of e-learning: reaching students without regard to time or location, so that a UC Santa Barbara sophomore facing a long wait for a key introductory economics class could instead take it immediately from a professor at UC San Diego.

The problem with implementing cross-campus enrollment is threefold, Williams explains. First, there is disagreement about where the money for the expense of teaching each student should come from. Second, there are problems transferring data between UC Online and different campuses in the system; every campus registrar has a different registration system, which creates difficulties in fulfilling reporting requirements for student financial aid. Third, autonomous academic senate policies mean that a course from one campus isn't automatically accepted toward major and degree requirements at another. All these bureaucratic difficulties notwithstanding, Williams says he is hopeful that the obstacles will be overcome by fall 2013. Registrars are amenable to creating more compatible data systems, he says, and campus leaders seem open to lowering credit transfer barriers. He also believes that opening up classes to non-UC students will help create some of the infrastructure needed to ease cross-campus enrollment within the system.

Empowering and Equipping Faculty

Williams readily acknowledges another significant problem: "the faculty is generally very skeptical." Well aware of the need to persuade professors that the new program has value, UC Online emphasizes that quality will be preserved by ensuring that each class is fully under the faculty's control. "UC Online is faculty-driven," the UC Web site's FAQ states. "Participating faculty work hand-in-glove with instructional designers to create courses tailored exactly to what faculty members want to teach, and how they want to teach it." In other words, there will be no effort to impose a one-size-fits-all template on each course. Williams contrasts this approach with the philosophy of most for-profits and extension programs (and places like UMUC), which have a high degree of comfort with standardization in teaching and curriculum. Those institutions "have a box they want everybody to fit within," he says. "We're trying not to put faculty in a box."

The result is a careful effort to create online classes in tandem with professors, deferring to their preferences while offering them technical and pedagogical assistance. Of course, not every professor passes muster in the first place. During the online project's first phase, eighty applied to teach classes, of which thirty made the initial cut and twenty-two ultimately went forward with courses. Mary-Ellen Kreher, the recently hired director of course design and development, observes would-be instructors with her team to assess their likelihood of succeeding in an online environment. Above all, they look for whether professors are engaging students. The most obvious example would be asking questions during lecture—"not just talk talk talk," says Kreher, who previously served as executive director of curriculum products at Kaplan Virtual Education.

Once faculty begin preparing a class, they're offered the help of instructional designers. Some have declined assistance and struggled more than they expected, Williams explains, while many have found the entire process more time-consuming than they anticipated. That is little surprise given the huge menu of options available to instructors. Modes of instruction include video segments of varying lengths; images, animations, or text accompanied by the instructor's narration; a Web tool called Piazza that lets students and instructors discuss and answer questions collaboratively; online office hours using AdobeConnect; weekly videos answering common student questions; and interactive whiteboards that let students see the teacher writing and ask questions via audio and video. Some classes are asynchronous, while others include synchronous, small-group discussion sections. Williams is confident that this menu of options is only going to expand and improve: "Everything's getting better. It's better now than it was two years ago, and it will be better in two years."

For their part, instructional designers try to ensure that each professor designs a course that includes clear learning objectives, well-articulated sequences of instruction designed to meet those objectives, and assessments that cover what students have learned. And courses must be sufficiently interactive to engage students with the content, with their instructors, and with one another, Kreher argues. "The highest level of learning is about the doing—the more you are engaged, that is when the most deep 'a-has' come," she says.

Competing with MOOCs

How will the emerging new world of MOOCs affect UC Online's nascent efforts? Williams draws numerous contrasts between the initiative he heads and the newcomers that have attracted huge attention over the past year. The most prominent MOOC ventures include MITx and a related entity, edX, a not-for-profit Harvard-MIT collaboration recently joined by UC Berkeley; and Coursera, created by a consortium of elite universities initially consisting of Stanford, Princeton, Michigan, and the University of Pennsylvania, then expanded to seventy other institutions. While all these courses are free, all involve automated delivery and testing with little or no personalized instructor feedback, Williams points out. They may be effective for students who can work well independently, and they're an important proving ground for elite universities to demonstrate that they can deliver effective online classes. But he contends that they don't offer the rich learning experience available through UC Online courses, which empha-size direct student-instructor and student-to-student interaction. There is also the most glaring distinction that, for now, gives traditional online pro-grams a decisive advantage over the MOOCs: course credit. As Williams explains, "Credit is much more useful as an educational achievement by current standards than a certificate."

Assessing Effectiveness, Making Improvements, and Revisiting Early Goals

For now, assessing which teaching technologies are most effective is a pri-ority for the UC initiative—an effort to build continuous improvement into its structure. John Yun, director of the UC Educational Evaluation Cen-ter at UC Santa Barbara, is leading the effort, which UC contends will involve "a degree of assessment unequalled in the offline environment."[5] To help make that happen, UC is monitoring students' academic results and also surveying them to find out which online experience they find most appealing. It also wants to use much more information about students' online interactions. Some current tools, such as AdobeConnect and Piazza, provide information on student participation in online discussions. But UC would like vastly more information: "Eventually we hope to have the ability to track what students did when on a Web page, what videos they watched and how many times, how much time they spent on different sec-tions of a unit or activity, how well they scored on nongraded embedded quizzes, problems, activities, etc.," says Williams.

Concerted efforts to measure and improve the quality of the student learning experience are crucial to making this initiative a success. But it is striking, and somewhat dismaying, that one key motivation behind the ini-tiative—to lower costs and expand educational resources in a time of finan-cial constraints—no longer seems front and center. The UC Online team is focused heavily on course development, quality of instruction, and navigat-ing bureaucratic and political obstacles (even the idea once floated by Edley of a two-year associate's degree is now off the table). Enrolled students don't save any money by taking online courses, and at $2,000 per course, the tuition for non-UC students is considerably more expensive than other online providers.

Still, as more students enroll both inside and outside the UC system, there should be economies of scale that will free up resources for other uses. "Because we're putting people in virtual seats, we can save money on real seats," Williams says. If the program can open up course access to many more students at modest marginal cost, it will have met one of its goals.

But this is still a big "if." Experience so far suggests that it may not be easy to expand and institutionalize even a high-quality program at a wary institution. Nevertheless, UC Online offers a precious commodity—credit from an elite public university—and the initiative's rocky start doesn't necessarily mean its goals are out of reach.

UDACITY

If scale is the key to cutting costs in higher education, the growing new world of MOOCs would seem to have the most far-reaching potential to upend the existing cost structure. MOOCs, which offer access to—but not traditional credentialing for—courses taught by top faculty, have been around for some time. But they attracted intense interest in 2011 and 2012 with the launch of Coursera, edX, and similar initiatives. One of the highest-profile ventures is Udacity, whose founding narrative has become emblematic of the possibilities MOOCs hold for changing how people think about college.

The story of Udacity, by now well known, starts with two cutting-edge computer scientists, Sebastian Thrun and Peter Norvig. The duo, who hold high-profile positions with Stanford and Google, started teaching Stanford's artificial intelligence class several years ago. In 2011, they decided to teach the class online, free, to students around the world. Despite minimal publicity, more than 160,000 students from 190 countries signed up to watch video lectures, take multiple-choice quizzes and exams, and participate in virtual office hours.[6] There were more students from Lithuania signed up for the class, its creators like to point out, than there are students enrolled at Stanford.

Some twenty-three thousand students made it to the final exam, with around two hundred fifty earning perfect scores.[7] No student earned Stanford credit, and the university insisted that its name not appear anywhere on the certificates of accomplishment that successful students received. Strikingly, the class proved appealing not just to the masses of far-flung students who enrolled, but to Stanford students themselves. By the time the class was over, just thirty of the two hundred who were taking the course in person were still showing up for flesh-and-blood lectures.[8]

Not long afterward, in early 2012, Thrun declared that he would no longer teach at Stanford (though he maintains a research affiliation). Instead, he announced that through Udacity he would spread the kind of learning experience he and Norvig had piloted in their introductory artificial intelligence class. (They had in fact created the for-profit company the previous year, under the name KnowLabs, with two colleagues. One was David Stavens, cocreator with Thrun and others of "Stanley," Stanford's driverless car and the precursor to Google's self-driving vehicle. The other was Mike Sokolsky, a Stanford robotics researcher.) In a massive show of ambition, Thrun announced the new venture in an oft-quoted statement at a January 2012 conference in Germany. "Having done this, I can't teach at Stanford again. I feel like there's a red pill and a blue pill [an allusion to the movie *The Matrix*], and you can take the blue pill and go back to your classroom and lecture your twenty students. But I've taken the red pill, and I've seen Wonderland."[9]

Innovating in Education

For now, Wonderland is very much a work in progress. Udacity's small Palo Alto offices, at the corner of El Camino Real and South California Avenue, look like a stereotypical Silicon Valley startup. There is no sign outside the building's exterior, and inside are a dozen or so twenty-somethings, their bikes, an open floor plan, whiteboards, and many computers. With $5 million in venture funding provided by Charles River Associates, plus $300,000 from Thrun himself (entrepreneur and author Steve Blank later put in $200,000), the company began by offering just two courses. Thrun taught a class on how to program a robotic car, while University of Virginia professor Dave Evans taught another on how to build a search engine.

Since then, nine more classes have been added, bringing the total to eleven. Most cover computer science topics, but classes in physics and statistics have also been introduced. All lend themselves to the automated (and inexpensive) computer grading that has so far been one of Udacity's defining characteristics. But a couple of classes on how to start a business, a topic that may bridge the purely quantitative academic world and more mainstream offerings, will soon follow, according to Stavens, now Udacity's president and chief operating officer. "We aspire to innovate in education," he says, "which means we have to teach everything eventually."

Personalizing the MOOC Experience

Udacity's classes thus far are marked by a stripped-down aesthetic inspired in part by the Khan Academy. As Steven Leckart recounts in his authoritative *Wired* magazine account of Udacity's founding, course videos feature close-ups of instructors speaking to the camera, followed by shots (taken by an overhead camera) that show their hands writing out diagrams and explanations on a tablet, with an accompanying voiceover explaining the material. As with most of the new generation of online courses, videos are broken into short segments, with questions interspersed that students can answer directly via their browsers.

Despite the lack of in-person interaction, Udacity leaders argue that there are pedagogical advantages to online instruction even in a mass format. While traditional lectures can certainly include live interaction, says Evans, who has now taken a leave from UVA to become Udacity's vice president of education, students who aren't quick to answer a professor's question can be marginalized. "One of the huge advantages of the online format is that every student gets the chance to answer the question. They can have as much time as they need—they can go back and watch the lecture segment if they don't get it." In conventional lecture settings, professors tend to overestimate how much students are able to learn by osmosis, adds Evans, rather than through actively tackling things like short programming exercises. "What students really learn from is by doing things and solving problems on their own." In a sense, then, even with a vastly larger class, "you're getting a much more personalized experience," he contends.

A related advantage, notes Stavens, is that constant small quizzes within each class unit, graded by computer, give instructors the kind of immediate feedback that is typically lacking in university classes. Where Thrun might lecture in a Stanford classroom for weeks without having a sense until the midterm of what topics students were or were not understanding, ongoing student feedback lets Udacity instructors know that 90 percent of students got a question on probability right, while just 40 percent correctly answered a question on SLAM (simultaneous localization and mapping). In the latter case, "that probably means we missed a step explaining, or the question was too difficult," Stavens says. Eventually, Udacity may develop adaptive learning that uses student responses to provide follow-up questions and exercises based on their individual strengths and weaknesses.

Recruiting and Developing Top-Notch Faculty

As the company begins to grow, it must not only expand course offerings but recruit faculty who can create high-quality classes. Picking new professors—even those with a proven track record in conventional classrooms—must be done carefully. The advent of mass online classes, Stavens suggests, is analogous to the beginning of the movie industry in the early twentieth century. "Not all actors who are talented on the stage will be talented on the screen. Not all professors who are great lecturers in the classroom will be great online." Candidates whose teaching seems most promising are flown to Palo Alto to be videotaped and vetted by Thrun, Stavens, and Evans to see whether they offer the right mixture of charisma and pedagogical skills. A large percentage are rejected. Those who do become Udacity instructors don't become wealthy: professors are paid from $5,000 to $10,000 per class.

The attention paid to teaching at Udacity contrasts starkly with Evans's experience at UVA. Like most major research universities, it hires faculty based on their research accomplishments. At Udacity, where recruiting and curriculum development are Evans's main responsibilities, professors are required to prepare assiduously for their videotaped lectures. This requires putting together a script that spells out each step of a lecture, including exact quiz questions, in much more detail than the outlined lecture notes that many professors at traditional institutions use. "We find that when people try to do a recording without that, it doesn't go very well." Even the best-designed lectures are heavily edited to ensure that students remain engaged. Udacity invests significant time and energy in video editing in order to create a watchable finished product.

During the preparation period, and once a class is under way, professors get help with class development, grading, and interacting with students from assistant instructors, who function much like traditional university teaching assistants, although they are full-time employees and not graduate students. Students also get a considerable amount of assistance from one another: many participate in online course forums where they can answer one another's questions. By the fall of 2012, groups of Udacity students had organized meetups in nearly four hundred fifty cities around the world; among the ten most popular sites are Coimbatore (India), Barcelona, Beijing, and Singapore.

Designing and Delivering Instruction Cost-Effectively

Udacity's financial model is a work in progress. The cost of developing and delivering Udacity classes is substantial, encompassing technology infrastructure, salaries for faculty and assistant instructors, and extensive video editing. But economies of scale have a way of putting those costs in perspective. "Our belief is that it's okay and it's necessary to put a lot of resources into developing a course, and that is amortized by having a large number of students," Evans says. Marginal costs are further lowered, of course, for the usual reason that technology can replace labor: far less professorial preparation and lecture time is required once a class has been thoroughly prepared. Stavens estimates that the company spends around $5 per student per class, a figure he believes will drop still further as enrollments increase. By comparison, he calculates, Stanford charges each student approximately $3,000 per class. "Yes, we're not accredited," he says. But for a student taking a Udacity class from a Stanford professor, sitting for the same final exam, proctored at one of the Pearson VUE global testing centers with which Udacity recently partnered, all at a cost vastly lower than at the elite university, "it seems like there's a value proposition there."

To become self-sustaining and even profitable, Udacity will need a business model that provides a reliable stream of revenue that comes either directly or indirectly from its hundreds of thousands of students. In addition to charging students modest fees to have their classroom performance officially certified (and given greater credibility) via one of the Pearson VUE testing centers, it may charge employers for introductions to Udacity's best students. These well-trained alumni are likely to be a valued commodity in markets where employees with excellent programming skills are much sought after. "We know some real rock stars who are as good as Stanford's best people," Stavens says.

In the end, this postaccreditation vision has much more far-reaching implications for lowering costs than efforts such as UMUC's or UC Online's. When free or low-cost online courses can provide students with credentials that have value in the labor market, conventional notions of selectivity and credentialing will in some cases be upended. "I love Stanford," says Stavens, who earned a PhD in computer science from the university. "But the idea that you can't get a great credential in computer science unless you're one of the few people they admit and who can pay $60,000 . . . Our classes show that there are talented people in Mongolia."

MOOCs have plenty of challenges and limitations of their own, of course. Even as they begin adding a richer variety of courses, they are in many cases likely to be a supplement or alternative to traditional higher education, not a replacement. "I totally agree that it's not a replacement for the traditional university experience," says Evans. "But there are millions and millions of people who don't have access to that—and that's where the real opportunities are." Particularly when the price is right.

CONCLUSION

Generalizations are difficult when describing today's online education landscape. The models offered by UMUC, UC Online, and Udacity illustrate just three of many possible approaches to course creation and delivery in a fast-expanding education marketplace. UMUC offers a fully accredited online degree; UC Online is developing online classes on a piecemeal basis with no fully online credential in sight; and Udacity is breaking new ground with unaccredited, specialized classes whose ultimate shape and value are still very much to be determined. What the three have in common is earnest attention to quality—from the length and form of videotaped lectures to the importance of instructor feedback to fostering the kind of student engagement that is increasingly recognized as crucial to a successful learning experience. They are also carefully attuned to creating cost structures over time that take advantage of the economies of scale made possible by technology.

Still, finding the sweet spot at the intersection of quality, scale, and cost is not easy. These and numerous other ventures, whether within traditional colleges or as freestanding initiatives, face continuing scrutiny about the legitimacy of the educational experience they offer. They are exploring the possibilities and limitations of their own work through constant trial and error. University-based programs, MOOCs, and fast-growing for-profits are all grappling with political and regulatory headaches, the need to make tradeoffs between personal attention and scale, and the quest for respectability.

It goes without saying that it is too soon to know how today's explosion of online initiatives will shake out. But it is noteworthy that online classes, despite the challenges they face, are rapidly losing some of the novelty and stigma once attached to them. Almost one in three college students is taking at least one online class, according to the Sloan Consortium.[10] Whether through hybrid classes, fully online degrees, mass-access ventures, adaptive learning modules, or as-yet-invented technologies, it is hard to believe that this phenomenon will not continue to spread. Already, there are promising signs that high-quality classes can be offered to growing numbers of students at modest cost. Such classes won't solve every problem facing U.S. higher education. But developing more of them—many more—is a goal well worth pursuing.

8

Beyond the Classroom

Alternative Pathways for Assessment
and Credentialing

Paul Fain and Steve Kolowich

Neera Grover, a successful working professional with a well-paying job, was stuck. A business analyst for an international consulting company, Grover, twenty-eight, was looking to make some changes. She had just moved from Connecticut to the Bay Area with her husband, who worked for Microsoft. Grover was looking to reorient her career accordingly. At her company, Grover's area of focus was health care. Now she wanted to shift her expertise to the Bay Area's main export: technology.

But Grover had a problem. She did not have the chops to handle a tech account. True, she had a bachelor's degree in technology and electronics from Punjab Technical University in her native India. But that was years ago, and anyway the modern software industry was a different animal. To make the lateral move, Grover needed more education.

So she enrolled in a continuing education program, Business Intelligence and SAS Analytics Software, at the University of California at Berkeley. The program comprised five courses and one hundred fifty hours of instruction. "This program is ideal if you are a post-baccalaureate business analyst wishing to gain a competitive advantage within companies with substantial information infrastructures," read a description on the Berkeley Web site.[1] The price worked out to about $1,000 per course for Grover.

She struggled to get her money's worth. The content was not as relevant to her goals as she had expected it to be, and commuting to Berkeley proved harder than she had hoped. The class met from 6 p.m. to 9 p.m., and Grover's work often kept her late. She enlisted her husband as a tutor, but he had his own busy schedule to keep. As the fall drew on, Grover wondered whether the whole plan was realistic.

So Grover started to shift her strategy. A friend of Grover's husband—a colleague at Microsoft—told her about an experiment some professors at nearby Stanford University were running. The professors were taking their Stanford courses, putting them online, and inviting anyone to enroll for free. Even Grover's husband and his colleague had been using the online course. "They just wanted to take a brush-up course to recollect the things that they don't use very often," she says.[2]

Grover registered for a course called Machine Learning, taught by Andrew Ng, the director of the Stanford Artificial Intelligence Lab. At the very least, Grover figured the course would help her fill the gaps in her Berkeley course. And if it didn't, no matter; it wasn't like she was paying for it.

As it turned out, the course suited Grover's needs perfectly. Ng, the professor, had broken his lectures into brief, video-recorded tutorials; Grover downloaded the videos to her smartphone and watched them on the train to and from work while taking notes. Her homework assignments and examinations were graded automatically by software that Ng and his Stanford colleagues had programmed into the course's online platform. Grover excelled, scoring 100 on every assessment. She dropped out of the Berkeley program.

In December, after passing the final examination in Ng's machine learning course, Grover got a letter from the professor. It was not a credential, exactly. It wasn't even a certificate in any usual sense. The name and seal of Stanford University appeared nowhere on the document; Stanford had firmly prohibited Ng and his colleagues from appropriating the institutional brand. What the letter *did* have was a signed note from Ng acknowledging that Grover had completed the machine learning course with flying colors.

Grover is confident that the course left her with a firm grasp of the basics of machine learning, an increasingly prevalent pillar of the software industry. But she has yet to learn whether the letter is enough to convince her consulting firm, and its tech-industry clients, that she has the chops to effectively analyze their business. Grover says she wants to accumulate a few more quasi-credentials before making her case. She hopes a potential employer or client will judge her based on the competency with which she is able to talk about tech issues in interviews—that is, if her cache of commendations manage to carry her that far.

"I'm not sure how things will work out," Grover says. "I will probably get to know once I start applying."

WIDENING THE GATE

Americans are unhappy about the price of college. Rising tuition and student debt levels have been labeled national crises. There's a simple reason for the increase in tuition levels in higher education: the cost of delivering an education in the traditional setting is growing just as fast as tuition. And for public institutions, state subsidies haven't kept pace with the expense side of ledgers.

But many in higher education feel the Internet may soon begin to deliver as a cost saver, where a high-quality course can be taught to far more students than can be crammed in any lecture hall. This form of course-delivery extension can add efficiency for colleges. The problem is, it can also undermine their traditional business model.

For substantial, systematic reductions in the cost of credentials and the time it takes to earn them, the academy will need to loosen its grip on the issuing of college credit. That won't be easy: colleges don't like to leave money on the table. They charge what they can, without really having to prove the value of their product. Change may be arriving, however, with the rise of massive open online courses (MOOCs), prior learning assessment, and competency-based higher education.

MOOCROECONOMICS

Neera Grover's story—and machine learning, the subject she chose when reorienting her consulting career to the software industry—is particularly relevant to the way technology could change the economics of higher education. The "Stanford course" Grover took for free online is a new species of education module known as a MOOC. This large-scale model for course delivery emerged in the late summer of 2011, when a cadre of Stanford professors decided to see if they could create an interactive educational experience for hundreds of thousands of learners at a time using advanced software that administers and assesses assignments and exams automatically.

The Massachusetts Institute of Technology soon followed. Several months later, Princeton University, the University of Pennsylvania, the University of Michigan, and the University of California at Berkeley pledged to adapt certain courses as MOOCs through Coursera, a company Ng—the Stanford professor who taught Grover's machine learning course—had started with his colleague, Daphne Koller, a fellow computer science professor. Harvard quickly joined forces with MIT on its platform, which became known as edX, and MOOCs were off to the races. By fall 2012, Coursera had signed up more than thirty brand-name universities and had more than two hundred courses in development.[3]

Online education has been booming for years, first among for-profit institutions and then among large public universities and community colleges, while the "elite" institutions have mostly stood by. Now they are scrambling to not be left behind, having decided, quite abruptly, that the medium has something to teach the standard-bearers of higher learning. "Online education is not an enemy of residential education," said Susan Hockfield, then the president of MIT, at the edX unveiling, "but rather a profoundly liberating and inspiring ally."[4]

The Scalability Advantage

So what makes MOOCs exceptional? In a word, scalability. While most online courses attempt to maintain a faculty-to-student ratio that's somewhat comparable to face-to-face courses, the MOOC platforms are designed to accommodate hundreds of thousands of students while keeping the number of faculty (one or two professors and maybe a few teaching assistants) the same. A typical online course at a traditional university might enroll between several dozen and several hundred students—the same as many traditional courses. MOOCs shift the ratio by orders of magnitude: last fall, two Stanford professors, Sebastian Thrun and Peter Norvig, taught an introductory course in artificial intelligence to one hundred sixty thousand people; twenty-three thousand of them completed the course, passing the same midterm and final exams as the two hundred Stanford students who took the face-to-face version in Palo Alto.

MOOCs endeavor to accommodate hundreds of thousands of students without hiring a proportional number of instructors by automating certain duties that historically have fallen to professors and their assistants both in face-to-face and typical online courses: assessing student work and answering their questions. Coursera, Udacity (a company started by Thrun and Norvig), and edX each have developed software that can promptly grade student assignments, hundreds of thousands at a time.

These systems often go well beyond tallying up multiple-choice answers. Many of the MOOCs that have already been through successful beta runs involve project-oriented assignments. For example, Udacity offers a Computer Science 101 course geared to teaching students how to build a search engine. Another teaches students how to program a robotic vehicle. Students in these courses are assigned to write programming code, and then the viability of their code is tested automatically. (Sample exam problem: "[B]uild a planner that helps a robot find the shortest way in a warehouse filled with boxes that he has to pick up and deliver to a drop zone.")

Not to be outdone, MIT professors have built a virtual circuitry laboratory for edX's inaugural MOOC, Circuits & Electronics. Anant Agarwal, a professor of computer science and electrical engineering at MIT and the president of edX, says he and his colleagues have built online labs where students can play with simulated circuit boards by clicking around their screens.[5] Because the software is running on MIT servers, even students without powerful computers can run the virtual lab as long as they have a good Internet connection.

Granted, the students in the MOOC version of Circuits & Electronics might not be getting practice handling physical components, picking up sensory cues ("Say, does anyone smell burning?"), and avoiding electrocution. But the architects of these virtual labs can write glitches and obstacles into the platform to simulate what electrical engineers might experience when dealing with actual circuit boards, says Agarwal. "At the end of the day, a simulation may not completely replicate a real live lab experience," he says, "but it can come pretty close."[6]

The virtual labs are expensive to develop, but over time and at scale Agarwal expects them to cost less than physical labs. The university spends money on the physical space and equipment in direct proportion to the number of students it serves; with virtual labs, the cost of the simulation software would theoretically go down as more students register. (The first iteration of the course drew one hundred twenty thousand registrants at the outset, and its overseers reported no capacity problems.)

Cross-Discipline Assessment

The MOOC developers seem confident that they can assess students' programming and engineering skills using robots. But the extent to which these platforms stand to shift the economics of higher education may depend in part on how broadly they can be applied across a curriculum. Math, engineering, and computer science involve problem-solving processes that are particularly amenable to automated grading. But as MOOCs expand into the humanities and social sciences, the question remains as to whether assessment in these disciplines, which tends to be more qualitative, can be carried out effectively at scale.

Robotic essay-reading software has grown in sophistication in recent years, but it can still be fooled or confused by unconventional prose. On MIT's own campus Les Perelman, the director of the writing center, has carried the flag for the anti-automatons, conducting a number of studies that have demonstrated, among other things, that popular essay-scoring software from the Educational Testing Service would have flunked the Gettysburg Address.[7] And while software developed for standardized writing tests does a good job of judging the coherence of a (short) piece of writing, nonhuman readers still have a hard time assessing the veracity of claims the writer is making.

To address this, Ng and Koller, the Coursera cofounders, have tried to turn the scale problem against itself with a method called *calibrated peer review*. Similarly to Web 2.0 projects that use their users both to generate and moderate content, the instructors of essay-intensive MOOCs may deputize its students as teaching assistants. The instructors can give these students a grading rubric and, using incentives, ask them to grade a number of short-answer essays. Each essay is scored by multiple readers, and then the scores are averaged to produce the essay grade. Koller has predicted that such a system could score student work at least as well as a "pretty good" teaching assistant.[8] At minimum, calibrated peer review posits a plausible model for using technology to assess nonquantitative student coursework at scale without relying on automatons.

Of course, the viability of this approach depends on the instructor's ability to enlist a critical mass of volunteer readers, and it remains to be proved whether MOOC instructors can incentivize such a system successfully.

Cost, Currency, and Credits

So what exactly do MOOCs have to do with stretching the higher education dollar? The answer depends on whose dollar you are talking about.

As far as student dollars, MOOCs provide obvious savings in that they enable students to take entire courses, while getting the opportunity to demonstrate their mastery of the material on assessments that are at least somewhat credible, without paying a dime. All of the MOOC providers say they plan to give students the opportunity to earn some sort of credential by paying a small fee.[9] At Coursera, deserving students might pay between $30 and $190 for a signed letter from their instructor certifying that they have passed the same exams as students getting Ivy League credit. (Compare that to the $1,000 Neera Grover was paying to take a similar course at the Berkeley extension school.)

Udacity and edX recently signed deals with Pearson Education that would let them hold proctored exams at Pearson's ubiquitous testing centers, a move that could give those certifications more credibility.[10] If MOOC credentials become accepted currency among employers, then students with certain educational goals—such as gaining the skills to transition from health care to the tech industry—might be able to do so without dipping too deep into their bank accounts. However, that is still a very big "if." The "alternative credential movement" has some buzz, but the current infrastructure for sorting résumés and assessing job skills remains oriented to traditional indicators—in particular, documents that bear the seal of a traditional university. "At the end of the day, you've got to have something that employers really believe in," said Bill Gates in a recent interview with the *Chronicle of Higher Education.* "And today what they believe in by and large are degrees."[11]

It seems more likely that MOOC participants will redeem their learning for college credits. Although most institutions that have signed up to offer MOOCs have said they will not offer credit for students who perform well on exams, other colleges and universities might end up doing so. In February, the American Council on Education, a membership group for college presidents, announced it had reviewed five MOOCs from Coursera and decided that students who pass them deserve formal credit.[12] Prior to that, Colorado State University's Global Campus, its accredited online arm, announced that it would begin granting credits to students in a Udacity computer science course who score well on proctored exams.[13] And California may soon offer an inexpensive pathway to credit for students at public universities and colleges who succeed in certain MOOCs.[14]

There is no guarantee that these early experiments will lead to broad change. But the movement to bridge the gap between MOOCs and the existing structures of higher education credentialing has plenty of momentum.

The Quality Question

As far as stretching institutional dollars, the promise of MOOCs lies in the scalability of quality education. The tricky part seems to be assessing the quality of MOOCs. So far, the most popular ones are taught by well-respected professors at reputable universities, which promise that the rigor of the online courses will be equivalent to those being held in classrooms in Princeton, Cambridge, Palo Alto, and Ann Arbor. But there is an important distinction to be drawn between the rigor of the assessment and the rigor of the instruction. The purported achievement of MOOCs is their ability to evaluate complex student work hundreds of thousands of assignments at a time. But the rigor of instruction has to do with the vigilance with which the instructors, human or otherwise, usher students from ignorance to mastery. MOOCs can measure what students know. But can they measure what students learn? And can they measure the extent to which that learning is attributable to the quality of instruction and support available in the Coursera, Udacity, and edX platforms?

Currently, MOOCs operate on Darwinian principles. When Norvig and Thrun held their first artificial intelligence MOOC, less than 15 percent of the one hundred sixty thousand people who registered for the course wound up completing it.[15] Udacity's subsequent courses in introductory computer science and robotic car programming have yielded similar retention rates, according to David Stavens, the company's chief operating officer. The success rates at Coursera have been similar: more than one hundred thousand people registered for Andrew Ng's course in machine learning last fall; thirteen thousand completed it with a passing grade.[16] Neera Grover was the exception, not the rule.

So it stands to reason that a provost at such an institution would not want to throw the majority of her students to the wolves by eliminating certain existing courses and directing students to MOOCs instead. To the extent that other universities might adopt a MOOC into their curriculums, they would likely do so in a way that would apply additional layers of instructional rigor. These layers would likely consist of instructor-led discussions, tutoring support, and other resources that might boost student success, but would add to the cost of delivering a MOOC solely through software and recorded tutorials.

Where technology might stand a better chance of stretching the higher education dollar is through a less massive kind of interactive online course, where automatons are enlisted not primarily to assess whether students have learned course material on their own, but rather to hold their hands through the entire learning process.

RISE OF THE TEACHING MACHINES

If Neera Grover's decision to abandon a traditional avenue of continuing higher education and take a MOOC was portentous, so was her choice of what MOOC to take. Machine learning is not only ascendant in the tech industry, it is also increasingly relevant to conversations about the cost of delivery in higher education.

As defined by Ng, machine learning is "the science of getting computers to act without being explicitly programmed."[17] In other words, it is the science of teaching a computer, or a software program, to learn things about its environment or about a person with whom it is interacting—her habits, her flaws—and then adapt without being given a specific directive by some human overseer.

Machine learning is the principle at the foundation of what researchers at the nonprofit Ithaka S+R have referred to as "highly interactive, adaptive, online learning systems."[18] In recent studies, the Ithaka researchers have taken to calling them *ILO systems*, short for "interactive learning online."[19] These ILO systems theoretically stand to increase the number of students each faculty member can effectively usher through a course, while still giving each student a modicum of personal attention.

While current examples of ILO fall short of human tutelage in some ways, they may exceed it in others. Candace Thille has been developing ILO systems for years through Carnegie Mellon University's Open Learning

Initiative, where she serves as director. The idea is to build courses that walk students through concepts and then drill them, all the while intuiting how well they understand the material, recognizing where they are getting tripped up, and nudging them accordingly. Ideally, it is like giving each student a private tutor—who, though unable to talk through problems orally, is incredibly observant and skilled at collecting data.

This, as it turns out, is an economical way to get people to learn. In a study of students taking an ILO statistics course that excised human instruction, conducted in fall 2005 and spring 2006, Thille and her colleagues found that removing living, breathing instructors from the course did not harm student performance; the hand holding provided by the artificially intelligent Carnegie Mellon software was enough to perform as well as their human-led counterparts on three midterms and a final exam.[20]

In another study, conducted in spring 2007, Thille and her colleagues studied what would happen if ILO systems were used in concert with human instructors. The students in the "blended" trial performed as well or better than the control group, with one major difference: they learned the material in half the time. A follow-up 2010 study by Marsha Lovett, associate director of Carnegie Mellon's Eberly Center for Teaching Excellence, found that students taking the blended statistics course (i.e., ILO systems taking the place of most classroom time) were able to master in eight weeks what their peers in the traditional version took fifteen weeks to learn.[21]

So the data so far suggests that deploying ILO systems at traditional universities would indeed stretch the higher education dollar with respect to how much it costs to deliver a course with a modicum of hand holding. Exactly how far these systems can stretch that dollar remains unknown.

LEARNING WHAT YOU ALREADY KNOW

One way higher education can become more efficient is for colleges to spend less time teaching students something they have already learned. Indeed, many colleges already do this through *prior learning assessment*, which is the awarding of college credit for learning that occurs outside the traditional academic setting, and before students even enroll. The appeal for students is that they get to graduation quicker by earning credits for previous experience and training. And by taking fewer courses, they also spend less on a degree.

But prior learning assessment's potential impact is bigger than just a handful of credits for adult students. The process's broader acceptance, which is still a work in progress, would mean that students, employers, and the academy itself all acknowledge that learning outside the academy is worthy of college credit. And prior learning assessment hinges on determining what someone has learned, with less value placed on how or where he learned it. That philosophical shift would help further open the door for competency-based learning models, like Western Governors University (the example du jour for education reformers), and other nontraditional approaches, where students can prove what they know in self-paced, online environments.

As a result, some higher education insiders think prior learning could be as disruptive as the Internet to higher education's current model.

"Prior learning is the next phase," says Ed Klonoski, president of Charter Oak State College, an online, public institution in Connecticut with a deep prior learning repertoire. "It's the next disruption."[22]

Prior learning assessment is hardly new, with roots in the post–World War II return of GIs, many of whom earned credits for their military training. This might be its moment to break into the mainstream, however, thanks to the college completion push and the recession's wake, which has driven a growing number of working adults back to college for second or third careers.

"No one ever took an interest in this until this whole completion agenda took hold," says Pamela Tate, president and CEO of the Council for Adult and Experiential Learning (CAEL).[23]

One in five Americans of working age has some college credits but no degree, according to the Lumina Foundation.[24] And those 40 million or so adults are the best place to start on the completion agenda. More than half of adult students with prior learning credits earned a college degree within seven years, according to a study conducted by CAEL, compared to only one in five who didn't get prior learning credits. And those much higher completion rates held when the study controlled for risk factors, like whether a student received financial aid.[25]

But don't expect to hear much about prior learning. The news media isn't particularly interested in adult students who attend nonstatus colleges, fixating instead on four-year, residential colleges—a much smaller, but wealthier piece of the higher ed pie.

Furthermore, colleges themselves aren't keen on advertising that corporate and military training, or other forms of experiential learning, can count for credits in the same way as faculty-taught courses. Therein lies prior learning's biggest remaining barrier: faculty members and traditional colleges that haven't bought into the process. Without colleges honoring prior learning credits, those credits don't count toward degrees. More than half of colleges accept some form of prior learning credit, but often in small doses, such as for extension programs. And the going is slow to get more colleges to sign on, given their wariness about prior learning and the persistent notion that it is merely exchanging cash for credits.

"There are some PLA programs out there that look like credit laundering," says Melanie Booth, an expert on prior learning and the dean of learning and assessment at Marylhurst University.[26]

Molly Corbett Broad, the president of the American Council on Education (ACE), says prior learning does have seedy examples in its past, but argues that the practice has matured. She compares reluctance about prior learning to major universities' long refusal to accept transfer students from community colleges. That stance has largely faded, and so will skepticism about prior learning, she predicts.[27]

Many professors, however, will be a tough sell. Johann Neem, an associate professor of history at Western Washington University, has written critically about prior learning assessment, giving voice to a widely held view that it is a "shallow measure." Neem doubts any testing-based assessment can adequately gauge the most important aspects of learning, like sophisticated thinking, original ideas, and creativity.[28]

"Can they evaluate the kind of experiences and work that go into a senior thesis, a lab experiment, or an artistic performance?" he asks. "Can they assess whether or not students are inspired? Or do they, in practice, end up rewarding much simpler things?"[29]

Assessments are not even the biggest problem, according to Neem and other faculty critics, who point to conflating the "certification" role of college with more important educational goals. While tests and grading are clearly important, the primary purpose of college is to educate, Neem says, and assessment is only one part of the learning process that happens in college.

"Now that we are told that everyone must go to college, there is a lot of pressure to find ways to make college fast and cheap," he says. "And that's why we are under pressure to award credit for prior learning."[30]

Also at play is the real threat that prior learning assessment poses to faculty members, both in their control of teaching students and, potentially, their job security. When a college recognizes that a student's prior learning covers a particular course requirement, that's one more class the student won't have to take—and an empty seat in that professor's class.

Prior learning assessments and accompanying credit recommendations have become a valid substitute for course work at a college, says David Moldoff, an expert on prior learning, who is founder and CEO of AcademyOne, a company that works on academic credit transfer and degree portability. And that is a bitter pill for some faculty members. "It's very hard for academics to say 'we're going to outsource this,'" he says.[31]

ACE IN THE HOLE

Prior learning is the Wild West of higher education in many ways. Adult students must do plenty of research to figure out the steps of getting credit for their work experience. And standards vary at the growing number of colleges that have begun accepting those credits. "The challenge is they all do it differently," Moldoff says. "The industry still is going to be very fragmented," at least for a while.[32]

Trust in the process also remains fleeting for students, colleges, and employers. As a result, respected national authorities, particularly nonprofits, have an opportunity to step into that void and set rules that people respect. That's where CAEL and ACE have an advantage over other prior learning players. Both groups have more work to do to fully assume those roles, however, particularly ACE.

As the primary umbrella group for higher education, ACE's membership includes leaders of sixteen hundred colleges and universities as well as two hundred other associations.[33] Taken together, the association represents 80 percent of higher education's total enrollment. Getting such a large group to move in the same direction is tough, particularly on something controversial, and even threatening. And some observers think ACE will fail to get its most powerful members to back prior learning, or will take too long to capitalize on the opening created by the completion agenda.

The association, however, has the most national clout on what learning should count for credit. Beginning with its work with the military, ACE has done credit evaluations for training programs offered by six hundred corporations, professional associations, labor unions, and government agencies, ranging from Starbucks and Jiffy Lube to the Federal Aviation Administration Academy and the National Security Agency. Each evaluation costs around $25,000 for a few course equivalents, with added fees for more credits, and is typically renewed every three years for the base fee. The programs then get ACE credit recommendations, which can be used at a growing number of colleges.

"ACE is really at the center of this," says John Ebersole, president of Excelsior College.[34]

One of the most established ACE corporate training reviews is of McDonald's Hamburger University, in an arrangement that goes back forty years. Hamburger U trains five thousand employees a year, some of whom walk away with substantial credit recommendations.[35] For example, restaurant manager training yields an average of twenty-three credits, including three credits in business management and one credit in delivery skills for presentation.

McDonald's has recruited partner institutions to grant those credits, including the University of Phoenix and online branches of Penn State and Drexel Universities. But most traditional colleges still exercise judgment in deciding which credits to accept from Hamburger U, and many do not accept all of ACE's recommendations.

The reason is that worries about quality in prior learning persist. Tate says some institutions' prior learning portfolio reviews are not up to snuff, particularly at certain community colleges, which she declines to identify. And more corporations may try to fly solo on prior learning programs, following Walmart's lead in developing an exclusive deal with a partner college with limited outside review. The American Public University System (APUS) hired a college president steeped in prior learning to kick the tires on the partnership. And while the two companies say they leaned heavily on guidelines from ACE and CAEL, they have not formally worked with either group. "I did not give them a blessing," Tate says. "They didn't go through us."[36]

POLICY HURDLES

Prior learning appears to have growing support from lawmakers. In perhaps the biggest sign that the process has gained policy traction, the Obama administration earlier this year announced that community colleges would need to use prior learning assessment to be eligible for $2 billion in grants from the Department of Labor. The support from Washington is also bipartisan. Senator Marco Rubio, a Florida Republican, gave prior learning assessment a plug in his televised response to the 2013 State of the Union address.

John Ebersole has worked on competency-based education and prior learning assessment for thirty years. He believes the time for both has finally arrived, but that the Department of Education has stymied progress. He says it's not that the feds don't want to help adult students, like Excelsior's average student, who is thirty-nine years old and enrolls at the private institution with transcripts from five different colleges. But the regulatory framework, much of which has been bulked up to crack down on for-profit colleges, makes innovation hard to bring to market, he says, and expensive.

"They're trying to demonstrate to the American public that they're stewarding Title IV dollars," Ebersole says, referring to federal financial aid. "But I do not believe they've done their homework."[37]

Ebersole cites ongoing struggles over federal aid policy and the state authorization process—the complicated approval hoops online colleges must jump through in each state where they enroll students. To operate in Florida, for example, Excelsior had to give state regulators a CV for all of the college's nearly one thousand adjunct faculty members. And those CVs had to be notarized, Ebersole says, which isn't easy for professors who live overseas.

States have taken their marching orders from the federal government, but also are motivated by protectionism—meaning the desire to keep outside colleges from entering the state—and by revenue from registration fees.

Another policy hurdle is the federal government's approach to competency-based education. Western Governors University (WGU), like Excelsior, is a nonprofit that caters to adult students and features relatively cheap tuition. But the university's much-heralded contribution is that it measures students' academic progress through their successful completion of a series of assessments, rather than through credit hours or how much time they spend in class. The university offers no classes or lectures in its bachelor's and master's degree programs, and does not operate on a fixed academic calendar. Students get credit when they can prove competency by passing examinations. And for what they can't pass, they are given learning materials and some light guidance.[38] The university charges tuition every six months, ranging from $2,890 to $4,250, depending on the program. And students can take exams whenever they feel they are ready.

Education reformers like the idea of breaking the link between seat time and credit, which is what competency-based education offers. "I want them to be the norm," U.S. Secretary of Education Arne Duncan has said of competency-based models.[39] And WGU's relatively pure competency focus, coupled with its students' qualification for federal financial aid, is what many reformers like about the university.

For example, its eligibility to participate in federal Title IV aid programs is a key difference between the university and StraighterLine, which is another emerging, low-cost model for online education. Spun off from an online tutoring service in 2010, StraighterLine offers about sixty online courses for $99 per month, or $399 for six months. Students get ACE credit recommendations when they complete StraighterLine courses. The coursework is self-paced, and takes about forty days on average to finish. But StraighterLine students have passed courses in a single week, meaning $99 can lead to three credits.[40] Even more tantalizing, StraighterLine recently announced that free online courses offered by the Saylor Foundation could be used for ACE credit through StraighterLine, which sounds a bit like MOOCs for credit.

Unlike WGU, however, StraighterLine is not a Title IV institution. But even WGU's federal aid status is a bit misleading, and not as unique as many in higher education believe.

A 2005 law, created specifically for the university, created a path for colleges to participate in federal aid programs by directly assessing how much students are learning, without requiring a link to credit hours. But WGU never pursued that authority. And no other college has successfully received the green light for direct assessment. So a model that truly disconnects learning from the classroom—taking prior learning and competency to the next level—while also serving students who benefit from financial aid, has yet to get off the ground.

Excelsior has tried, and failed. The college has a competency-based associate's degree program in nursing, which the Stanford Research Institute has praised for its academic quality.[41] To be admitted to the program, applicants must have a medical background, so Excelsior can skip the clinical skills courses that remain difficult to teach online.

Ebersole says the college had asked the Education Department to classify a new, online nursing degree program as competency-based, "as we understood they were willing to do for WGU."[42] But Excelsior was denied. "This has forced us to spend over a million dollars" to create a program that will not be aid-eligible, he says, "which will cost students at least five times more than the assessment-based approach."

Competency-based learning, particularly when coupled with prior learning credits, can substantially reduce the cost of a college degree. But for now, the higher education establishment and federal regulators are not quite sold on, as Ebersole says, "accepting ways of learning other than in the classroom."

A PATCHWORK PATH

The three emerging forms of college-level learning outside of college—MOOCs, prior learning assessment, and competency-based education—could all be used together. And that convergence may be happening now.

Let's start with a hypothetical situation, based on a real-life example. The *Milwaukee Journal Sentinel* reported that a surprisingly large number of students at local two-year colleges already hold bachelor's degrees, sometimes from the state's prestigious flagship, the University of Wisconsin–Madison. The reason is that the job market remains tough in Wisconsin, and some college graduates are enrolling in community colleges to pursue associate's degrees with hard skills. For example, 5.5 percent of recent graduates at Madison Area Technical College already held a bachelor's degree, according to the newspaper.[43]

So let's say student A graduated from the flagship at Madison in 2011, with a degree in English. He wanted to work in journalism (a tough field) and got a job working at a startup Web site, which attempted to do local reporting and lifestyle-oriented writing about Milwaukee's hipster set. The office was small, with only a few employees, and Student A's bosses quickly realized he had a talent—all self-taught—for Web site design. So he spent a good chunk of his time helping the company's one full-time IT employee. Then, two years after he was hired, the Web site folded, and Student A moved in with his parents.

While on the couch at home, Student A heard about Coursera, and decided to indulge his growing curiosity about computer programming. He took four Coursera MOOCs: Algorithms, Part I, taught by two Princeton professors; Algorithms: Design and Analysis, Part I, a Stanford professor's course; Software Engineering for SaaS, from a Berkeley professor; and Internet History, Technology, and Security, taught by a Michigan professor. He completed all the courses with flying colors (but no grades), receiving certificates for them.

CAEL's Tate says successfully completed MOOCs can and will garner credit recommendations through portfolio-based prior learning assessment. That will no doubt be put to the test soon, as over a million people registered for Coursera classes in the month or so after the venture announced its expanded offerings.[44]

Student A is one of the first to try, at least according to this fiction. He signs up for Learning Counts, and takes the three-credit portfolio course. At the same time, he enrolls at Madison Area Technical College, and decides to begin working toward an associate's degree in applied science, in the IT-programmer/analyst track, which is designed to land entry-level IT jobs in manufacturing, government, and insurance, to name a few. The technical college is a Learning Counts partner, and has therefore agreed to accept the program's credit recommendations.

He takes the course from CAEL, spending about $750 on it. The faculty advisor recommends nine credits for the Coursera courses he completed, and the college approves those credits. Student A is on his way, but hasn't saved too much money. At $116.90 per credit, those courses would have cost $1,052 if he had taken them at the technical college. But the Coursera classes, which ran over six to ten weeks, were more convenient than the standard face-to-face courses he would have taken. Even better, Student A was able to give Coursera a whirl risk-free, and the courses helped him decide to dive into the associate's degree program.

Another fictional story offers a glimpse of how to add the third leg of the stool: competency. Student B has no college degree. She has worked for twelve years as an administrative assistant at a food delivery service in Utica, New York, but dreams of starting her own catering company. She's heard about Excelsior College, where she could probably get some credit for her work experience, thanks to Excelsior's competency-based examinations and its partner status with Learning Counts.

Student B is ambitious and an intrepid researcher—obviously so, given that she found Excelsior, which doesn't have the highest national profile. She also read about the Khan Academy, and had taken several mathematics tutorials on its Web site—including ones on statistics and college-level algebra. She wants to earn an associate's in applied science in administrative/management studies from Excelsior, or maybe a bachelor's, eventually. Excelsior offers credit by examination in several courses that could apply to that associate's degree. So Student B takes two course exams, using knowledge she earned on the job. She passes one, in the three-credit interpersonal communications, which she learned well dealing with her company's drivers and often-persnickety customers. She also trims her time-to-degree by receiving fifteen credits for her Learning Counts portfolio.

As Student B quickly progresses through the associate program, she often uses Khan Academy videos as tutoring guides. It's a habit she takes with her, after graduating in two years. She had to keep working at her job to pay the bills, but the online format is flexible enough that she can work around those hours. She also graduates with little debt, and decides to enroll at Western Governors University to pursue an online bachelor's in business management, where competency can get her to graduation within eighteen more months of study. Along the way, she continues to take MOOCs from a growing number of top-flight universities.

THE ROAD AHEAD

Neera Grover recently enrolled in her second MOOC: an introductory programming course taught by a pair of professors at the University of Toronto. She still wants to piece together several technology-oriented credentials from Coursera to help get her next job. But like everyone else, Grover is not sure how much pull those documents, signed by professors but not endorsed by the brand-name universities where they teach, will have with potential employers or clients.

This gets to an important point. For all the buzz generated by the companies and nonprofits that are spearheading innovative credentialing pathways outside of the traditional college campus, the power of those innovators and their ideas to change the way credentialing works, and how much it costs, still depends on the extent to which they are co-opted by the existing higher education system. If Grover were to redeem her work with Coursera for college credit with Colorado State University's online arm, she could put something on her résumé that employers would immediately recognize. By contrast, credentials that bear the name of companies or consortia or unaccredited educational entities do not have, to borrow the words of Eric Rabkin, "a well-understood meaning"—or, to put it in economic terms, a well-understood value.[45] Until they do, the coin of the realm—degrees and the credits they comprise—will be secure.

Meanwhile, the bridge between outside education providers and the traditional higher education system remains under construction. Hypothetical students A and B, the ones described in the previous section, have no proxy in reality. Patient Zero has yet to emerge. And to follow these paths to degrees would require a breadth of knowledge about how to navigate the system that few possess, even these two higher education reporters. But in this game of connect-the-dots, more solid lines will emerge. The reason, put simply, is that millions of adult students need to earn degrees in their limited spare time. And a growing number of colleges and companies—both traditional institutions and outsiders—want to meet that demand.

Also a safe bet is that colleges, particularly those on the innovative edges, will continue to push the envelope to find ways to serve those huge numbers of adult students. Companies like Pearson will be there, too. The ones that succeed will take some of the best ideas from for-profit colleges and other online veterans. For their part, the federal government and accreditors have given tentative backing to online learning's next expansion. State regulators are more of a wild card. But with increasing demand from students and employers, growth seems inevitable. A backlash remains possible, however. Progress could halt if low-quality approaches run unchecked, particularly ones that have access to federal financial aid.

Traditional colleges will continue to thrive in the near future, and beyond. But in the emerging posttraditional era of American higher education, students will have more control in cobbling together their pathway to graduation. And at the end of that path will be credentials that say more about what students know than where they learned it.

9

Disruptive Technologies and Higher Education

Toward the Next Generation of Delivery Models

Paul J. LeBlanc

" **I**nvent the next delivery model that might put our growing online educational programs out of business." That is the charge to the Innovation Lab at Southern New Hampshire University (SNHU), where I serve as president, and even as our College of Online and Continuing Education (COCE) experiences meteoric growth in offering conventional online programs, the Innovation Lab, essentially our Research and Development group, is working on the College for America project. College for America means to harness competency-based learning models, social networking theories and methods, self-paced learning, open educational resources, and strong assessment to offer a radically new degree program—radical in terms of price (our target is $4,000 for a two-year associate's degree), precision of learning outcomes, and assurance of quality and mastery. It is a model that would have been unthinkable just ten or maybe even five years ago.

Many colleges and universities are announcing new online offerings ranging from systemwide and conventional efforts such as the $50 million University of Texas Virtual Camps to MIT and Harvard's joint venture into MOOCs (massive open online courses), the awkwardly named edX.[1] Many are doing so as a rear-guard attempt to fend off new online competitors or to reassure worried boards of trustees that they are being responsive to the changes in higher education. Indeed, the recent and implicit blessings of online education by our nation's most elite universities are a signal that large-scale online learning has fully emerged, is here to stay, and will be increasingly accepted as a respectable pathway to a degree. It may even signal that online learning can no longer be considered a "disruptive innovation," even if many institutions feel threatened by it and unprepared to compete for online students.[2] What we now know with certainty is that well-designed online education provides *improved* learning, *better* service to students, *greater* access to programs and resources, and *improved* economics to the provider institutions (though often little savings to students).[3] In that sense, online learning improves, extends, and *sustains* existing models more than it actually disrupts them.

However, even as much of traditional higher education is catching up with online learning as a sustaining innovation, next-generation models are poised to more fundamentally change and disrupt higher education as we have always known it. Our industry, critical to the nation's health and future in so many ways, is moving into a phase of disruptive innovation not dissimilar to what happened in the world of print journalism and the music industry. Those industries, like education, are fundamentally about the creation, curating, and consumption of information. Technological innovations thoroughly reshaped delivery systems, business models, and economics in those industries in ways that are still in progress and not fully worked out. Education, however, is a more complex endeavor that is highly regulated and subsidized, and its paradigm shift is likely to be slower. But it doesn't feel that way to a world that has remained largely unchanged since the 1400s.

Online education, as it has largely taken hold, is an evolution that may be giving way to a revolution in how we think about education. What follows is an attempt to provide context and a theory of change, to share some insights into large-scale online education, and to explore the next-generation changes now gaining traction.

HOW DID WE GET HERE?

Higher education has become an "above the fold" topic of national discussion, debate, and hand wringing. We live in a time of innovation, entrepreneurship, and invention driven by

- The emergence of new technologies
- An access and cost crisis
- Frustration over the sector's slow response to its critics
- The growing influence of a large for-profit sector that encompasses massive corporations and entrepreneurial startups

Reformers and educational insurgents often cite Clayton Christensen's theory of disruptive innovation to provide a framing narrative and theory for the change under way. The opportunity to rethink the delivery of education especially lies in theories of *disaggregation*, the process by which mature industries begin to unbundle all the value-added activities that were once vertically integrated.[4] Michael Staton has ably described how that might look within higher education and cited many of the new third-party providers now on the educational landscape.

Disruptive innovation, and the associated business-model reengineering it implies, is a powerful heuristic for change. More often ignored is Christensen's thinking around the "jobs to be done" theory, outlined in his 2002 book *The Innovator's Solution*.[5] The theory invites us to be far more precise in identifying what jobs our customers (students, in our case) are trying to get done when they buy from us and then urges us to use technology and build business models that deliver those solutions in the most effective way possible, removing the "pain points" and being thoughtful about where we add value. The new wave of higher education insurgents often criticizes higher education, but is imprecise about what higher education "job" supposedly is not getting done. After all, American higher education gets a lot of different jobs done. Just a sampling:

- In its research functions higher education drives improvements, new knowledge, and breakthroughs across a wide variety of fields (no one really is asking to disrupt this area).
- Residential undergraduate education provides a safe "coming of age" space where students inhabit a learning/living ecosystem in which they ostensibly grow up (and the *demand* for getting this job done remains robust, even as the ability or willingness to pay for it erodes).
- Higher education plugs students into a value-added network of alumni and fellow graduates that probably reaches its highest expression in the blue-chip selective institutions and has its payoff mostly *after* graduation.
- Workforce development functions provide job and career opportunities for learners, feed a talent pipeline to employers, and support economic well-being in local communities.
- Higher education helps adult learners without a degree and increasingly cut off from meaningful and well-paying work find a pathway to better earnings when they achieve that sought-after credential.

There are other jobs that higher education gets done, but the real point here is that *what we disaggregate and how we disaggregate has a lot to do with the problems we think need solving and what jobs need doing.*

One illustrative example: three-year programs are a much-discussed topic, and they theoretically reduce the cost of an undergraduate degree by 25 percent, especially if institutions genuinely reengineer the curriculum rather than simply adding more courses to a shorter time period and charging the same per-credit fee.[6] However, despite the substantial savings, SNHU has struggled to attract more than seventy or eighty new students per year to its long-established three-year program. Then it dawned on us: the job we thought we were doing so well, saving a lot of money for families, is *not the job* our traditional-age undergraduates wanted done. They had waited eighteen years and worked hard to get onto a campus. The job they wanted done was a combination of finding freedom, reinventing themselves, living with other young people, socializing, playing sports and joining organizations, and, yes . . . getting an education. Our three-year program offered *25 percent less* of what they mostly wanted, and while parents often appreciate the savings, students usually make the final purchase decision. We were essentially offering *less value* than the norm when viewed through the more precise lens of the jobs students wanted doing. We are now marketing the program differently, as a 3+1 that gives them all they want from campus life, but graduates them with a master's degree, not just a bachelor's degree, in four years.

The "jobs to be done" theory is also helpful in imposing a kind of discipline on institutions. There has been a great deal of mission drift in higher education as institutions try to be more things to more people, often chasing status, Christensen would argue, and almost always adding expense.[7] Does a community college need a gym and health clinic? Does a university focused on teaching need to decrease faculty course loads to support more scholarly activity? Does a four-year residential college that helps young people grow up need to launch an online program? Disaggregation opens the door to creating more specialized learning environments, with each attending to some more highly defined part of the overall learning landscape. New competency-based providers like Western Governors University or our College for America are explicitly career- and vocational-focused, for example.

Turning to large-scale online learning, where most higher education innovation is taking place, we should recognize that the job most adult learners want done is built around the Four Cs:

- Convenience—can you provide it in a way that fits my busy life?
- Completion—how quickly can I get my degree?
- Cost—how affordable is the degree I seek?
- Credential—is it a degree or credential that will help me improve my life?

These are not exactly inspiring educational ideals, but they reflect the reality facing millions of Americans. Life and the labor market are finally telling these students to get a degree. In reality, with the erosion of the traditional liberal arts over the last decades, these adult learners are not so very different than millions of their younger peers studying business, nursing, or education.

In our increasingly have and have-not world, getting and keeping a good job has a pronounced urgency, especially for poor and working Americans. In SNHU's online programs, 66 percent of the students are Pell-eligible. The for-profit sector accounts for about 45 percent of Pell Grant dollars. The point is that online education serves a disproportionate percentage of poor Americans because those students have few other choices, illustrating another aspect of disruption theory. As Christensen points out, disruptive innovation often takes hold where the customer's *next best choice is nothing else.* Poor Americans are least well served by traditional higher education and so have increasingly turned to online education (though some unscrupulous for-profits have certainly sought them out as well). Because of one or more of the Four Cs (often all), the great majority of online students are not well served by their local on-the-ground providers or have options that just don't work very well for them. The ways in which they are not well served has come to shape how successful online programs think about disaggregation. Online providers get very focused on the jobs that need to be done, jobs not often well addressed by traditional higher education. As online education has improved, more and more adult learners are flocking to it.

Convenience

In terms of convenience, nontraditional-age students of the type just described have voted with their feet and moved from evening and weekend programs to online alternatives by the hundreds of thousands because we have essentially *decoupled learning and student service from place and time constraints.* As recently as five years ago, our site-based students would occasionally take online courses, but usually go back to their center for more of the traditionally delivered courses with which they began. Today, when students start at a center and then take an online class, they usually do not return to the face-to-face format because of convenience. Because it can be decoupled from location or schedule, online education simply works better for busy learners juggling jobs, family, and soccer practices.

There is another dimension to convenience we too often neglect: comfort. We easily forget how intimidating the traditional campus can be for those not accustomed to it. Once we consider office hours that don't align well with student needs, indecipherable acronyms, and a feeling of not fitting in, suddenly the campuses we love are often intimidating to this student demographic who are often *unconfident learners*. This notion of the unconfident learner extends to issues of preparedness and basic skills, as discussed later, but it begins with the simple feeling of not fitting in. Couple ill fit with poor or inadequate service levels, and students can easily feel they do not matter and will interpret that feeling as a reflection of *their* inadequacy, not our institutional shortcomings. Online education removes the hurdle of coming to campus and provides superior service (at least in the best cases) to create an easier on-ramp to learners.[8]

The brick-and-mortar impact of the shift to online delivery is enormous. Consider that our online operation at SNHU serves twenty-two thousand students, but has an annual facilities cost of just $1.076 million (lease costs, utilities, and operations), while our traditional main campus serving roughly three thousand five hundred students will cost us $25.9 million in debt service and operations this year. Parents often ask, "Is there a food court?" or "Can we see the fitness center?" or "How long before my son or daughter gets into the newest dorm and has a single room?" and in the very next breath, "Why is tuition so high?" Because online education does not seek to perform the coming-of-age job, it is relieved of the facilities burden and the enormous attendant costs.

Completion

In terms of completion, the real question being asked is "How quickly can I get my degree?" *Large-scale online programs* (LSOPs) have more aggressively accepted prior learning credits, have more transfer-credit-friendly policies, and are more ready to accept ACE credits and give credit for training than are more traditional campus-based programs. More importantly, they have moved to shorter term lengths—eight weeks is common—speeding students to degree completion and improving their own cash flow in the process (six term starts per year effectively doubles revenue flow over the traditional three-semester schedule).

Cost

In terms of cost, after the aforementioned capital savings, most of the savings in educational delivery come from significantly lower faculty costs made possible by disaggregating the traditional role of the faculty member. Until recently, the act of creating a course, building a syllabus, identifying and assembling necessary content, outlining learning activities, delivering instruction, intervening when students struggle, assessing student learning, and perhaps revising the course on occasion rested with one person: the faculty member. Collections of faculty members essentially mirrored that set of actions at the program level, bringing their courses together in a cohesive whole—in essence, a vertical integration of functions. It has, with little exception, always been thus since the cathedral schools of the Middle Ages, precursors to the earliest universities.

A closer look is merited. Most online education is provided in the third-generation delivery models refined by the for-profit sector over the last ten years (the first generation was closer to correspondence schools and based on mail and later television/videocassette recorders; the second generation was the short-lived video-based systems of the 1980s and 1990s). Since for-profits first set the stage, LSOPs, for-profit and nonprofit, are now disaggregating the delivery of instruction with a vengeance. Subject matter experts (SMEs) working with expert instructional designers are creating high-quality courses that will be taught by *other* faculty members acting as facilitators. With a more top-down business model in terms of academic oversight (as opposed to traditional campuses with traditional governance), and a displacement of faculty roles as just described, most LSOPs operate with few full-time faculty members and rely on adjuncts to deliver courses. In turn, the key emotional ties between students and the institution are more likely to be through advisors than through faculty members. Advisors, taking on a role now disaggregated from those traditionally performed by faculty, are usually assigned scores of advisees (one advisor to three hundred students is a widely accepted benchmark) and work from a call-center-like environment. They are paid much less than traditional faculty members, but often deliver superior support to nontraditional students.

Table 9.1 illustrates the comparison of the two models and makes clear where most LSOPs disaggregate.

Consider the cost savings that accrue when we move from the traditional to the new model of delivery. For example, using an average full-time

TABLE 9.1 **Comparison between traditional and third-generation higher education**

Traditional higher education	Third-generation online
Full-time (FT) faculty creates courses and programs.	Subject matter experts are hired to create courses and programs.
FT faculty delivers most courses.	Part-time faculty delivers most courses.
FT faculty provides advising.	Advisers provide advising.
FT faculty and staff provide learning support.	Third-party tutoring is often employed.
Expensive campus facilities are typical.	Office space is minimal.

faculty cost of $116,000 (salary and benefits across a seven-course load per year), a course release to work on a new course—not unusual in supporting course development—costs approximately $16,571. In contrast, our online operation employs SMEs for approximately $3,000. While we pay another $10,000 to develop the actual course, when it comes to the delivery of the course, the standardized course design allows us to effectively use adjunct faculty at $2,500 to $3,500 per course versus a full-time faculty cost of $16,571.

Credential

LSOPs do no better or worse in offering credentials to this student cohort—with two notable exceptions. On the positive side, online learning often provides access to programs not available on the ground through traditional providers, effectively expanding choice. Early-generation distance education was designed to serve the geographically isolated. On the negative side, unscrupulous for-profit providers have been accused of granting near-useless certificates and degrees, spurring calls for "gainful employment" legislation to curb the abuses.

What about the quality of that credential? LSOPs have found a way to better deliver on the Four Cs—convenience, completion, cost, credential—while driving out a great deal of cost. That success automatically raises concerns about quality for many critics of online learning. However, we have more mechanisms for quality improvement in online delivery than in traditionally delivered higher education, and there is much research to reassure us about quality. For example, at SNHU we have built tools that monitor classes 24/7, we collect data even at the assignment level, and we reinvest in improving courses (spending over $2 million in course revisions, for example) and faculty performance.

There are other ways in which disaggregation is shaping online learning. LSOPs often turn to third-party providers for tutoring support, 24/7 technical support, call center services for inquiry management, and, increasingly, IT infrastructure. Disaggregation theory posits not only the opportunity to use third-party entities for those functions previously integrated, but also that those third-party entities are usually more expert or effective in their respective functional areas. Well-defined service metrics and reporting can ensure that service to students is maintained at a high level while at a cost lower than the institution can achieve. There are some signs of a trend to tie compensation to eventual student performance on assessments, the real test of vendor efficacy. Traditional ground-based institutions can similarly outsource, but the online providers have tended to do so more aggressively.

Now it is important to remember what jobs LSOPs tend not to do well. For now anyway, they do not address the research job, the coming-of-age job, or the value-added network job. More importantly, they also do not address the cost job as well as they might. Many for-profits charge as much or more than their more traditional peers on a cost-per-credit basis, and most nonprofits use the surpluses of their online operations (typically running anywhere between 25 and 35 percent even after the assignment of indirect costs) to provide a cross-subsidy to their traditional operations. At SNHU, our online program provides a hefty surplus that in FY11 covered the nearly $4 million operational deficit on the traditional campus, provided substantial increases in grant aid to our traditional-age students (a 50 percent increase from 2009 to 2011), allowed for a revision of 211 existing courses, and added to our small endowment. We could have offered the online programs at even lower price points, but chose to instead create a subsidy to be used in the ways just described.

We would also argue that online programs have not done a good enough job solving the unconfident learner challenge, a fact reflected in dismal retention rates for much of the sector and especially many of the large for-profits (though not much worse than many of the community colleges that serve the same students). All of that said, LSOPs by and large address the needs of nontraditional-age learners better than traditional programs and have used disaggregation to create new business models that improve quality while cutting cost. Online learning is here to stay because it works.

THE NEXT GENERATION OF EDUCATIONAL DELIVERY MODELS

While many nonprofit institutions see large-scale online programs as a *new* paradigm for serving nontraditional-age students, they are in fact now well established and well understood, and the challenge for most nonprofits will not be technical or structural. It will be a combination of hurdles that include cultural change, talent, and capital.

If not pressed by cuts in state funding, loss of enrollments, and/or downward pressure on tuition increases (and upward pressure on discount rates), many, if not most, nonprofits would happily ignore online learning. That said, delivering high-quality online programs with excellent service to students is not truly innovative any longer, though it is disruptive in the sense that students have decided it gets the job done for them in more effective ways, and online programs will continue to grow and displace longstanding programs using more conventional delivery methods.

The next wave of truly disruptive innovation is emerging through an even more aggressive disaggregation of the business model than the one just described with LSOPs. Western Governors University (WGU) has moved emphatically in this direction with its self-paced, $6,000-per-year online delivery model, which unpacks the traditional faculty role by allowing sets of faculty to operate in more highly specialized and functional silos, turning to scores of third-party content providers instead of creating its own, and decoupling learning from time, allowing students to demonstrate mastery as quickly as they can and to move on to their next course. For the non-traditional student, WGU addresses the Four Cs exceedingly well.

A group of new educational startups is opening up avenues for thinking about all or parts of the teaching and learning enterprise. A few examples:

- New companies like StraighterLine and New Charter University (NCU) are now offering self-paced courses and programs in the "all you can eat" pricing models. For example, StraighterLine offers its courses at $99 per month no matter how many courses a student takes.
- Others are substituting peer-to-peer learning for the traditional role of the faculty in either delivering instruction or helping students struggling with a concept or task. For example, OpenStudy offers a free peer-to-peer environment of over one hundred thousand users helping one another across a range of topics, with questions typically answered in less than five minutes and the wisdom of the crowd correcting misguided counsel.
- Alternative credentialing systems are starting to replace courses with competencies as units of knowledge. The "badges" movement is perhaps the best known, but elite MOOC providers are offering courses with "certificates" that are less than credit worthy, but still a signal of successful completion.
- More streamlined, online prior learning assessment (PLA) services like the Council for Adult and Experiential Learning's Learning-Counts are helping students get credit for what they already know.
- The open education resources movement is aggressively making content available for free, as are the MOOCs provided by elite universities (though there is every chance that these will be monetized in some way).

By combining these innovations, most of which are made possible by technology, new delivery and business models will emerge that stand to more dramatically disaggregate and disrupt the traditional delivery models.

A further word on MOOCs is merited. While MOOCs remain very much in the news, there are four issues for them to deal with: MOOCs seem to confuse delivery of content with education and learning and all the human complexity involved; no MOOC provider has outlined a persuasive business model; MOOCs seem to confuse brand value with actual credentialing; and MOOCs seem very unclear about whom they serve and what job they think they are doing. If MOOC providers can work through those four challenges, they *might* emerge as a new force in higher education, but they are far from there now.

COLLEGE FOR AMERICA: SNHU'S NEXT-GENERATION LEARNING MODEL

College for America is an attempt to create a new, very low-cost, high-quality educational model; the program launched in January 2013. College for America offers a two-year associate's degree (assuming the equivalent of full-time enrollment) for just $2,500 per year and uses a very different educational model. Its key components include

- Replacing courses with competencies as units of learning and the curriculum with the Knowledge Map, 120 competencies across nine domains and at three levels
- Giving students smaller, more easily mastered competencies at the outset to build skills and confidence
- Assigning badges to each competency, certificates to the first two levels, and an associate's degree at the completion of the third and final level (plans are to expand to a full four-year degree)
- Self-paced learning that takes faculty almost entirely out of the learning experience, relying instead on "learning guides" (mentors in the workplace or day-to-day lives of students) and peer-to-peer environments
- More radically breaking the seat-time/learning outcomes relationship, allowing students to go as fast as they like, à la WGU, but also to take *as long as they need* to master a competency
- An insistence on open source materials and no textbook costs
- A strong focus on evidence of mastery including clear rubrics for evaluation, third-party assessments (we are partnering with the Educational Testing Service), and a portfolio to provide evidence of mastery

College for America disaggregates the traditional delivery model and moves a number of responsibilities to the learner—essentially a kind of cost shifting that allows for a dramatically lower price. The university "curates" the educational model, but once this is done it is infinitely scalable. We add value in designing and organizing the learning model (the aforementioned curating role), providing the platform and tools, overseeing the assessments, and awarding the accredited degree. We can do all that for $2,500 per student per year and be self-sustaining—at least we think so.

Returning to the "jobs to be done" heuristic, College for America tries to better address two jobs that most LSOPs don't do well (in addition to lowering the price of a degree program). The program wants

- To better support unconfident learners by bringing education more fully to where they work and live through the use of corporate and community partners, by leveraging social networking theory and tools, and by giving students early small "victories" to build confidence
- To provide employers with greater reassurance about students' genuine mastery of competencies at a time when a degree is no longer an accepted proxy for even basic skills like communication, quantitative reasoning, or basic computer use

These are important jobs, and they receive too little attention in our national debates about access, completion, and quality. While we know that tens of millions of Americans need a postsecondary degree, we often forget that many are unconfident learners with a hundred good reasons not to enroll and two hundred to drop out once they start to struggle. They are not breaking down the door to attend and often bail out once enrolled. Yet self-paced models require drive and discipline that may elude many learners, and online learning can feel isolating; both contribute greatly to the often-poor persistence rates of LSOPs.

The new models of delivery have to be much better at addressing the challenge of the unconfident learner. Disaggregation can lower cost and improve quality, as outlined earlier, but most of the disaggregated delivery models have thus far ignored the support that their students require. College for America moves to more emphatically explore the ways in which self-paced learning models can drive persistence through the use of social capital and social network theories. Online learning is not the answer to our higher education challenge if it merely succeeds in enrolling students but then not graduating them.

Higher education is facing discomforting questions about how much students actually learn, most recently in Richard Arum and Josipa Roksa's much-discussed study *Academically Adrift*.[9] The book suggests that far too little learning actually takes place on American campuses. This unsettling notion confirms what many have come to believe: that a college degree can no longer be trusted as a proxy for a range of knowledge and skills—writing, critical thinking, quantitative reasoning—and too many students who graduate from college remain poorly prepared for the workplace no matter what their transcripts suggest (a longstanding and growing employer complaint about much of higher education). With College for America, employers get a detailed map of the student's competencies, excellent third-party assessments, and the ability to go into a portfolio and see for themselves the evidence of mastery. The great bulk of college transcripts cannot touch this level of transparency and reassurance. College for America launched in January 2013 and we are still refining the model, but if we have it right we will be able to better serve nontraditional learners, dramatically lower cost, and demonstrate genuine mastery of competencies that matter.

THE CHALLENGES AHEAD

The for-profit sector has led the way in online education, and a handful of nonprofits are getting to scale, but we are still early in the process of change. While most American universities and colleges are doing online courses and programs, few have yet developed large-scale online operations. Many are still grappling with online education as it has matured and not yet with the new emerging models. A number of formidable challenges face us as an industry.

What Happens When Online Technology Creeps onto Traditional Campuses?

This analysis has thus far focused on nontraditional-age learners and the jobs they need to have done, showing how disaggregation of the traditional delivery model, mostly enabled by technology, is dramatically reinventing educational delivery for *this* cohort. But innovation for one class of customers often makes its way to other cohorts. In Christensen's model of disruptive innovation, the new disruptive service or product improves in quality at a faster rate than the incumbent service or product so that the innovation starts to climb up market, displacing the incumbents at each successive level.[10] Consider that notion in the context of traditional-age students, and new possibilities for reconfiguring the business model start to emerge. For example, one might imagine intentional student communities decoupled from learning. Those communities could be where the coming-of-age job gets done, while the mastery of knowledge and competencies (the learning job) is provided online or through experiential learning models like our new College Unbound Program (where students do project-based learning in the workplace and the classroom is an as-needed supplement to their learning). Brigham Young University–Idaho has reimagined its residential campus experience and disaggregated the traditional faculty role, allowing it to redefine classroom time, use peer-to-peer learning, and focus faculty on learning "interventions." One can imagine more radical attempts at the exercise. Traditional campuses may very well be forced down that path by the new generation of students who have only ever known and navigated a world shaped by online technology.

What Happens to the Traditional Full-Time Faculty?

The new emergent models greatly displace the traditional role of the faculty. WGU creates subsets of faculty. BYU–Idaho removes the generative scholarship role. College for America shifts the role to a curatorial or learning design function. Peer-to-peer learning removes the faculty altogether. Every industry that has seen the large-scale deployment of technology has also seen a displacement of specialized labor. Higher education has seen a pretechnology wave of lower-cost labor (teaching assistants and increasing reliance on adjuncts), but the new disruptive models stand to dramatically shift the faculty's role to where their greatest value-add is realized: the *design* of learning, *evaluation* of content, and *creation* of new knowledge in research contexts. Increasingly absent will be teaching (at least at the first and second levels, while perhaps being available for the difficult learning interventions), assessment, and governance. Teaching at the highest levels within disciplines—at the doctoral level, for example—may very well continue as presently constituted. There will continue to be traditional residential campuses where faculty members play traditional roles—SNHU's main campus, what we call University College, is investing to further reify that model—but for the great bulk of higher education, the traditional model just doesn't get the job done at scale and acceptable cost. This is, in many ways, an existential threat to the traditional role of the faculty member.

How Do We Innovate in This Regulatory Environment?

While technology is making possible all kinds of innovative practices and the cost/access/quality crisis calls for change, higher education remains a highly regulated industry with deeply entrenched stakeholders fueled by their own powerful myths and narratives. Title IV funding can be made to better support alternative delivery models. The Department of Education (ED) is starting to think more openly about competency-based learning and alternatives to Carnegie units as the sole measure of learning. The idea that taxpayers pay for seat time, but not learning, is antiquated. Financial aid rules around artifacts like last date of attendance, satisfactory academic progress, and "learning activity" need to be broadened. Add to ED's focus on compliance the crazy quilt of state regulations regarding online learning, and we hardly have a government environment conducive to innovation.

Finally, if we want traditional higher education to be part of the solution, we have to give it room to experiment and operate differently. Yet regional accreditation tends to reaffirm vertical integration and traditional models. For example, in our 2012 ten-year reaccreditation, SNHU's innovation and success were praised, but the bias of the report was to have us more fully reintegrate, failing to recognize that it was by disaggregating our business units that we had become successful. Regional accreditation is fundamentally a reaffirmation of the status quo by incumbents. Both ED and the regional accreditors assert their support of innovation, but almost always within the rules as currently prescribed, and genuine innovation cannot take hold under those conditions.

How Do We Balance the Need for Lower Costs to Students with the Cross-Subsidy Pressure?

As has been outlined, LSOPs can deliver high-quality education at a much lower cost, but those cost savings have not usually been passed on to students. In the nonprofit sector, the public institutions use the healthy surpluses generated by online divisions to offset cuts in state support, while the tuition-dependent private institutions (that's most of them) use them to offset declining net student revenues from traditional-age, campus-based students. The for-profits, by their nature, seek to maximize profit and shareholder value. So while most of them have no cross-subsidy pressure, they seek to keep profits as high as the market will bear. As a result, LSOPs have not yet resulted in substantially lower costs for online students.

That may change. How so?

- Next-generation learning models are coming into the market at markedly lower price points. It is not yet clear that any of them have a sustainable business model, and almost all of them require a dramatic reinventing of the delivery model—none of them quite proven—and volume enrollments. If these models gain traction, there will be downward pressure on price to students.
- Competition in online education will also work its magic. With more and more nonprofits finally entering the online market and learning how to compete head-to-head with the for-profit giants, the latter will feel increasing pressure to compete on price. Fair or not, regulatory pressure and a harsh media spotlight have put the big for-profits back on their heels and have opened the window for savvy nonprofits to grow. For example, in June 2012, Apollo Group

(owners of the University of Phoenix) reported an 8 to 10 percent decline in enrollments for the fiscal year, while SNHU saw a 125 percent increase in its enrollment for the same period (and grew from 6,975 to 13,700 students in just two years).[11]

- The emergence of MOOCs may presage an era when instruction and content are wholly free and students pay for other "add-ons" including credentialing, tutoring, advising, and so on.

None of these scenarios is certain. The new models are still striving to establish themselves. The nonprofits have a host of institutional hurdles and cultural resistance, and MOOC providers struggle to develop a workable business model. In turn, many of the for-profit incumbents remain highly profitable, have expansive cash reserves, and are both smart and agile.

Can the Incumbent Model Disrupt Itself?

In his original work, Christensen found in industry after industry that the incumbent players were smart and well aware of the changes happening around and to them, but that their combination of business model, organizational structures, economic realities, and culture did not allow them to fend off the disrupting innovations that came to displace them. They weren't dumb—they were trapped. The best they tended to do was employ the innovations late in an effort to preserve their place, not advance it or lead. This may be where traditional higher education finds itself today. It seems unimaginable, but think about those amazingly smart and seemingly unassailable companies that were upended by disruptive technologies: Kodak and Polaroid by digital photography; Digital Equipment Corporation and Wang by low-cost desktop technology; myriad music store chains by iTunes; Borders and Barnes & Noble by Amazon—and the list goes on.

Higher education is admittedly more complex, as mentioned before. But aside from the elite institutions and flagship research universities, the great majority of colleges and universities stand to be disrupted. As Christensen found in other industries, the leaders of these colleges and universities know it and feel similarly trapped or at least challenged. In meeting after meeting I hear my colleague presidents grappling with the dramatically changing environment, yet they face the incumbent challenge.

The strategy is straightforward in many ways and essentially outlined by Christensen (who, incidentally, sits on the SNHU Board):

- Create a new business unit or separate the one you hope to leverage and give it the "breathing space" to grow and compete within the new paradigm. Breathing space for most institutions means more flexible governance (minimally), policies and processes that make sense for it, and license to rethink the business model.

- Be unequivocally clear about whom you serve and what jobs they need done, and build the business model to do those jobs.
- Hire the right talent, clear roadblocks, and get them resources.
- Serve the underserved markets first, ideally those for whom the next best option is nothing at all.

It is easier to do those things during healthy fiscal times, but then the pressure to innovate is not so keenly felt; when financial pressures do mount, there are fewer resources to divert to the new venture and a lot of resistance from stakeholders who are already feeling financially squeezed. It is easier if the institution is further down the status ladder. Institutions that enjoy high status within the industry—or in their own minds—tend to resist innovations that are admittedly inferior at their start (as was early online education), fail to accept the improvements, and overestimate the security of their position. Faculty members, correctly recognizing their displaced roles in the new online business models, tend to resist the change or burden it with demands that prevent it from being successful.

SNHU has become an increasingly prominent player in online education because at least some of our ostensible weaknesses became strategic strengths. As a nonselective institution that had seen hard financial times and learned to be scrappy, we had less of the aforementioned status consciousness to get in the way. While the 2009 recession hit us hard, it also created a greater sense of urgency, and we actually doubled our investment in growing online programs even as we made cuts elsewhere. We also had some strengths. We had been early developers of both continuing and online education, and while those programs were modest in size, they gave us experience and a commitment to adult learners alongside our traditional campus programs. Many of our full-time faculty had taught in those programs and became supporters and participants. Timing helped. We started to grow just as the for-profits came under fire and the recession drove people back to school for retooling. We also worked hard to educate the campus, garner board support, share the gains (we have an award-winning benefits plan, give healthy raises year after year, and have reinvested in the traditional campus). We were willing to hire great talent, pay more for it, and shamelessly borrow best operational practices from the for-profits (working with students at their preferred times, tracking and using data, delivering quick turnaround times, and actively monitoring classes) while eschewing those that earned that sector considerable and well-earned criticism.

The process was not without its tensions, and there are still some skeptics on campus, but our traditional campus has benefited greatly from the success of our online program, and our online program has benefited from leveraging the assets of the traditional program. Keeping the two separate allows each to flourish in the ways it needs to in order to serve its distinct student markets. While we would eagerly compare our quality controls and efforts to any of our peers, we still hear the "SNHU is becoming like Phoenix" barbs from some of our more traditional competitors. There is the occasionally voiced, "Is the tail wagging the dog?" concern, but in truth, any objective analysis would show considerable investments in a traditional campus that in many ways is becoming *more* traditional, not less. Of course, that then raises the question of "Are we making that traditional model even less sustainable and more dependent on online's cross-subsidy?"

In reality, the operational prowess of our online group, much borrowed from the for-profits, is influencing operations on the main campus and making it more efficient, service-oriented, and able to support more students with scalable systems. The online program's large marketing footprint has raised overall SNHU brand awareness and has had a halo effect, producing record numbers of applicants to the traditional campus-based program. While there will likely be an ongoing cross-subsidy, we are nearing the point where it is established as a set amount and the traditional campus works to a greater level of self-sustenance within that budget discipline.

SEVEN QUESTIONS INSTITUTIONS MUST ASK THEMSELVES ABOUT ONLINE DELIVERY

Every institution is different (it is tempting here to paraphrase the opening line of *Anna Karenina*), so will forge its own answers to a set of somewhat vexing questions:[12]

1. *How much savings will you pass on?* Online learning is undoubtedly less costly to offer and with *scale* there can be considerable margins. At SNHU we do a number of things. We provide a subsidy to the traditional campus. We reinvest in growing and improving the online operation (largely to the benefit of students). We build the endowment. We also address cost to students, providing millions more in scholarship aid and holding down tuition increases to CPI or less.

2. *How will you enter the online market?* The word *scale* is emphasized in the prior paragraph for a reason. Not so long ago, an institution could enter the market with modest programs and small enrollment goals. However, the cost of offering online programs has risen for a number of reasons, including:

a. Higher service levels that have become the industry norm (for example: like many others we pay the $10 transcript request fee for our prospective students and chase down their transcripts, removing for them that hurdle to entry—but it requires money and staff).

b. The cost of compliance is climbing as ED has invoked state registration rules, adding hundreds of thousands of dollars in fees as the market expands to more states, as well as legal fees (we have hired a general counsel and a full-time assistant to simply administer the processes, each wildly different from the next).

c. Cost of student acquisition remains high and is likely to climb as more competitors vie for leads. Student acquisition costs often hover around $3,000 when the full cost of marketing is accounted for and includes the advertising now required to break through the "noise."

d. Talent is more expensive if you intend to compete with the for-profits.

There's more, but it comes down to capital and the ability to make the necessary investment. SNHU was lucky in terms of timing, entering the market when it could still do so at more modest levels of spending and then using growth to self-fund expansion. The cost and complexity of entry is now much higher.

3. *Will you launch your online program within the institution's organizational structure or as a largely separate business unit?* It is no surprise that many of the most successful online nonprofits have been launched as standalone or separate entities. Think about WGU or the University of Maryland University College or SNHU. Yet governance, the desire to leverage existing resources (separation does mean some duplication of expense), and politics often steer institutions to integrated models.

Maybe most challenging are the four questions that are situated in the messiness of human nature and culture:

4. *Do we know what we do not know?*

5. *Do we have the people we need to lead and deliver on the initiative?*

6. *Do we have a culture of accountability, urgency, data (most higher education institutions do not), and a true passion for student success?*

7. *Is it consistent with our mission, what we see as the institutional job we are trying to do?*

The first three questions can be answered with money and business planning, but what we know about organizational change is that human nature, culture in the collective, is the most complicated and daunting of factors. The final four questions map out some of that murkier landscape.

All of the above begs the central question for any institution: why should we offer online programs? If it is to learn more about the possibilities that come with new technologies, to improve teaching and learning, or to offer some additional choices for existing students, then even a modest online program can prove useful and possible. If it is to protect or gain market share and provide substantially new revenue streams to the institution, then the task is not an easy one any longer. And finally, again: who are you trying to serve? Online learning is a long way from disrupting traditional campuses serving eighteen-year-olds (it doesn't do that job very well), and if that's the job you do, relax. If you educate adults, then you need to get busy.

Finally, why have we at SNHU chosen to work on College for America even as our online program grows nationally and allows us to dramatically improve the institution as a whole? Because the lesson in Christensen's work and the one currently being played out across much of higher education is that at some point new disruptive innovations will come about. We think LSOPs have years of growth ahead of them given the enormous need for higher education and the comfort most people feel with a delivery model that largely mimics traditional education, albeit in a virtual space. That said, we want SNHU to be part of the next disruptive wave when the time comes. That means finding resources to support what is essentially our R&D effort, serving new markets that are not well served by LSOPs, and giving the new business unit license to rethink not only what the traditional campus does, but also what our successful online operation does. In that sense, the Innovation Lab's charge is to disrupt the disruptor. As Bill Gates suggested once, the changes we will see in the next two years will probably be far less than the enthusiastic national discussion presumes, but in ten years we are likely to see higher education redefined, expanded, and improved in ways that are almost unimaginable.[13] Traditional higher education providers have an opportunity to shape that future, but must remember the most basic rule about the flying trapeze: to get to the other side of the circus tent, you have to let go of the handle that got you halfway there, even as you reach for the one coming your way.

10

Public Mandates, Private Markets, and "Stranded" Public Investment

Burck Smith

Dating back to the American Revolution, the United States Postal Service (USPS) has been a trusted and cherished American institution. Who doesn't associate the Pony Express with the opening of the American West or the slogan of "neither rain, nor sleet, nor snow . . ." with American perseverance? With a mandate to provide access to mail service to anyone, anywhere, the USPS let a polyglot citizenry communicate across a sprawling country. It was a nation-building need that the private sector would not fill. In the nearly two hundred fifty years since Ben Franklin served as the first Postmaster General, the U.S. population has grown from under 3 million to over 300 million, and the need for communication has grown exponentially.

The USPS experienced nearly constant growth until its peak of 208 billion pieces of mail delivered in 2001.[1] However, by 2010, the number of items delivered dropped to 171 billion, an 18 percent reduction, and the number of higher-profit first-class letters dropped by 25 percent.[2] The decreased mail volume resulted in a $10 billion loss in 2011. The response of the USPS to such losses has been to increase stamp prices and cut services (and appeal to Congress). However, raising prices and reducing services only drives more customers away, which results in even higher prices and greater service reductions—a business model death spiral.

Key Points

- The market and product characteristics of higher education are fundamentally different than they were sixty years ago due to demographic and technological changes.

- Today's taxpayer subsidies for higher education accessed through accreditation are based on a legacy regulatory model.

- The application of a legacy regulatory model to the new market results in significant "profiteering" for many accredited colleges.

- The legacy regulatory model cannot be adapted to the new market because the changes would undermine the revenue structure of those that control it.

- Because of the mismatch between the legacy regulatory model and the characteristics of the new market, none of the higher education cost-reduction strategies currently discussed are likely to succeed.

- Principles of new regulatory models should focus on outcomes, student choice, and model innovation.

- Possible models range from consolidating all postsecondary subsidies into a consumer Lifetime Learning Account to "do no harm" where existing structural tensions lead to stranded public investment.

With an insatiable demand for communication in an exponentially growing marketplace, what happened to the USPS? First, e-mail, cheap long-distance calls, and online billing made personal communication essentially free. Second, the percentage of the United States population that can't be reached by either new technologies or private delivery services is extremely small. Put simply, the market for personal communication—previously unprofitable and requiring public support—became profitable and diversified, just not for USPS. Today, messaging options that are free—like e-mail and long-distance phone service—are bundled with other services that customers will pay for—like Internet access, cell phone access, and search engines (for search engines, customers "pay" by being advertised to). Messaging options that are expensive—like overnight delivery—are now offered by providers who are able and willing to absorb losses from a small percentage of deliveries by profiting on the much larger number of deliveries. The evolution of the personal communications market from monolithic, unprofitable, and publicly supported to competitive, profitable, and privatized has brought massive innovation and savings to consumers, but it also erodes the economic justification for a publicly subsidized communication system.

Another publicly subsidized market where customers can choose their provider and whose foundation is built upon information sharing and communication is higher education. In the name of access to higher education, a scarce resource in the twentieth century and all centuries before it, new colleges were built and operated with public money. To continue to spur demand for college education, publicly sanctioned financial instruments were created to purchase what we think of as "college" at already subsidized prices. Due to greater supply and an even greater demand for skilled workers, annual college enrollment has grown tenfold over the last sixty years to over 21 million students.[3] Starting in 2001, some students began learning online. The growth in online learning coincided with increases in the number of transfer students, nontraditional students, certificate programs, and, increasingly, unaccredited alternatives to the traditional notion of college. As with the postal service, the arrival of new and cheaper options allows students/customers to differentiate themselves by type and by need. Institutions negatively affected by such differentiation are raising prices while reducing services—again, the business model death spiral. Lastly, "access"—the original justification for public mandates and taxpayer subsidies—is no longer limited by geography or by a scarcity of providers. It is limited by price and technological infrastructure. The mechanisms used to subsidize higher education, and possibly the subsidies themselves, no longer fit the market that they serve.

Some will argue that the USPS and public higher education are too dissimilar to draw meaningful conclusions; that e-mail is qualitatively better than snail mail while online learning is better than traditional higher education only in certain circumstances. Admittedly, the "product" of higher education is far more complicated than the delivery of a simple message. However, we should remember that e-mail was not qualitatively better than the postal system when e-mail first became widely available in the mid-1990s (almost a decade prior to the precipitous decline in first-class delivery). Too few people had e-mail addresses, computing devices were scarcer and deskbound, bandwidth was limited, and file format incompatibility made attachments an adventure. However, as more users signed on, the technical limitations were solved and the necessary infrastructure expanded such that now, in 2012, e-mail seems qualitatively better than snail mail. Further, snail mail remains a preferred method of delivery, but for a small subset of uses. For instance, messages for which more emotional weight is desired—like birthday cards from relatives, letters from lovers, and advertisements for products—are best sent by post. A better question for postal and higher education regulators is: "Is the relative value of physical mail delivery and place-based education sufficient to justify the taxpayer investment in it? If so, in what parts and by how much?"

Unlike the postal service, the higher education regulatory and financing model creates barriers to competition that have slowed the ability of customers to self-differentiate. These barriers prevent new providers and new models from emerging, which keeps prices high. To extend the analogy, if the postal service acted like higher education, it would have asserted its exclusive authority to offer e-mail and charged first-class rates for the messages. However, the recent growth of alternatives to traditional credentialing (e.g., StraighterLine, edX, and Udacity), service delivery (e.g., SMARTHINKING, InsideTrack, Piazza, and OpenStudy), and content creation (e.g., Flatworld Knowledge, Carnegie Mellon's Open Learning Initiative, and the Saylor Foundation's open courseware) point to an accelerating fragmentation of our historical definition of college. Simultaneously, and not coincidentally, the issues of ever-rising college prices, student debt, and diminishing return on investment (ROI) for an undergraduate degree are becoming mainstays of media and public policy.

The advent of more course- and component-level choices for students is crashing headlong into the self-interest of providers of "college"—threatening the business models of incumbent providers. The problems of price, debt, and ROI will not be solved until we confront the realities of a higher education market where the founding assumptions embedded in our regulatory and financial structures are no longer valid. In this chapter, I explore how these founding assumptions will stunt the current effort to lower prices and suggest some new approaches to reform that can encourage low-cost providers to emerge and flourish.

WHY ARE MARKETS SUBSIDIZED?

Governments intervene in private markets to protect consumers, fix market failures, protect local industries, redistribute wealth, or provide for the common good. For instance, without the FDA, dangerous drugs and foods would be easier to purchase, thereby harming consumers. Without public utilities commissions, electricity providers would evolve into monopolies with too much pricing power, thereby distorting the market for electricity. Without agricultural subsidies, our (arguably) critical agricultural industries would be at risk to foreign competition. Without a progressive tax code, those who benefit the most from society's rules and mores would contribute the least. Without the Department of Defense, our nation's protection would be in the hands of other people who might not have the same interests as the country as a whole.

The primary justification for government intervention in higher education has been that students, particularly rural students, could neither access nor afford college—a personally uplifting and publicly democratizing institution. Therefore, public colleges were built in rural locations, and student aid and other financial instruments were created to subsidize both the supply and demand for college. Frequent secondary justifications for public investment in higher education include income redistribution through grants and subsidized loans, the provision of spillover social benefits above and beyond those that accrue for individuals, and consumer protection through the federal accreditation and state licensing system.

However, like the role of the postal system in the personal communication market, the public role of higher education needs to be rethought in a market whose characteristics have fundamentally changed. Today, the price of college courses taken online should be much lower than those taken in a face-to-face environment. Further, the number of students desiring a college degree has exploded due to population growth and the increased demand for postsecondary training. Lastly, the education options available to any single student have multiplied due to the ability to learn online. Access, the principle justification for public higher education, is no longer limited by providers but by price and high-speed bandwidth.

Other justifications, like consumer protection, are increasingly debatable. The ability of the current postsecondary regulatory apparatus to protect consumers is dubious. College tuition has risen four times faster than inflation, grade inflation is rampant though students are studying much less than they used to, studies indicate that students are learning very little, per-student debt is skyrocketing, profit margins for online courses are substantial, and the federal government felt it necessary to reregulate already accredited for-profit institutions.

If access and consumer protection are not being served by the existing regulatory and financial structure, the lone remaining justification for public investment is simply investment in an enterprise whose social benefits accrue to more than just the individual. These benefits would be threefold: (1) the creation of an educated citizenry benefits the civic infrastructure and is the lifeblood of a democracy, (2) college subsidies generate research and knowledge creation that would not be generated by the private sector, and (3) colleges create local cultural and employment centers.

Though it can be argued that the public benefits of higher education warrant market intervention, markets with surplus public benefits are not, by default, worthy of public investment. For instance, bicycle use (health improvement, pollution reduction, road use reduction) and newspaper publishing (education and community building) create significant public benefits but are not subsidized markets. Also, some activities with public benefits are funded by usage fees rather than broad-based taxpayer subsidies. For instance, airport security and 911 telephone service are paid for by user surcharges. To the extent that the public benefits of private education deserve subsidies, these should be negotiated and delivered on their merits. For instance, direct student subsidies might make sense to increase the percentage of the population that takes advantage of higher education, thereby increasing the public value, but institutional subsidies do not serve the same purpose. Much of the research function in higher education is already funded by nontuition revenues like grants and contracts, and there is a spirited debate about the value of much of the research that is generated by academia. So, the research function of education is already well equipped to argue for its own subsidies. Lastly, the cultural and community benefit offered by colleges are questions of public resource allocation rather than student learning. Public subsidies for these functions should be justified accordingly.

Nevertheless, the public belief in the social benefits of higher education is sufficiently widespread to assume that some kind of public support of higher education is warranted. However, what is the right instrument for public support? Today's chaotic mix of customer and provider subsidies through direct payments and tax code adjustments has created a regulatory Frankenstein's monster whose perverse consequences are profoundly distorting a higher education market that should be much more affordable than it currently is.

HIGHER EDUCATION'S CURRENT SUBSIDIZATION AND REGULATORY STRUCTURE

Access, the other side of the coin to scarcity, is the single most common justification for public funding of higher education. Indeed, throughout history, access to the individuals and materials necessary to learn has been limited and precious. As eloquently described by Peter Smith, current vice president at Kaplan University, former president of Cal State University–Monterey Bay, and former congressperson:

> Our system of higher education is based on and organized around the principle of scarcity, that the resources needed to provide an education must be collected in one place—a campus—because there is an insufficient supply of those resources in the general community. Not enough faculty members. Not enough classrooms. Not enough laboratories. Not enough library books. There was no other way to "do" higher education . . . Scarcity was a reality in the world of information, teaching, and learning until the early 1990s when the Web was born. Essentially, the principle of scarcity says that for an institution to be valuable to the community around it, it must offer a service that community members can't get more

cheaply or with higher quality somewhere else. The scarcity, based on an inability to duplicate the resource, controls the market.[4]

Scarcity has been the underpinning of the organizational and business model of "college" since "college" first started in the Middle Ages. Because subject matter experts were scarce and real-time communication options were limited, it made sense to build impressive campuses to attract professors and enable teaching. With such large fixed costs, adding a few more professors was relatively cheap. A critical mass of professors attracted a critical mass of students, who attracted more professors, and so on. This model—substantial fixed costs with low marginal costs (the cost to offer one more class)—became the only and preferred economic model when it was "hardwired" by tying a college's accreditation status to substantial direct and indirect public subsidies. By awarding significant taxpayer subsidies to course providers that adhere to a high-fixed-cost, low-marginal-cost economic model that is enshrined by accreditation, these providers have a preferred position in the marketplace. Such a position makes it difficult for alternatives to emerge.

Students get a wide variety of taxpayer support to go to college. Taxpayer subsidies flow to public, private, and for-profit colleges through both state and federal channels, as shown in table 10.1.

These subsidies include federal grants, federal loan subsidies, federal loan guarantees, federal tax-favored savings plans, federal tax credits, state grants and subsidized loans, state subsidies of colleges, and the nonprofit tax status of colleges. Though impossible to fully calculate, a partial calculation yields $163 billion annually, not including the value of federal tax-exemption and government endorsement. Divided by 21 million students (full- and part-time), this yields a taxpayer subsidy of over $7,750 per student per year.

To be accredited, a college must meet a variety of criteria, but most of these deal with a college's inputs rather than its outcomes. Furthermore, only providers of entire degree programs (rather than individual courses) can be accredited. And even though they are accredited by the same organizations, colleges have complete discretion over their "articulation" policies—the agreements that stipulate the credits that they will honor or deny when transferred from somewhere else. To better make the point, if a student wanted to take a course from the world's best and cheapest provider of any given course, she would not be able to pay for the course with any of the taxpayer subsidies available to purchase courses from accredited colleges. Then, if the student purchased anyway, she would have to persuade the college she attends to award credit for the course even though the college

TABLE 10.1 **Higher education subsidies**

	Annual direct subsidies	**Annual indirect subsidies**
Demand side (student subsidies)	• $8.5 billion (student state and local aid, FY2011)[1] • $41.5 billion (federal Pell Grants, FY2012)[2] • $2.07 billion (lost revenue from subsidized Stafford loans at 3.4 percent interest rate, FY2012)[3] • *Total: $52.07 billion*	• $25 billion (government revenue losses from higher education tax provisions, FY2010)[4] • $9.6 billion (student loan defaults, FY2010)[5] • $6.7 million (Perkins loan cancellations, FY2010)[6] • *Total: $34.6 billion*
Supply side (institutional subsidies)	• $73 billion (state and local appropriations to colleges and universities, FY2011)[7]	• Property tax exemption for nonprofits, $2.8 billion (1997)[8] • Federal tax exemption for nonprofits • Land grants • De facto student loan guarantees

Note: This table is not intended to provide an authoritative value on the total higher education subsidy. There is undoubtedly a wide variety of subsidies and credits that are not included. It is an attempt to list the multiple sources and an order of magnitude for taxpayer support for higher education.

---

[1] State Higher Education Executive Officers, *State Higher Education Finance FY2011* (Boulder, CO: State Higher Education Executive Officers, 2012), 18.

[2] National Association of Student Financial Aid Administrators, *National Student Aid Profile: Overview of 2012 Federal Programs* (Washington, DC: National Association of Student Financial Aid Administrators, 2012), 5.

[3] Based on Chase Select Private Student Loan maximum starting interest rate (see http://www.chasestudentloans.com/apr-example.html). Multiply difference in student loan interest rates by total loan subsidized Stafford loan volume (8.62 percent − 3.4 percent × $39.7 billion). Calculated using data from National Association of Student Financial Aid Administrators, *National Student Aid Profile*, 6.

[4] U.S. Government Accountability Office, *Improved Tax Information Could Help Families Pay for College*, (Washington, DC: U.S. Government Accountability Office, 2012), 5.

[5] Kelly Field, "Government Doesn't Profit From Student-Loan Defaults, Budget Analysis Shows," *Chronicle of Higher Education*, February 14, 2011, http://chronicle.com/article/Government-Doesnt-Profit-From/126373/.

[6] "Federal Campus-Based Programs Data Book 2010," U.S. Department of Education, http://www2.ed.gov/finaid/prof/resources/data/databook2010/databook2010.html; "Federal Campus-Based Programs Data Book 2011," U.S. Department of Education, http://www2.ed.gov/finaid/prof/resources/data/databook2011/databook2011.html.

[7] State Higher Education Executive Officers, *State Higher Education Finance FY2011*, 18.

[8] Joseph J. Cordes, Marie Gantz, and Thomas Pollak, "What Is the Property-Tax Exemption Worth?" in *Property-Tax Exemption for Charities*, ed. Evelyn Brody (Washington, DC: Urban Institute Press, 2002).

has a strong financial disincentive to do so. Lastly, to further tip the scales toward incumbent providers, accreditation bodies are funded by member colleges, and accreditation reviews are conducted by representatives from the colleges themselves. The "iron triangle" of input-focused accreditation, taxpayer subsidies tied to accreditation, and subjective course articulation (shown in figure 10.1) ensures that almost all of the taxpayer funds set aside for higher education flow to providers that look the same. And by giving these models such a preferred position in the market for higher education and making it difficult to alter the form of higher education, the legacy regulatory structure prevents the kind of innovation necessary when market conditions change.

LEGACY REGULATORY STRUCTURES, NEW MARKET CONDITIONS, AND "PROFITEERING"

And the market has changed—dramatically. Between 1950 and today, the number of enrolled postsecondary students per year has grown tenfold while the overall population has only doubled.[5] Also, the revolution that began in the mid-1990s in the technologies of information transmission and communication—the underpinnings of education—is accelerating exponentially today. With information and communication changing from scarce to free, the necessity of a physical location to share information, ideas, and discussion has diminished. In fact, as the cost of content, learning management software, and telecommunications plummets toward zero, the only remaining direct cost for online courses is the cost of a professor's

FIGURE 10.1   **Subsidies, accredation, and barriers to innovation**

Subsidy	• State allocation. • Federal student grants/subsidized loans. • Nonprofit tax status. • Tax preferred plans. • Competitive advantages.
Accreditation	• Only degrees can be accredited, not courses. • Accreditation measures inputs, not outcomes. • Colleges set own, subjective articulation policies. • Accrediting agencies are staffed and financed by colleges.
Competitive barriers	• Colleges cannot easily be disaggregated. • Colleges must look similar to each other. • Standards are set and enforced bu those that would be undermined by changes.

time. With this kind of cost reduction, some of the elements of the college business model are now vastly cheaper to deliver. By combining newly viable customer segments with new technologies, some student segments and some segments of the college experience should be *much* cheaper to serve. But which segments?

When colleges began offering online courses and programs as academically equivalent to face-to-face offerings, they created course-level economic substitutes with much lower cost structures. With courses and credits already interchangeable among many accredited colleges, online learning creates a global market for courses (instead of a geographic monopoly). The availability of cheaper substitutes within a global marketplace gives students a level of purchasing power and consumer choice that was previously unavailable. Under these conditions, a less regulated market would see prices plummet for those elements of college that are affected by lower cost structures (see figure 10.2) and revenue would migrate to new providers. However, such pricing would dramatically undermine the revenue models of many existing colleges that rely on the subsidies generated by higher-priced face-to-face courses. Instead, colleges, with the protection of the accreditation and financial aid system, have kept course prices constant across all methods of delivery. By keeping pricing constant, colleges avoid a migration of students from a high-revenue course option to a low-revenue course option that might undermine their business model (on a side note, this is why the cable television industry fights so hard against

FIGURE 10.2   **Market segments susceptible to disruption**

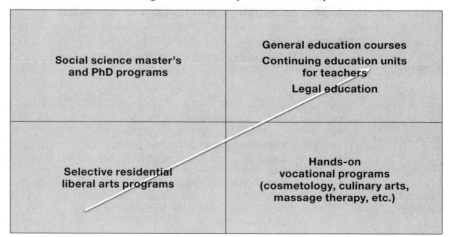

channel-specific purchases). Going one step further, some colleges have realized that constant pricing not only prevents revenue erosion, but it can also be a big money maker. By developing online programs, the savings that are possible from online learning are captured by the college rather than delivered to the student. Indeed, 93 percent of colleges price online courses the same or higher than face-to-face courses.[6]

According to Clayton Christensen and his seminal work on market disruption, there are three generic business models: solution shops, value-adding process businesses, and facilitated user networks.[7] Solution shops solve unstructured problems. Examples include consulting firms or advertising agencies. They typically charge on a fee-for-service basis. Value-adding process businesses bring in items that are incomplete and add value. Examples include manufacturing and restaurants. They typically charge on a per-unit basis for the output of their work. Facilitated user networks are enterprises in which the participants exchange things with each other. Examples include insurance companies or telecommunication companies. They usually charge a fee for membership or a fee for use. Due to the economic logic of scarcity, colleges perform all three functions. For instance, imparting critical-thinking skills and civic responsibility are unstructured problems that universities profess to be good at solving. Workforce preparation and content delivery are value-added solutions for students. Membership in an alumni community and access to the physical campus itself are facilitated user networks. Colleges sometimes perform these functions together and sometimes in isolation, but more importantly, due to accreditation, a college *must* perform all of them. Due to colleges' incentive to avoid customer segmentation, they offer constant prices across all delivery models.

Though the stereotypical 18- to 22-year-old student likely benefits from the conflation of these three business models, many do not. Due to increased demand for skilled workers, the largest segment of today's college students are adults, working or attending college part-time.[8] These students may have already developed critical-thinking skills, civic responsibility, and effective work habits; therefore, they do not need the solution-shop element of higher education. Similarly, they may have gained the skills that would be taught in a value-adding process, but simply need proof to take elsewhere. Lastly, their work participation or obligations to other facilitated user networks may limit their desire to participate in the campus experience. Any given student may need only one of these permutations. More importantly, some of these are more appropriate for different parts of a degree program. The consumer demand possibilities not only vary by business model, but by elements within a degree program.

In a better-functioning market, these students would be able to choose by business model, by level of granularity, and by service offering at a wide variety of price points from a wide variety of providers. However, such choice is constrained by the distorting effects of market subsidies and the lack of an objective definition of college used by accreditors. In most industries, new technologies yield productivity improvements and price reductions because consumers vote with their dollars, and providers that don't adopt new technologies ultimately go out of business. However, in higher education, colleges use their preferred market position and existing subsidies to capture the price reductions that should flow to students. It's not an accident that most colleges are looking to online learning as a way to deal with budget woes.

Many colleges' distance education programs are cash cows whose profits are maintained by the ability to keep prices high, allow students to access federal debt, and exert selective credentialing authority. For instance, Arizona State University Online, a revenue-sharing relationship between Pearson and Arizona State University, yielded $6 million in profit in 2011. Projections are that it will yield $200 million in profit by 2020.[9] Similarly, Southern New Hampshire University, a private nonprofit college, is justifiably proud of the seven thousand students (up from one thousand seven hundred in four years), $73 million in annual revenue, and 42 percent profit margins generated by its online program.[10] However, back-of-the-envelope math shows that each student generates over $4,000 in profit per year for this nonprofit. By definition, online students are being overcharged to subsidize face-to-face students.

At most universities, these profits—whether derived from online learning, big-time sports, or outsourced services—are heavily invested in university facilities and personnel, rather than the students themselves. For instance, "between 1993 and 2007, the number of full-time administrators per [one hundred] students at America's leading universities grew by 39 percent, while the number of employees engaged in teaching, research, or service only grew by 18 percent. Inflation-adjusted spending on administration per student increased by 61 percent during the same period, while instructional spending per student rose 39 percent."[11] Colleges have also committed to significant facilities construction, reflecting a belief in the continued and escalating flow of revenue. According to Jeff Selingo, editor of the *Chronicle of Higher Education*, in a 2012 *New York Times* op-ed, "Students were not the only ones to go deeper into debt. So did schools, building lavish residence halls, recreational facilities, and other amenities that contributed little to actual learning. The debt taken on by colleges has risen 88 percent since 2001, to $307 billion." As the market begins to adjust to price points that more accurately represent the cost of delivery for courses that are academic equivalents, many colleges' budgets will no longer be supportable, and they will have stranded fixed and personnel expenses.

Some will argue that the reduction of course delivery costs does not translate to a reduction of college expenses because the college experience is greater than the sum of its constituent courses. While this is true at some colleges, student behavior at most others proves that students see at least a significant portion of "college" as interchangeable. Over one-third of all students transfer, and nearly half have taken at least one online course. This does not include courses and credits earned from alternative sources like dual enrollment, AP, CLEP, ACE Credit recommended courses, prior learning assessment, and credit imported from other colleges.

LEGACY REGULATION PROTECTS COLLEGES RATHER THAN CONTROLLING PRICE

Because of the market distortions caused by an outdated regulatory and subsidy structure and the limitations on product innovation created and maintained by accreditation, there is no effective price-setting mechanism in higher education. Without effective price setting in a market with thousands, rather than a few, providers for any given student, cost control will never be realized. Accordingly, almost all current cost-control policy suggestions that protect existing colleges are likely to be unsuccessful.

When markets are working properly, their benefit is that they set prices efficiently. To work properly, markets need sufficient buyers, sellers, and available information about the product to be purchased. In the past, there weren't sufficient buyers (students) or sellers (colleges), and the only way to organize and deliver "college" was a time-delimited stint in a physical place with other buyers. "College" was well defined, but the market wasn't. Accordingly, the public stepped in to subsidize the market. Today, the market is well defined, but "college" isn't. There are plenty of buyers and sellers, but "college" could be delivered in all sorts of ways. Yet, the price is either set by government mandate (public colleges), varies depending on the buyer characteristics (net tuition), or both. The product—a college degree—is defined by the college and accreditors, and information about its value for any given provider is not only not available, but also not tracked and certainly not communicated. In short, despite having sufficient buyers and sellers, market pricing cannot flourish because the product ("college") is defined by its providers, preserved by the government's financial backing, and difficult to measure because of the paucity of interprovider information. The result is little innovation in the elements of the product, coupled with continued price growth despite lower-cost means of delivery. When providers can combine strong demand with strong pricing power emanating from limited competition, the result is rapid price growth. It is also the textbook definition of a cartel. Like all profit-maximizing entities, colleges want to maintain this preferential market positioning. However, because they are being funded and protected by government dollars and policies, they must respond to criticism about rising prices.

When asked about ways to reduce the high price of college, colleges almost always point to cost-reduction—rather than price-reduction—strategies. Examples include Course Redesign (a proven way to reduce the cost of delivery of high-enrollment classes while improving student outcomes), the promotion of free content through open courseware initiatives, and greater use of online learning.[12] Unfortunately, even if every college in the country adopted Course Redesign principles for all of its general education courses (it's a crime that more haven't done so already), used all available open courseware, and offered a full list of online courses, higher education tuition would continue to rise unabated.

To understand why the cost of course delivery can fall but price can continue to rise, it's helpful to look at a college's course-level revenue and cost structure. For instance, in Massachusetts (other states have comparable cost structures), the average tuition and fees charged by the two- and four-year systems (not including the University of Massachusetts) are roughly $540 and $872, respectively (I derived these by dividing the tuition and fees for a full-time student by ten courses). The portion of two- and four-year systems' budgets that are subsidized by the state is roughly 32 percent and 21 percent, respectively.[13] This means that the average all-in revenue for a course delivered to an in-state student at a two-year college is $792 and $1,108 at a four-year college. Depending on the college and course, the direct instructional costs (not overhead and fixed costs) of an introductory-level course are somewhere around $100 per student. (For back-of-the-envelope calculations, assume that an adjunct makes $3,000 per course with thirty students.[14] There are few other direct instructional costs.) Courses redesigned using Course Redesign principles have demonstrated an average 37 percent reduction in the cost of delivery. For a $100 per-student course, this represents a $37 savings. Though this cost reduction adds up to real dollars, it represents only a 5 percent potential price reduction for that course at a community college and a 3 percent potential price reduction at a four-year college for that particular course. The most likely candidates for Course Redesign are the forty or so general-education courses. These represent about one-third of all enrollments in higher education. So, even if

Course Redesign principles were applied to all applicable courses, the total price reduction would be 1.6 percent at a community college and 1 percent at a four-year college.

Another often-touted cost-reduction strategy is greater use of open and free content. Indeed, many foundations, state governments, and the federal government have subsidized the creation of open and free content. The rather nebulous justification is that, if content is free, then somehow college costs will be reduced. However, open and free content has zero impact on college prices. This is because (1) professors already build courses with their own materials as part of their compensation, and free and open online materials do not change this cost equation; (2) the cost of the digital materials in course development, when amortized over all the students taking the course, is trivial; and (3) students pay for textbooks separately from tuition, which lets professors get digital materials from major publishers for free. What's more, any cost savings derived from Course Redesign or the use of open courseware are often promised to the departments that adopted the innovation to get their buy-in. These savings may be used to support lower class loads, hire additional personnel, or support additional research. While these activities may be useful, they don't result in lower prices.

If cost-saving strategies won't reduce the price of college, can policy makers focus on price-based strategies? Successful price-based strategies must incorporate all of the necessary elements of efficient markets. There must be sufficient sellers, sufficient buyers, sufficient transactional information, and a product definition that is consistent between the buyer and the seller. The following is a list of the price-based strategies that are most often discussed, but unfortunately, these are all lacking one or more elements:

- *Performance funding.* Performance-funding initiatives tie taxpayer support to higher completion rates. Though not exactly a price-reduction strategy, it aims to get greater value for the existing price. Performance funding is elegant in theory, but without objective, course-level outcome assessments, it is likely to further diminish the credibility of a college degree. Grade inflation is already rampant in America's colleges, and students are already studying 40 percent less than they did twenty years ago. Without a consistent and public definition of the product between the buyer and the seller, performance funding is more likely to harm than help.
- *Shaming.* Shaming is the practice of publicly listing the colleges with the highest tuition and tuition growth. For the most part, this is relevant only to those colleges that are the most selective or that use tuition as a proxy for quality. Because these colleges are selective,

the students who apply are not particularly price-sensitive and represent the smaller portion of the college-going population; thus, such a policy is not likely to have a material impact on college behavior.

- *Pricing transparency of full-time enrollment.* Colleges were recently required to put "net price calculators" on their Web sites. These calculators are supposed to allow students to input financial information to determine what their net price would be. The theory is that, by creating greater pricing transparency, these calculators will prompt students to make choices based on net price and force colleges to reduce the overall price of tuition. Unfortunately, most colleges are not able or willing to give a complete view of the true cost because many financial decisions won't actually be made until enrollment. Further, the net price calculator doesn't allow for the possibility of completing some parts of a college in one place (like at a community college or StraighterLine) and completing the rest of college at the school. Lastly, there are multiple versions of a net price calculator with varying inputs and outputs.

CREDENTIALING AUTHORITY IN A POST-ACCESS WORLD

Colleges and universities have a private-sector business model with a public-sector mandate. Despite a degree being a uniform measure of achievement, it has different measures and value depending on the institution. Until the notion of a degree is more artfully explained, unbundling within the accreditation system will remain difficult.

The authority to award a degree derives from either public or private sources. Consider a typical graduation ceremony: the long robes, silly hats, multicolored sashes, and the solemnity of the occasion create a sense of continuity, extending all the way back to the Middle Ages. In this model, where one group welcomes a new member, the granting of a credential is a "private" asset, meaning that the decision to award or withhold the credential lies with the group, and the group determines the standards. The private credentialing model resembles the inclusion in a guild or the completion of an apprenticeship. It is also the model around which the accreditation structure is organized. Accreditation assumes that all colleges are awarding credentials derived from a private authority.

While this iconic model continues to thrive, particularly among small liberal arts colleges, many students now have a very different college experience. For them, proofs of course completion (i.e., credits) are increasingly accumulated from multiple sources. Students may get college credit while in high school, continue at a community college, move to a public university, and take coursework from an employer (or, now, from many alternative providers of college courses). To the extent that they're transferable, these credits, or "stackable credentials," are eventually assembled into a publicly recognized degree that is conferred by one of the colleges, usually the last one the student attends.

With stackable credentials, the authority to grant a degree or course credit becomes a "public" asset, meaning that the student has met standards that apply to a wide variety of institutions. Getting a diploma is like getting a building permit, earning a driver's license, or passing a bar exam. Individuals who meet the standard are entitled to the credential—unlike the private credential, which is determined by the group that accepts its graduates. Most students and colleges are operating under a public credentialing model, yet are regulated as if they have a private one.

As free or low-cost online courses that are comparable to a college's own online courses become widely offered by many providers outside of the accredited environment, the credentialing element of a college's mission becomes more important than the course delivery element. Because alternative providers of college courses are not allowed to participate in the existing accreditation system, they must rely on the good faith of those with public credentialing authority. This tension will require colleges and policy makers to think much more carefully about where degree-granting authority originates and the responsibilities that it entails.

Though colleges are not accustomed to seeing themselves as licensers, the explosion of possible providers of online courses changes the public's requirement of many of the nation's colleges. Colleges are no longer the sole provider of college coursework. More than ever, they are needed as a credentialer of others' coursework. This new role requires the kind of objectivity and transparency expected from licensing agencies and written into government contracting processes. Without these basic safeguards, the degree will be less a measure of student accomplishment and more a tool to drive revenue.

POST-ACCESS REGULATORY SUGGESTIONS

Today's subsidization and regulatory structure is ill suited for a market with myriad product options at a wide variety of price points. Course providers with preferred market status—public and nonprofit colleges—can use this status to drive profits at the expense of the student. Examples range from substantial overpricing of online courses, to big-time college sports, to entering partnerships that end up charging fees to students for the delivery of financial aid.[15] Clearly, institutions of all stripes are engaged in profit-maximizing behavior, which is typical in an efficient market where all entities are expected to maximize profits. However, nonprofit and public colleges are given taxpayer subsidies under the expectation that they *will not* maximize profits. When working well, markets—and well-designed subsidy systems—pit provider self-interests against each other to the benefit of the consumer and taxpayer.

If the existing regulatory model is no longer appropriate for a market with an abundance of suppliers, demanders, and tools that could provide greater transactional transparency, what is? The answer for online learning might be none—or very little, anyway. The answer for all of higher education might be a model that focuses its subsidies only on consumers, rather than subsidizing both providers and consumers.

Given that today's students and technology create a vastly larger array of supply and demand possibilities, what would a "post-access" higher education regulatory structure look like? How would it meet the core elements of an effective market: sufficient suppliers, sufficient consumers, sufficient transactional information, and shared definition of the product?

- *Shift supply-side subsidies to the demand side.* To encourage innovation in business model and price, supplier subsidies need to be shifted to consumers and consumer subsidies need to be consolidated. The overall subsidy amount can remain constant, yet the structure would be radically clearer. $163 billion per year in annual higher education subsidies divided by the number of students equals at least $7,750 per student annually. This is likely an underestimate. Such a voucher (call it a Lifelong Learning Account) can use the same data currently used by federal financial aid to adjust the total voucher, its value could diminish over time, it could be inherited by children or family members (like current 529 dollars), and it could be subject to other modifications. By delivering this to students, enabling equal competition, better defining the product, and making outcome information public, we can raise the value of higher education dramatically.
- *Institute a minimum objective outcome assessment.* Like open source operating systems, colleges should award equal credit for equal courses, no matter where the course is taken. They could accomplish this by setting uniform outcome standards for commonly taken courses and/or creating an independent review mechanism for course providers. Though not authorized to confer the same market benefits as accreditation, some reviewing entities already exist like ACE's Credit Recommendation Service, the National

College Credit Recommendation Service that serves the state of New York, and, to a lesser extent, the College Board's Advanced Placement review service. Similarly, require assessment to be separated from instruction wherever possible—at least one-third of all college courses are relatively standard across colleges. There is no reason why statewide or even nationwide pools of assessors can't evaluate student work independently and impartially.

- *Provide an escape hatch.* As with the Distance Education Demonstration Program it conducted in the middle part of the previous decade, the Department of Education (ED) could grant accreditation on a case-by-case basis for postsecondary models that seem promising. To be effective, however, such a program must allow for a much wider variety of organizational models than those offered previously. The original Demonstration Program simply changed the locus of delivery from face-to-face to online without changing the basic prerequisites of accreditation. Today's emerging models are much more granular, engage faculty in entirely new ways (if at all), and are far cheaper. A Demonstration Program today would need to look at course-level rather than degree-level accreditation and ROI rather than completion.

- *Choose your own outcome.* Today, accreditation applies to over four thousand colleges with widely divergent missions. Clearly, all colleges should not be required to meet the same outcomes. Today, the closest we've come to setting a desired outcome is Foundation and ED focus on degree completion. However, even degree completion is problematic due to the dilution of a degree's rigor nationally, the inability to compare degrees across schools, and the selection bias among students attending any given college. One way to overcome this is to create a finite set of outcome measures from which a college could choose. Once it has chosen one, the education provider would be evaluated by its ability to meet its metric. Examples might include:
  - Average ten-, twenty-, and thirty-year income of graduates
  - Value added on a predetermined critical-thinking-skills measure like the CLA or ETS iSkills
  - Job placement rates
  - Cohort default rate
  - Individual course pass rate and price

- *Discharge student loans at bankruptcy.* Arguably, one of the drivers of higher education price increases is the availability of guaranteed money. Private loans are effectively guaranteed by the federal government because it is extremely difficult to get a student loan discharged. If lenders faced risk, then they would be more likely to evaluate the investment. As in the mortgage industry, formulas that evaluate student, provider, occupation, and interest rate would quickly emerge. To guard against "redlining," the federal or state government could provide interest rate subsidies for desired socio-economic groups using the data already collected by the FAFSA. While such an approach does not focus on outcome measurement or encourage new organizational models, it lets the market determine the best financial risk. This might include students taking courses outside of the accredited environment prior to enrollment to demonstrate the aptitude and attitude for program completion.

- *Do no harm.* Without doing anything, the existing regulatory and financing structure of higher education will begin to collapse. College prices will continue to rise because of structural inflation, the withdrawal of state support, and the defection of high-margin customers to lower-priced offerings. Concurrently, sources of student aid will continue to dwindle, and the ROI for college will continue to come under attack. Combined, rising prices and declining aid will accelerate the growth of parallel markets, which will accelerate price increases, and so on. By simply avoiding bailouts, additional loan burdens for students and additional anticompetitive regulation, the "do no harm" scenario avoids political confrontation and allows incremental change. It also creates a politically favored and taxpayer-subsidized service without a viable business strategy, like the USPS.

CONCLUSION

Whether it is black-market products during wartime, speak-easies during Prohibition, or jitney cabs at the airport, when a government-regulated market becomes too dysfunctional, new ones emerge. In the United States, the demand for higher education has grown dramatically and the cost of delivery has fallen, yet prices continue to rise despite massive public subsidies. With the proliferation of viable, affordable, and unsubsidized providers of college courses emerging outside of the accreditation system, parallel markets are emerging. With the advent of these new markets, policy makers need to decide whether to subsidize higher education or subsidize accredited colleges.

Historically, because the brick-and-mortar college was the only scalable organizational model to combine information, communication, and reflection, colleges were synonymous with higher education. The rationale for subsidizing colleges was to create access for learners. The subsidization of learners came with tangential benefits like the subsidization of research and scholarship and the contribution of service and culture to local communities. However, as this rationale unravels—brick and mortar isn't the only scalable organizational model, ergo colleges are not synonymous with higher education, ergo the rationale and model of subsidies needs to be rethought—the continued subsidies of these tangential benefits need to stand on their own merit.

However state and federal governments choose to respond to the now-obvious presence of ultra-affordable online courses, it should be clear that colleges cannot keep raising their prices while lowering the cost of delivery forever. As former British Prime Minister Margaret Thatcher famously remarked, "The problem with socialism is that you eventually run out of other people's money." As state and federal governments turn off the spigots, family assets plummet, and students become unwilling to go into dramatic debt, other people's money is drying up. Eventually, even the best-protected markets buckle under these conditions.

Conclusion

Andrew P. Kelly and Kevin Carey

The growth in college costs is not a new story. Since the first year of the Reagan administration, the sticker price of tuition has grown faster than the rate of inflation; over the last ten years, it has grown at two to four times that rate.[1] Even after adjusting for inflation and growing enrollments, colleges are spending more money than they have in the past.

During good times, when pockets are full and governments more generous, the trend does not look as frightening. But each time the country hits an economic trough, policy makers, journalists, and families raise doubts about the value of higher education and the sustainability of the system. For their part, higher education leaders have had few encouraging answers, claiming that they are just as powerless to curb the cost of college as the families they are pricing out.

But there is a growing sense that things are different this time, and not just because the fiscal and economic challenges facing governments and families are graver than ever before. Today the opportunities for a bold way forward have never been so apparent. New ventures—a groundbreaking MOOC provider, an agreement to accept prior learning credits, a new competency-based degree program—are emerging at an ever-increasing rate, definitively changing the higher education landscape in the process. Even more surprising: the drive to innovate has not only come from Silicon Valley startups, but also from some of the country's oldest and most august institutions.

Advances in technology and entrepreneurial energy are only part of the story. We have also entered a new political moment, one in which high-profile leaders on the left and the right have come to recognize that the current path is not financially sustainable. Republican and Democratic policy makers in states like Texas, Indiana, Missouri, and Washington have vocally challenged their higher education systems to do more with less, while simultaneously opening up space for innovative higher education models. This trend starts at the top, with President Obama famously telling colleges and universities in his 2012 State of the Union address, "We can't just keep subsidizing skyrocketing tuition; we'll run out of money . . . So let me put colleges and universities on notice: if you can't stop tuition from going up, the funding you get from taxpayers will go down."[2] While the president's plan to tie campus-based student aid to measures of net price and access stalled, it was still a high-profile shot across the bow.

For all the energy around reforming the cost structure of higher education, there are still significant barriers to change. Foremost among them is the lack of a coherent policy agenda that systematically attacks the college cost problem instead of just coping with it. Newfangled ways of delivering content and instruction may make headlines in the *New York Times*, but they are still the exception rather than the rule. The vast majority of students still pay top dollar (or, more accurately, borrow top dollar) to attend traditional institutions. Meanwhile, the recent emphasis on maintaining low student loan interest rates and creating more generous repayment options mistakes the symptom of the problem for the problem itself. It is natural to be sympathetic to the struggles of young borrowers. But making the terms of borrowing easier may relieve whatever incentive colleges have to lower their prices in the first place. Focusing on student debt and ignoring its source is good politics, but bad policy.

Of course, there are those who argue that it may be better to do nothing; that the system will collapse under its own weight; that the popular theory of "disruptive innovation" is under way, and higher education will resemble the computer, steel, and airline industries in ten years.

But these arguments underestimate the ability of incumbents to protect the policy environment that allows them to maintain their dominant position. It's difficult to dislodge existing providers in regulated markets not only because of their market share, but also because they can use that position to stack the rules of the game in their favor. Powerful higher education interest groups, risk-averse federal regulators, and protectionist state licensure boards will all have something to say about who gets disrupted and when.

Rather than waiting around for a new, more affordable higher education market to emerge on its own, reform-minded leaders can seek out opportunities to coax it along. The chapters in this volume identify many of those opportunities. Collectively, they suggest that college costs and prices are a complex but tractable problem. But our contributors are not Pollyannaish about the challenge ahead. Rather, looking through the contributions here, we see five important lessons for leaders looking to lay the groundwork for a new, cost-conscious era of higher education policy.

COST CONTAINMENT IS POSSIBLE

There is some truth to the tale colleges weave about rising costs: highly educated labor *has* become more expensive, while the basic technology of undergraduate education—the lecture—has not changed much. This is a recipe for growing costs and declining productivity.

But colleges are far from helpless when it comes to containing their costs. In fact, they are often directly responsible for the growth in spending and the accompanying tuition increases. In chapter 2, Robert E. Martin finds that the "revenue model" (or the Bowen hypothesis) of college spending—raise all the revenue you can, spend all the revenue you get—provides a better explanation for the dramatic rise in costs than do factors from outside the university, such as government mandates or increases in labor costs.

Martin and Jeffrey J. Selingo (chapter 5) both highlight one culprit in particular: spending on an increasingly large and byzantine administrative layer. While colleges are complex organizations that require some amount of administrative support, the massive and continuous increase in the size and cost of administration defies any utilitarian logic. Selingo's profile of Bain's efforts at the University of California at Berkeley, the University of North Carolina at Chapel Hill, and Cornell University suggests that much of the administrative hierarchy is redundant; Bain analysts found that most university administrators functioned as mid-level managers, often with fewer than five subordinates reporting directly to them. Not surprisingly, this "bureaucratic entropy," as Martin calls it, has led spending on administrative overhead to increase faster than spending on academics, and the growth in administrative positions has outpaced the growth in student enrollments. All of this leads to higher costs without a proportional increase in output.

Beyond cutting back administrative bloat, colleges and universities must move away from the revenue model of spending and think hard about cost-effectiveness. As Douglas N. Harris argues in chapter 3, higher education leaders, researchers, and policy makers actually know very little about what programs and policies are cost-effective. As a result, when budget deficits require reallocation of resources, leaders often opt for across-the-board cuts rather than a more strategic approach. But it is difficult for campuses to simply cut their way out of budget difficulties, Ari Blum and Dave Jarrat argue in chapter 4. Across-the-board cuts, while less controversial, eliminate productive and unproductive investments alike. Reallocating resources toward cost-effective programs like counseling can boost student success at a reasonable cost, which in turn lowers the cost per degree produced.

The cost disease is not destiny. Harris provides leaders and policy makers with some useful advice on how to implement cost-effectiveness analysis in their own decision making. And the later chapters give a glimpse of how unbundling can lower costs and maintain quality. But these are not simply technical questions; they require a shift in culture. Whether college leaders choose to do more than simply nibble around the edges while waiting out the storm will depend on whether they have incentive to do so.

LOWER COSTS DON'T ALWAYS LEAD TO LOWER PRICES

Even if most colleges adopt far-reaching reforms to their cost structure and become more efficient, it is not a foregone conclusion that cost savings will translate to lower prices for students. The mapping between cost and price has never been straightforward in higher education; state subsidies, endowment earnings, and student aid have typically allowed colleges to "sell" higher education for less than it costs to produce. When colleges take steps to reduce the cost of delivery—say, by adding adjunct faculty—there is little or no pressure to pass on those savings to consumers in the form of lower tuition. Instead, savings are typically used to cross-subsidize the things that generate prestige—research, administration, and student life.

Online courses, like adjunct faculty before them, allow colleges to substitute an inexpensive mode of delivery for costly faculty time. After significant up-front investment, online courses are generally less expensive to deliver than the in-person version. But, as Burck Smith argues in chapter 10, very few colleges charge lower tuition for their online courses. Indeed, recent research has found that more than 90 percent of colleges charge the same price or higher.[3] At these tuition rates, online courses are mostly profit, and the additional revenue cross-subsidizes the traditional campus.

Even a forward-thinking president like Paul J. LeBlanc admits that this is the model at Southern New Hampshire University. The university's online arm charges comparable tuition to the brick-and-mortar campus, generating revenue for cross-subsidy. To the school's credit, Southern New Hampshire uses much of that revenue to provide aid to on-campus students (thereby lowering the net price for these students). And its new College for America program will buck the trend by providing an inexpensive, online associate's degree. But as LeBlanc points out in chapter 9, college leaders have the freedom to decide what to do with the cost savings that arise from online delivery. By and large, the online higher education market looks a lot like the brick-and-mortar one: competition has not yet forced online programs to compete on price.

Of course, less spending per student is a positive outcome from a tax-payer perspective, even if tuition remains unchanged. Decreasing the cost per degree can allow colleges to serve more students with the same amount of state subsidy or endowment income, producing more human capital at the same cost to taxpayers. But for students and families, dramatic improvements in affordability will require that lower-cost modes of delivery translate to lower prices.

NEW MODELS ARE TAKING ROOT, BUT BARRIERS TO ENTRY REMAIN

Outside of the existing system, lower-priced higher education is not only possible, it is already happening. Entrepreneurs have developed new models that stand to threaten the traditional, high-cost model of postsecondary education—low- or no-cost course providers like MOOCs, new methods of awarding credit for prior learning, and competency-based degrees, to name a few. Once these challengers enter the market, the argument goes, competition will force traditional institutions to lower their prices or lose market share. As Michael Staton argues in chapter 6, entrepreneurs are turning their attention to the higher education market because they see an opportunity to do it better and cheaper.

But despite the buzz, these new models still face an uphill battle in competing with incumbent colleges. Foremost among the barriers is an antiquated regulatory system that measures inputs and processes rather than student outcomes. In the absence of objective, agreed-upon measures of quality, regulators like accreditation agencies and state licensure boards rely on proxies that favor traditional models—things like site visits, faculty credentials, and whether facilities are adequate to support student learning. Because winning state and federal approval is key to attracting students and the federal financial aid that comes with them, these barriers tilt the playing field against new, more affordable challengers that may not look like colleges at all.

The open question is whether employers will become convinced that credentials from these new ventures provide a signal of student competency that is as good or better than a diploma from a traditional university. Traditional colleges are able to charge such high prices in part because they have a monopoly over what students want: a credential with labor market value. If upstarts like Udacity, Coursera, or College for America can challenge that monopoly, they will threaten incumbents' main comparative advantage.

Will this happen? Only time will tell. Optimistic observers, including some of our contributors, believe that it is only a matter of time. But the broader policy context suggests that the tidy "disruptive innovation" narrative, whereby traditional universities go the way of the newspaper and record store, will be considerably more complex. So long as the regulatory system and labor market favors the traditional model, existing institutions will maintain a powerful position.

NOT EITHER/OR, BUT BOTH/AND

Existing colleges and universities are unlikely to disappear overnight, but they *will* have to adapt in important ways. In contrast to the futurists who have already declared traditional higher education on the verge of extinction, our contributors suggest that opportunities for lower-cost education are present within and outside the existing sector. Indeed, the most tantalizing opportunities may rest in a complementarity between innovation and tradition. Reforming the cost structure of higher education is not an either/or endeavor.

The contributions in this volume highlight several opportunities for these two agendas to work in tandem. Paul LeBlanc's firsthand account reveals how far a forward-thinking institution can go in creating new, low-cost pathways. But he also notes that the process has been aided by Southern New Hampshire's heritage as a traditional brick-and-mortar institution. In LeBlanc's view, the online program has "benefited from leveraging the assets of the traditional program" and vice versa. Ben Wildavsky's profile of University of Maryland University College in chapter 7 echoes the notion that existing institutions can help lead the way in higher education innovation. UMUC currently provides more bachelor's degrees to African Americans than Maryland's entire set of historically black colleges and universities, thanks in large part to its advances in online learning.

Even among more traditional brick-and-mortar institutions, the emergence of an unbundled market may not kill them off, but it will force them to focus on their comparative advantage. Michael Staton's continuum of unbundling suggests that existing colleges should not focus their energy on competing over the components of higher education that are easy to unbundle and provide at scale, like content and instruction. Instead, traditional institutions should double-down on the facets of the college degree that low-cost, no-frills competitors cannot provide as easily, like the invaluable social networking and "coming of age" functions of the traditional college campus. Even in this unbundled world, traditional universities can still have a role to play, albeit a more limited one than in the past.

Likewise, many of the low-cost "pathways to credit" outlined by Paul Fain and Steve Kolowich in chapter 8 are also positioned as a complement rather than a substitute to the traditional model. For now, the promise of prior learning assessments and MOOCs hinges on how widely accepted these credits become at institutions that grant credentials. Similarly, StraighterLine's main selling points are its articulation agreements with thirty-six accredited colleges and its American Council on Education (ACE)-accredited courses. As these innovations take root, more cost-conscious students will be able to opt for a lower-cost route to credit, but those credits will likely have to be "redeemed" at a traditional college. In this world, existing institutions will continue to serve an important credentialing function, aggregating credits and certifying student learning.

LIMITED POLICY LEVERS

The contributions to this volume do not offer any silver-bullet policy solutions that will "fix" the college cost problem. The Gordian knot of governance structures that Robert Martin describes is not easily solved: pulling on one set of incentives may only wind the other pieces of the knot tighter. In isolation, traditional policy levers—top-down regulation, student aid policy, and use of the bully pulpit—may not be well suited for the job at hand.

Sure, policy makers can opt for a top-down approach, telling colleges and universities that they must keep their tuition prices below a certain level or limit tuition increases to inflation. This is already the model in some states, though higher education institutions have often found ways around such rules, using "fees" and other charges to raise additional revenue. More generally, attempts to compel lower tuition prices via fiat have given rise to charges of "price controls," sparking faux-libertarian objections from higher education trade associations.

Even President Obama's modest proposal to link the small campus-based aid programs to measures of affordability and value was a nonstarter. In a particularly striking rhetorical flourish, David Warren of the National Association of Independent Colleges and Universities warned the president that higher education interests will "use every wise and effective political action to say, 'You cannot go there'" and march "shoulder to shoulder in defense of the principles of our independence."[4]

Setting aside Warren's histrionics, there are reasons to doubt that federal efforts to regulate tuition will get us very far. Tying eligibility for federal aid to tuition rates may help to slow growth in the short run, as colleges scramble to limit tuition increases to "only" a couple percentage points above inflation. Such a policy may even lead colleges to move further into lower-cost models of delivery. But it is unlikely that such a top-down strategy would generate the kind of price competition that can drive down costs over the long term.

To their credit, federal policy makers have taken steps to cultivate more cost-consciousness with better information about higher education prices. As mandated under the 2008 reauthorization of the Higher Education Act, the Obama administration created the College Affordability and Transparency Center, which publishes an annual list of the schools with the highest tuition prices and the most growth in tuition over past years, as well as information on the net price of attendance. Informed consumers are a necessary component of a healthy market. But after years of tuition increases, it seems unlikely that public shaming will affect institutional behavior outside of the most egregious offenders.

At the state level, leaders have used the bully pulpit to push for lower-cost degree pathways. Rick Perry's $10,000 degree challenge is perhaps the most well known, but there are others. Leaders in Indiana, Washington, and Texas have created state-level branches of Western Governors University, while Wisconsin governor Scott Walker has borrowed from WGU's model in his push for a competency-based degree awarded by the University of Wisconsin system.

These new degree options will help to make the case that lower-cost higher education is possible. But these strategies are likely to produce islands of affordability, not systemic pressure to make education more affordable across the board. For instance, Western Governors typically serves working adults with some credits but no degree, those students who have been underserved by the existing system. Traditional campuses are often ill equipped to serve this demographic, meaning that state branches of WGU will not so much compete for students with the traditional campuses as carve off a distinct clientele. And while the $10,000 degree has promise, most of the entrants have thus far opted for conventional ways to reduce the net price to $10,000: targeting a small handful of programs, providing college credit for courses taken in high school, or using scholarships to directly subsidize students.[5] For now, the $10,000 degrees are better thought of as niche programs than a broad, sustainable solution.

To be sure, these policy ideas indicate an important rhetorical shift: after years of focusing on student aid to promote access, top political leaders have come to call on colleges and universities to do more with less. But policy has not yet caught up to the rhetoric. Existing efforts often feel more like retrofitting than reinvention: they aim to compel or entice existing institutions to get more efficient and lower their prices. This approach is not wrong-headed, but it will be hard-pressed to generate the kind of innovation and competition that has driven down costs and improved quality in other sectors. Doing so will require a more forward-thinking approach to reform.

PRINCIPLES FOR A WAY FORWARD

If many popular reforms are insufficient, what policies *can* make a dent in the soaring price of higher education? This is the trillion-dollar question. The good news: the country is having a very different conversation at the dawn of 2013 than even two years ago (when our *Reinventing Higher Education* book was published).[6] College costs are on the political agenda and new models are attracting students, media attention, and the imprimatur of elite colleges. How can policy makers capitalize on the recent wave of entrepreneurship and innovation to dramatically reduce the cost of degrees?

The key is to seek out reforms that create an environment in which providers of all stripes—existing institutions, online universities, standalone course providers—compete with one another to provide high-quality postsecondary education at the lowest possible price. Rather than thinking of the cost of college as a problem to be solved with a particular policy, leaders would be wise to consider how current policy may stunt the incentives for cost containment, innovation, and competition. We outline four basic areas of reform.

Give All Providers Reason to Pay Attention to Cost and Price

Robert Martin's chapter reminds us that existing policies have given colleges almost no incentive to spend money wisely. But it does not have to be that way. Existing institutions must be given a reason to spend resources effectively, experiment with new modes of delivery, and seek out opportunities to partner with lower-cost providers.

Some states have built measures of productivity into their accountability systems, explicitly focusing the energies of institutional leaders on responsible spending and efficiency. For instance, policy makers can learn from the National Governor's Association's Policy Academy, where six states—Colorado, Connecticut, Kentucky, Missouri, Nevada, and Utah—are working to develop measures of efficiency and cost-effectiveness to include in their respective accountability systems. The goal is to link those measures to budgeting decisions.[7] These policies are still taking root, but the six participants have developed new productivity metrics from which others can learn.

At the very least, accountability policies like these will prompt the institutions subject to them to pay attention to their costs. They will also encourage reform-minded leaders to experiment with lower-cost modes of delivery. Whether developed in-house or through partnerships with new ventures, these innovations can help streamline students' path to a degree and reduce the investment necessary to get to the finish line. Consider the Kentucky Community and Technical College System's Learn-on-Demand program, which allows remedial students to pay for only the online learning modules they need and progress as quickly as they can, rather than sit through an expensive, semester-long course. As this book was going to press, the state of California had just announced a partnership with Udacity to provide MOOC-like remedial and introductory math courses to four-year and community college students.[8]

Such opportunities to stretch our higher education dollars are out there, but institutions need a reason to seek them out. Asking tougher questions about where money goes, and why, can provide such an incentive while allowing institutions the autonomy to come up with their own solutions.

Encourage Competition via Smart Deregulation

Improvements at existing institutions are a start, but competition from new ventures is key to driving down prices over the longer term. As one of us testified to the Senate Committee on Health, Education, Labor, and Pensions, "the higher education market needs many new, high-quality, low-price competitors to act as a counterweight to traditional colleges and universities bent on increasing prices forever."[9]

Current regulatory policies have erected significant barriers to these kinds of competitors. Up to now, federal regulations around student aid have precluded both course providers and institutions that are purely competency-based from accessing federal aid (though Paul LeBlanc's new program will test this). And at the state level, licensure boards are often staffed by representatives of existing colleges and universities and operate as cartels that seek to minimize competition. In the latest and most absurd example, the State of Minnesota barred Coursera from providing *free* courses to state residents. In their embarrassment, state regulators reversed the policy soon after it came to light.[10]

Policy makers can learn from experiences in trucking, airlines, and telecommunications, where deregulation cracked open closed markets, encouraged new entrants, and fostered competition. This does not imply a laissez-faire approach to higher education, but one where regulators would privilege outcomes over inputs and processes, moving away from existing rules that reify the traditional model and protect incumbents. Smart deregulation, based on outcome data, would make it possible for all manner of low-cost postsecondary providers to enter the market and compete on price and value.

A worthwhile first step would be to open up the federal financial aid system to low-price entrepreneurs who are willing to be transparent about and accountable for the quality of the services they provide. This policy would include educators and companies who provide only individual *courses*. If you can specialize by providing the world's greatest college calculus class, and only that, why should you be excluded from the student aid system? New providers would be held to outcomes-based standards and evaluated on a regular basis.

At the state and institutional level, leaders should consider Oklahoma State University professor Vance Fried's proposed "corporate venturing" model, where states or institutions set up new, autonomous higher education ventures.[11] These new providers would be insulated from the rest of the state system and allowed to organize and operate in new ways. In exchange for the freedom to innovate, new ventures would be held to strict performance contracts. Southern New Hampshire's Innovation Lab is one model of institutional venturing; state-sanctioned branches of WGU and no-frills campuses like the University of Minnesota–Rochester reveal what is possible at the state level.

Measure Outcomes, Not Processes

Deregulation and healthy competition will require more systematic measurement of student outcomes. Without objective indicators of quality and value, new providers that look nothing like a traditional college have a hard time competing even if they can enter the market. Rigorous measures of student outcomes like learning and graduate success are needed to level this playing field. With this outcome data in hand, low-cost providers can convince regulators that they deserve to be in the market and students that they deserve their business.

The federal government has traditionally played the role of data collector in higher education via the Integrated Postsecondary Education Data System (IPEDS). But student outcomes reported to IPEDS are notoriously incomplete, and the entire system is built around a bundled, institution-centric view of the world. This data is not well suited to evaluate and regulate the emerging higher education market. Congress has made reform even more difficult. In 2008, at the behest of the higher education lobby, an amendment barred the federal government from collecting student-level data. The policy limits our ability to systematically measure the outcomes we care about. A more muscular federal role in coordinating longitudinal data collection would lay the groundwork for the kind of outcomes-based regulatory process that could lower barriers to entry while maintaining consumer protections.

An unbundled world also requires that we think on a much more granular level about student outcomes. In a world where organizations provide bite-size doses of postsecondary education, the relevant unit of analysis will be the course or the badge rather than the degree. New ventures must take the lead on collecting and validating these kinds of granular outcomes.

Inform the Cost-Conscious Consumer

Consumer choices do the "work" in competitive markets, rewarding the sellers that best fit their needs and collectively putting pressure on those that do not improve. This process not only requires that consumers have a range of providers from which to choose, but also that they have the information about price, quality, and value they need to sort through them. Any effort to cultivate a more diverse and competitive higher education market must take this consumer information requirement seriously. In particular, comparable information about the likely return on investment from one pathway versus another is a prerequisite to the kind of beneficent competition envisioned here.

Policy makers are already working on these questions. Leaders in states like Florida, Texas, Tennessee, and Virginia have linked postsecondary and wage records to produce basic data on the labor market success of graduates from particular programs at particular institutions. In an effort to capitalize on this state-level activity, U.S. Senator Ron Wyden (D-OR) introduced the Know Before You Go Act in 2012, which would replace IPEDS with state-collected longitudinal data that tracks individual students into the labor market. And while their capacity is still developing, it seems likely that unbundled providers will have to collect and publicize data on the success of their students if they wish to compete.

The beauty of providing better data on the costs and benefits of particular options is that it can accommodate consumers with very different preferences, allowing individuals to make their own trade-offs regarding price and quality. Students who are not price-sensitive could continue to shop for the boutique program that best fits their intellectual needs, while the value-conscious can find one that provides sufficient student outcomes at the lowest possible price. It is this latter group that is both underserved by the current market and increasing in size. Empowering this growing segment to make informed choices will help create a more competitive higher education market.

GUARDED OPTIMISM

Together, the chapters in this volume reveal more reason for optimism than pessimism. The pace of higher education innovation has been remarkable, particularly for a sector known for its hostility to change. Indeed, even the most prestigious institutions are dipping a toe in the sea change. In just a few short years, entrepreneurs have proven that high-quality higher education can be delivered at scale and at very low cost to students. These new players, evolving outside of traditional higher education, are already challenging our traditional notions of college. If the cost of college continues its inexorable rise, it may not be long before these upstarts put much of the existing sector out of business.

But policy makers should not underestimate the work that remains. Leaders must not be content to highlight the pockets of innovation and islands of affordability that have emerged around the country while leaving the rest of the sector to grow more and more expensive. Instead, reformers should identify the policies that allow most institutions to rest on their collective laurels and those that discourage entrepreneurs from taking their place. If leaders do not take on this challenge, America's higher education system will be hard-pressed to maintain its place as both the best and most accessible one in the world.

Notes

Introduction

1. Rates quoted based on those provided by a bank in Washington, DC; accessed on December 20, 2012.
2. Richard Arum and Josipa Roksa, *Academically Adrift: Limited Learning on College Campuses* (Chicago: University of Chicago Press, 2010).
3. Sarah Lacy, "Peter Thiel: We're in a Bubble and It's Not the Internet. It's Higher Education," TechCrunch.com, April 10, 2011, http://techcrunch.com/2011/04/10/peter-thiel-were-in-a-bubble-and-its-not-the-internet-its-higher-education/.
4. Harold A. Hovey, *State Spending for Higher Education in the Next Decade: The Battle to Sustain Current Support* (Washington, DC: National Center for Public Policy and Higher Education, 1999).
5. State Higher Education Executive Officers, *State Higher Education Finance FY2011* (Boulder, CO: State Higher Education Executive Officers Association, 2012), 18.
6. Steven Hurlburt and Rita J. Kirshtein, "Spending, Subsidies, and Tuition: Why Are Prices Going Up? What Are Tuitions Going to Pay For? A Delta Data Update, 2000–2010," Delta Cost Project at American Institutes for Research, http://www.deltacost-project.org/resources/pdf/Delta-Subsidy-Trends-Production.pdf.
7. "Trends in Instructional Staff Employment Status, 1975–2009," American Association of University Professors, http://www.aaup.org/NR/rdonlyres/78594C4C-2E73-4714-8DB8-9608726C7CD6/0/2009trends.pdf.
8. Robert B. Archibald and David H. Feldman, *Why Does College Cost So Much?* (Oxford, UK: Oxford University Press, 2011).
9. Robert E. Martin and R. Carter Hill, "Measuring Baumol and Bowen Effects in Public Research Universities" (working paper, Centre College, Danville, KY, and Louisiana State University, Baton Rouge, LA, 2012), http://ssrn.com/abstract=2153122.
10. "Trends in College Pricing 2012," College Board, http://advocacy.collegeboard.org/sites/default/files/college-pricing-2012-full-report_0.pdf.
11. Archibald and Feldman, *Why Does College Cost So Much?*, chapter 5.
12. I. Elaine Allen and Jeff Seaman, "Going the Distance: Online Education in the United States, 2011," BABSON Survey Research Group, http://www.onlinelearningsurvey.com/reports/goingthedistance.pdf.
13. Kevin Carey, "Rick Perry is a Higher Education Visionary. Seriously," *New Republic*, August 25, 2011, http://www.tnr.com/article/politics/94172/rick-perry-higher-ed-reform.
14. Lara Seligman, "Did Texas Just Discover the Cure for Sky-High Tuition?" *Atlantic*, November 26, 2012, http://www.theatlantic.com/business/archive/2012/11/did-texas-just-discover-the-cure-for-sky-high-tuition/265571/.

15. www.coursera.com.

Chapter 1

1. Mark Kantrowitz, "Total College Debt Now Exceeds Total Credit Card Debt," http://
www.fastweb.com/financial-aid/articles/2589-total-college-debt-now-exceeds-total-
credit-card-debt; Eyder Peralta, "AP Analysis: Half of New Grads Are Jobless or
Underemployed," *The Two-Way* (blog), *National Public Radio*, April 23, 2012, http://
www.npr.org/blogs/thetwo-way/2012/04/23/151217630/ap-analysis-half-of-recent-
college-grads-are-jobless-or-underemployed; Sandy Baum and Jennifer Ma, *Trends in
College Pricing 2011* (Washington, DC: College Board Advocacy and Policy Center,
2011).
2. Charley Stone, Carl Van Horn, and Cliff Zukin, *Chasing the American Dream: Recent
College Graduates and the Great Recession* (New Brunswick, NJ: John J. Heldrich
Center for Workforce Development, 2012).
3. Ibid.
4. Leslie E. Linfield, *2010 Annual Consumer Bankruptcy Demographics Report: A Five
Year Perspective of the American Debtor* (South Portland, ME: Institute for Financial
Literacy, 2011); Stone et al., *Chasing.*
5. Anya Kamenetz, *Generation Debt: How Our Future Was Sold Out for Student Loans,
Bad Jobs, No Benefits, and Tax Cuts for Rich Geezers—and How to Fight Back* (New
York: Riverhead, 2006).
6. Ibid.
7. Kelly Sheehy, "10 Medical Schools That Lead to the Most Debt," *U.S. News and World
Report Education*, May 22, 2012, http://www.usnews.com/education/best-graduate-schools/
the-short-list-grad-school/articles/2012/05/22/10-med-schools-that-lead-to-the-most-debt.
8. Ryan Lytle, "10 Law Schools That Lead to the Most Debt," *U.S. News and World
Report Education*, March 22, 2012, http://www.usnews.com/education/best-graduate-
schools/the-short-list-grad-school/articles/2012/03/22/10-law-schools-that-lead-to-the-
most-debt; Thomas E. Chase and Fabian Gonnell, *Law School Debt and the Practice
of Law* (New York: Committee on Legal Education and Admission to the Bar of Association of the Bar of the City of New York, n.d.), http://www.nycbar.org/pdf/report/
lawSchoolDebt.pdf; Joe Palazzolo and Jennifer Smith, "Law Grads Claim Schools Mis-
led," *Wall Street Journal*, February 2, 2012, http://online.wsj.com/article/SB100014240
52970203920204577197471843581532.html.
9. "Credit Background Checks," Society for Human Resource Management, http://shrm
.org/surveys.
10. Michelle Dotson, "TransUnion Selling Credit Reports to Employers," *Examiner*, May 4,
2012, http://www.examiner.com/article/transunion-selling-credit-reports-to-employers.
11. Stone et al., *Chasing.*
12. Joshua S. Weiner, John M. Bridgeland, and John J. DiIulio, Jr., *Achievement Trap: How
America Is Failing Millions of High-Achieving Students from Low-Income Families*
(Leesburg, VA: Jack Kent Cooke Foundation, 2007), http://www.jkcf.org/assets/
files/0000/0084/Achievement_Trap.pdf.
13. Pathways to Prosperity Project, *Pathways to Prosperity: Meeting the Challenge of Preparing Young Americans for the 21st Century* (Cambridge, MA: Harvard Graduate
School of Education, 2011), http://www.gse.harvard.edu/news_events/features/2011/
Pathways_to_Prosperity_Feb2011.pdf.
14. Mary Nguyen, "Degreeless in Debt: What Happens to Borrowers Who Drop Out,"

Education Sector, February 23, 2012, http://www.educationsector.org/publications/degreeless-debt-what-happens-borrowers-who-drop-out.

15. Sara Murray, "The Curse of the Class of 2009," *Wall Street Journal*, May 9, 2009, http://online.wsj.com/article/SB124181970915002009.html.

16. Stone et al., *Chasing.*

17. Alan B. Krueger and Mikael Lindahl, "Education for Growth: Why and for Whom?" *Journal of Economic Literature* 39 (2001): 1101–1136.

18. Riel Miller, *Education and Economic Growth: From the 19th to the 21st Century* (San Jose, CA: Cisco Systems, Inc., 2007).

19. "History," American Legion, http://www.legion.org/history.

20. "Fast Facts," National Center for Education Statistics, http://nces.ed.gov/fastfacts/display.asp?id=98.

21. Kamenetz, *Generation Debt*, 52.

22. Ibid.

23. "High-Growth Entrepreneurs Plan to Continue Growing," Ewing Marion Kauffman Foundation, http://www.kauffman.org/newsroom/high-growth-entrepreneurs-plan-to-continue-growing.aspx.

24. Tom Morrison et al., *Boiling Point? The Skills Gap in U.S. Manufacturing* (Washington, DC: Deloitte, Inc., and The Manufacturing Institute, 2011), http://www.deloitte.com/assets/Dcom-UnitedStates/Local%20Assets/Documents/AD/us_PIP_2011SkillsGapReport_01142011.pdf.

25. Martha Kantor et al., "Meeting President Obama's 2020 College Completion Goal" (speech, U.S. Department of Education, Washington, DC, July 21, 2011).

26. "2008 Annual Report," American Colleges and Universities Presidents' Climate Commitment, http://www.presidentsclimatecommitment.org.

27. Cristian Deritis, "Student Lending's Failing Grade," *Moody's Analytics Regional Financial Review*, July 2011, http://image.exct.net/lib/fefb127575640d/m/2/Student+Lendings+Failing+Grade.pdf.

28. "Trends in College Spending 1999–2009," Delta Cost Project, http://deltacostproject.org/resources/pdf/Trends2011_Final_090711.pdf.

29. William J. Baumol and William G. Bowen, *Performing Arts: The Economic Dilemma* (New York: Twentieth Century Fund, 1966).

30. "Trends in College Spending."

31. Ibid.

32. Craig Bicknell, "Beaver College Not a Filter Fave," *Wired*, March 22, 2000, http://www.wired.com/politics/law/news/2000/03/35091.

33. Clark Kerr, *The Uses of the University* (Cambridge, MA: Harvard University Press, 1963).

34. Daniel Fulks, *NCAA Revenues and Expenses Division I Report 2004–2009* (Indianapolis, IN: National College Athletics Association, 2010), http://www.ncaapublications.com/productdownloads/REV_EXP_2010.pdf.

35. Baum and Ma, *Trends.*

36. "Trends in College Spending."

37. Ibid.

38. Stacey Patton, "The Ph.D. Now Comes with Food Stamps," *Chronicle of Higher Education*, May 6, 2012, http://chronicle.com/article/From-Graduate-School-to/131795/?sid=at&utm_source=at&utm_medium=en.

39. "Trends in College Spending."

40. Susan Aud et al., *The Condition of Education 2011* (Washington, DC: National Center for Education Statistics, 2011), http://nces.ed.gov/pubs2011/2011033.pdf.

41. Baum and Ma, *Trends*.

42. Christina Chang Wei et al., "2007–08 National Postsecondary Student Aid Study" (Washington, DC: National Center for Education Statistics, 2009), http://nces.ed.gov/pubs2009/2009166.pdf.

43. James B. Lockhart III, "Statement of FHFA Director James B. Lockhart" (press release, Federal Housing Finance Agency, Washington, DC, September 7, 2008).

44. Dennis Cauchon, "For-Profit Colleges Focus of Student Loan Issue," *USA Today*, October 18, 2009, http://www.usatoday.com/news/education/story/2011-10-18/student-loans-for-profit-college/50819470/1.

45. "Historical Loan Limits," FinAid.org, http://www.finaid.org/loans/historicallimits.phtml; "Federal Student Aid Information for Parents," FinAid.org, http://www.finaid.org/loans/historicallimits.phtml.

46. Andrew Martin, "Slowly, as Student Debt Rises, Colleges Confront Costs," *New York Times*, May 14, 2012, http://www.nytimes.com/2012/05/15/business/colleges-begin-to-confront-higher-costs-and-students-debt.html.

47. Ibid.

48. Ben Rooney, "Ohio State Is No. 1—in President's Pay," *CNN Money*, January 18, 2010, http://money.cnn.com/2010/01/18/news/economy/university_executive_compensation/index.htm.

49. Howard Bowen, *The Cost of Higher Education* (San Francisco: Jossey-Bass, 1980).

50. Clayton Christenson, "Key Concepts in Disruptive Innovation," http://www.clayton-christensen.com/disruptive_innovation.html.

51. Gordon Moore, "Cramming More Components Onto Integrated Circuits," *Electronics* 8, no. 38 (April 1965).

52. "US IT Expenditures by Category and Education," Compass Intelligence, http://www.marketresearch.com/Compass-Intelligence-v3311/Education-Expenditures-Category-Level-6379299/.

53. "Top Software Companies Survey,"Amplicate, http://amplicate.com/software/778-top-software-companies/.

54. Student-faculty ratio: 41:1. About.com, collegeapps.about.com/od/collegeprofiles/p/university-of-phoenix-online.htm.

55. Ibid.; "Tuition, Billing, and Payment," University of Iowa, http://www.continuetolearn.uiowa.edu/ccp/de/derules/tuition.htm#1.

56. Anya Kamenetz, *DIY U: Edupunks, Edupreneurs, and the Coming Transformation of Higher Education* (New York: Chelsea Green Publishing, 2010), 90.

Chapter 2

1. "Economic performance" refers to higher education's historical record in terms of cost and quality of services rendered.

2. Robert E. Martin and Andrew Gillen, "Measuring College Affordability" (working paper, Centre College, Danville, KY, and Center for College Affordability and Productivity, Washington, DC, 2011), http://papers.ssrn.com/sol3/papers.cfm?abstract_id=1734914. This research reveals that when the dollar increase in the net attendance price exceeds the dollar increase in household income, the household's original higher education quality choice is no longer within the household's budget constraint, household utility declines, welfare declines, and the household must choose a lower-quality

education experience. This problem is aggravated by trends in student subsidies over the past four decades. Institutions committed more and more student support to merit scholarships over this period, and state governments directed more student scholarships to merit support. Since student performance is directly related to household income, more support is going to higher-income families than to traditional middle-class families.

3. This body of evidence includes graduation rates, student study time, test scores, grade inflation, and adult literacy. For more information, see Robert E. Martin, *The College Cost Disease: Higher Cost and Lower Quality* (Cheltenham, UK: Edward Elgar, Ltd, 2011); William F. Massy, *Honoring the Trust: Quality and Cost Containment in Higher Education* (Boston: Anker Publishing Company, Inc, 2003); Derek Bok, *Our Underachieving Colleges: A Candid Look at How Much Students Learn and Why They Should Be Learning More* (Princeton, NJ: Princeton University Press, 2005); Richard Hersh and John Merrow, *Declining by Degrees: Higher Education at Risk* (New York: Palgrave Macmillan, 2005); Richard Arum and Josipa Roksa, *Academically Adrift: Limited Learning on College Campuses* (Chicago: University of Chicago Press, 2011).

4. Martin, *College Cost Disease*, 16–22; Malcolm Getz and John J. Siegfried, "Costs per Student over Time," in *Economic Challenges in Higher Education,* ed. Charles Clotfelter (Chicago: University of Chicago Press, 1991), 357–392; William J. Baumol and William G. Bowen, *Performing Arts: The Economic Dilemma* (New York: Twentieth Century Fund, 1966); Howard R. Bowen, *The Costs of Higher Education: How Much Do Colleges and Universities Spend per Student and How Much Should They Spend?* (Washington, DC: Jossey-Bass Publishers, 1980).

5. This is in contrast to for-profit firms who expand output only if there is a reasonable prospect of higher profits.

6. The current dominance of higher education by nonprofit institutions is an example of the *survivor principle*—that is, evolved structures that persist tend to be optimal. Hence, the flawed nonprofit character of higher education may be less flawed than a comparably regulated for-profit solution. This does not mean that for-profit institutions cannot improve competition at the margin; it does suggest, however, that an unregulated for-profit industry is likely to be worse than what we have now.

7. Consumers have enough information to distinguish between labor market signals produced by elite institutions over the signals sent by institutions in the lower-quality tiers. Hence, the "quality" tiers in higher education are based on labor market signals, not human-capital value added.

8. The people employed in higher education are neither more nor less prone to agency abuse than any other group of people. The point here is that the constraints on agency problems one expects to find are simply not there in higher education.

9. Robert E. Martin and R. Carter Hill, "Measuring Baumol and Bowen Effects in Public Research Universities" (working paper, Louisiana State University, Baton Rouge, LA, 2012).

10. Mark Bauerlein, "Professors on the Production Line, Students on Their Own" (working paper, AEI Future of American Education Project, Washington, DC, 2009).

11. Ibid.

12. In addition to the National Survey of Student Engagement (NSSE), part of the metric system must include feedback from students through evaluations or online resources such as RateMyProfessor.com, pre- and post-testing, intercollegiate peer-reviewed teaching, and more local and national prizes for exceptional teaching. In order to

establish a market for senior teachers, the information will have to come from third parties (not the candidates or their home institutions) the same way that information about scholarship comes from third parties.

13. Martin and Gillen, "Measuring College Affordability."

14. See, for example, Lynn O'Shaughnessy, "A New College Rankings Scandal," *CBS News*, November 21, 2012, http://www.cbsnews.com/8301-505145_162-57547972/a-new-college-rankings-scandal/.

15. Jay P. Greene, Brian Kisida, and Jonathan Mills, *Administrative Bloat at American Universities: The Real Reason for High Costs in Higher Education* (Phoenix: Goldwater Institute, 2010), http://goldwaterinstitute.org/article/administrative-bloat-american-universities-real-reason-high-costs-higher-education.

16. Robert E. Martin and Andrew Gillen, *How College Pricing Undermines Financial Aid* (Washington, DC: Center for College Affordability and Productivity, 2011).

17. William Bennett, "Our Greedy Colleges," *New York Times*, February 18, 1987, A27, http://www.nytimes.com/1987/02/18/opinion/our-greedy-colleges.html.

18. Michael McPherson and Morton Owen Shapiro, *Keeping College Affordable: Government and Educational Opportunity* (Washington, DC: The Brookings Institution, 1991); Michael Rizzo and Ronald Ehrenberg, "Resident and Nonresident Tuition and Enrollment at Flagship State Universities," in *College Choices: The Economics of Where to Go, When to Go, and How to Pay for It*, ed. Caroline M. Hoxby (Chicago: University of Chicago Press, 2004), 303–354; Bradley R. Curs and Luciana Dar, "Does State Financial Aid Affect Institutional Aid? An Analysis of the Role of State Policy on Postsecondary Institutional Pricing Strategies" (working paper, University of Missouri, Columbia, MO, 2010), http://ssrn.com/abstract=1641489; Bradley R. Curs and Luciana Dar, "Do Institutions Respond Asymmetrically to Changes in State Need- and Merit-Based Aid?" (working paper, University of Missouri, Columbia, MO, 2010), http://papers.ssrn.com/sol3/papers.cfm?abstract_id=1702504; Judith Li, "Estimating the Effect of Federal Financial Aid on College Tuitions: A Study of Pell Grants" (unpublished manuscript, Harvard University, Cambridge, MA, 1999); Bridget Terry Long, "How Do Financial Aid Policies Affect College? The Institutional Impact of the Georgia HOPE Scholarship," *Journal of Human Resources* 39, no. 4 (2004): 1045–1066; Larry Singell and Joe Stone, "For Whom the Pell Tolls: The Response of University Tuition to Federal Grants-in-Aid," *Economics of Education Review* 26, no. 3 (2007): 285–295.

19. Martin and Gillen, *College Pricing*.

20. Federal Reserve Bank of New York, *Quarterly Report on Household Debt and Credit* (New York: Research Statistics Group, 2012), http://www.newyorkfed.org/research/national_economy/householdcredit/DistrictReport_Q42011.pdf.

21. Every dollar spent per student has an opportunity cost—that dollar could be spent on other public and private goods and services. Therefore, the total social cost per student is the total cost per student, while the net price of attendance includes only part of the total cost: the cost paid by private households with children currently in college.

22. John D. Hutcheson Jr. and James E. Prather, "Economy of Scale or Bureaucratic Entropy? Implications for Metropolitan Governmental Reorganization," *Urban Affairs Review* 15, no. 2 (1979): 164–182.

23. Dale W. Jorgenson, Mun S. Ho, and Kevin J. Stiroh, "A Retrospective Look at the U.S. Productivity Growth Resurgence," *Journal of Economic Perspectives* 22, no. 1 (2008): 3–24; William J. Kettinger, T. C. Teng, and Subashish Guha, "Business Process

Change: A Study of Methodologies, Techniques, and Tools," *MIS Quarterly* 21, no. 1 (2008): 55–80.

24. Thomas H. Benton, "Graduate School in the Humanities: Just Don't Go," *Chronicle of Higher Education*, January 30, 2009, http://chronicle.com/article/Graduate-School-in-the/44846; Suzanne B. Clery, "Part-Time Faculty," *NEA Higher Education Research Center Update* 7, no. 4 (2001); Maureen Murphy Nutting, "Part-Time Faculty: Why Should We Care?" *New Directions for Higher Education* 123 (2003): 33–39.

25. In the author's models of public research university cost from 1987 to 2008, academic, overhead, and total cost are all lower the higher the ratio of tenure-track faculty to administrators. Preliminary results suggest this is also true among private research universities. This evidence and other evidence suggest that economic performance improves the more balanced is shared governance.

26. Greene, Kisida, and Mills, *Administrative Bloat*.

Chapter 3

1. Note that here and elsewhere in the paper I use *productivity* and *efficiency* somewhat interchangeably, though, strictly speaking, the former refers to output per unit of input (e.g., labor hours), whereas efficiency has a broader meaning. I adopt *productivity* here to align the discussion with how policy makers more typically use the terms in this context.

2. Charles T. Clotfelter, *Buying the Best: Cost Escalation in Elite Higher Education* (Princeton, NJ: Princeton University Press, 1996); Arthur Hauptman and Young Kim, *Cost, Commitment, and Attainment in Higher Education: An International Comparison* (Boston: Lumina Foundation and Jobs for the Future, 2009).

3. Martha J. Bailey and Susan M. Dynarski, "Inequality in Postsecondary Education," in Greg Duncan and Richard Murnane, eds., *Wither Opportunity: Rising Inequality, Schools, and Children's Life Chances* (New York: Russell Sage Foundation, 2011); John Bound, Michael Lovenheim, and Sarah Turner, "Why Have College Completion Rates Declined?" (working paper #15566, National Bureau of Economic Research, Cambridge, MA, 2009).

4. This is an imperfect measure of productivity because, for example, the resources included in the four-year (two-year) sector expenditures are not all supposed to go toward BA (AA) production, but the nondegree roles of colleges have not changed significantly over this time period, so this probably influences the productivity level, but not the trend.

5. Productivity in 2006 was 81 percent of 1970 levels. Current expenditures in 2007 on four-year colleges were $196 billion (U.S. Department of Education, National Center for Education Statistics, 2003–2004 through 2006–2007 Integrated Postsecondary Education Data System [IPEDS]). Table 362: Expenditures of public degree-granting institutions, by purpose of expenditure and type of institution: 2003-04 through 2006-07, 2010). Assuming the trend continues, productivity in 2050 will be 81 percent of 2010 levels and this will require an additional $42 billion to generate the same degrees. This slightly understates the additional resources because the figure represents only 36 years rather than 40, so the extrapolated productivity would actually be slightly larger. These calculations exclude two-year colleges because productivity is largely unchanged in that sector. The calculations also exclude private colleges for which less data are available.

6. There were 6.1 million FTE undergraduates in public four-year colleges 2008. U.S. Department of Education, National Center for Education Statistics, Higher Education

General Information Survey (HEGIS), "Fall Enrollment in Colleges and Universities" surveys, 1969 through 1985; and 1986 through 2008 Integrated Postsecondary Education Data System, "Fall Enrollment Survey" (IPEDS-EF: 86–99), 2010. Dividing the $42 billion by this number yields $6,885. By comparison, according to the Delta Cost Project ("Trends in College Spending 1999–2009," http://deltacostproject.org/resources/pdf/Trends2011_Final_090711.pdf), tuition at public research universities was $6,741 ($5,004) in public research (public master's) institutions in 2006.

7. William J. Baumol and William G. Bowen, *Performing Arts: The Economic Dilemma* (New York: Twentieth Century Fund, 1966); Gordon C. Winston, "Subsidies, Hierarchy and Peers: The Awkward Economics of Higher Education," *Journal of Economic Perspectives* 13 (winter 2009): 13–36; Dan Black and Jeffrey Smith, "Evaluating the Returns to College Quality with Multiple Proxies for Quality," *Journal of Labor Economics* 24, no. 3 (2006): 701–728; Liang Zhang, "Do Measures of College Quality Matter? The Effect of College Quality on Graduates' Earnings," *Review of Higher Education* 28, no. 4 (2005): 571–596; R. B. Archibald and David H. Feldman, "Explaining Increases in Higher Education Costs," *The Journal of Higher Education* 79, no. 3 (2008): 268-295; R. B. Archibald and David H. Feldman, "Why Do Higher Education Costs Rise More Rapidly Than Prices in General? *Change*, May/June 2008: 25–31; Douglas N. Harris and Sara Goldrick-Rab, "The (Un)Productivity of American Higher Education: From 'Cost Disease' to Cost-Effectiveness" (working paper, Wisconsin Center for the Advancement of Postsecondary Education, University of Wisconsin–Madison, December 2010).

8. W. J. Baumol and S. A. Blackman, "How to Think About Rising College Costs," *Planning for Higher Education* 23 (summer 1995): 1–7; H. R. Bowen, *The Costs of Higher Education: How Much Do Colleges and Universities Spend Per Student and How Much Should They Spend?* (San Francisco: Jossey-Bass, 1980); D. W. Breneman, "An Essay on College Cost," in Alisa F. Cunningham, Jane V. Wellman, Melissa E. Clinedinst, and Jamie P. Merisotis, *Study of College Costs and Prices, 1988–89 to 1997–98, Volume 2* (Washington, DC: National Center for Education Statistics, 2001), 13–20; Ronald G. Ehrenberg, *Tuition Rising: Why College Costs So Much* (Cambridge, MA: Harvard University Press, 2000); Malcolm Getz and John J. Siegfried, "Cost and Productivity in American Colleges and Universities," in Charles T. Clotfelter, Ronald G. Ehrenberg, Malcolm Getz, and John J. Siegfried, eds., *Economic Challenges in Higher Education* (Chicago: University of Chicago Press, 1991), 261–392; Dennis Jones and Jane Wellman, "Bucking Conventional Wisdom on College Costs," *Inside Higher Ed*, July 20, 2009, http://www.insidehighered.com/views/2009/07/20/wellmanjones; Richard Vedder, *Going Broke by Degree: Why College Costs Too Much* (Washington, DC: AEI Press, 2004); Burton A. Weisbrod, Jeffrey P. Ballou, and Evelyn D. Asch, *Mission and Money: Understanding the University* (New York: Cambridge University Press, 2008); William G. Bowen, Matthew. M. Chingos, and Michael McPherson, *Crossing the Finish Line: Completing College at America's Public Universities* (Princeton, NJ: Princeton University Press, 2009).

9. Robert B. Archibald and David H. Feldman, "Explaining Increases in Higher Education Costs," *Journal of Higher Education* 79, no. 3 (2008): 270.

10. John Immerwahr, Jean Johnson, and Paul Gasbarra, *The Iron Triangle: College Presidents Talk About Costs, Access, and Quality* (San Jose, CA: National Center for Public Policy and Higher Education and Public Agenda, 2008). Direct quotations are not included in the cited paper, but were collected as part of the study and provided by the

cited authors.

11. Exceptions include: William F. Massy, "Productivity Issues in Higher Education," in William F. Massy, ed., *Resource Issues in Higher Education* (Ann Arbor: University of Michigan Press, 1996); Michael McPherson, Morton Owen Schapiro, and Gordon C. Winston, *Paying the Piper: Productivity, Incentives, and Financing in U.S. Higher Education* (Ann Arbor: University of Michigan Press, 1993).

12. Sara Goldrick-Rab and Josipa Roksa, *A Federal Education Agenda for Promoting Student Success and Degree Completion* (Washington, DC: Center for American Progress, 2008).

13. David H. Monk and Jennifer A. King, "Cost Analysis as a Tool for Educational Reform," in Stephen L. Jacobson and Robert Berne, eds., *Reforming Education: The Emerging Systemic Approach, 1994 Yearbook of the American Education Finance Association* (Thousand Oaks, CA: Corwin, 1993); Jennifer King Rice, "Cost Analysis in Education Policy Research: A Comparative Analysis Across Fields of Public Policy," in Henry M. Levin and Patrick J. McEwan, eds., *Cost-Effectiveness Analysis in Education: Progress and Prospects, 2002 Yearbook of the American Education Finance Association* (Larchmont, NY: Eye on Education, 2002).

14. Exceptions include Massy, "Productivity Issues"; McPherson, Schapiro, and Winston, *Paying the Piper.*

15. This is not the only way to think about costs. The discussion of costs here ignores the distinction between opportunity costs and budgetary costs that economists typically make. *Opportunity cost* refers to the value of a resource in its next best use. When markets are competitive, the market price accurately reflects opportunity cost. There are cases where the two notions of costs do not line up. Of particular relevance here is that financial aid programs are considered transfer payments and are costly in a budgetary sense, but not as opportunity costs.

16. This is not always the case. If the ratio is negative because a positive impact is generated with reduced (negative) costs, then this is an exception to the rule and the negative ECR is a positive indication of the social value of the program. But if the ratio is negative because the impact is negative and the costs are positive, this obviously reflects poorly on the program. Positive ECRs can also be generated with a combination of negative costs and negative effects. Such a program might be worthwhile if the sacrifice of lower outcomes is worth the lower costs, so that the resources could be redeployed to more cost-effective options.

17. Some programs or policies engage students prior to college entry, while others affect them after entry. The timing of the entering cohort aligns with the timing of the program—if the program begins in high school, then I consider a cohort of one hundred high school freshmen; if it begins in college, then I consider a cohort of one hundred college freshmen. This is all intended to make the ECRs as comparable as possible across programs.

18. Both figures account for a fringe benefit rate of 25 percent (U.S. Census, *Public Education Finances*, Washington, DC: Census Bureau, 2005). The four-year figure is somewhat higher than the $354,000 reported by Barrow and Rouse, partly because they chose a higher discount rate. See Lisa Barrow and Cecilia E. Rouse, "The Economic Value of Education by Race and Ethnicity," *Economic Perspectives* 30, no. 2 (2006).

19. Harris and Goldrick-Rab, "(Un)Productivity."

20. First, I consider evidence from the very small number of studies that report program impacts on multiple outcomes. For example, Susan Dynarski, "Does Aid Matter?

Measuring the Effect of Student Aid on College Attendance and Completion," *American Economic Review* 93, no. 1 (2003): 279–288, reports that the point estimates for financial aid impacts are about 25 percent smaller when the outcome is obtaining at least one year of college compared with when the outcome is entering college. This implies an entry-to-persistence multiplier of about 0.75. Eric Bettinger and Rachel Baker, "The Effects of Student Coaching: An Evaluation of a Randomized Experiment in Student Mentoring" (working paper #16881, National Bureau of Economic Research, Cambridge, MA, 2011) report effects of college coaching on retention twelve months from initial entry, as well as graduation. Their graduation effects are roughly 30 percent larger than the effects on persistence, suggesting that multipliers above 1.0 are realistic. I discuss these studies and the programs involved in greater detail shortly. The goal here is only to show how I am using the studies to identify plausible ways of translating effects on entry and persistence into effects on graduation. As a second approach, I combined a simple compounding model of persistence with evidence on typical persistence and graduation rates from the Beginning Postsecondary Study (BPS:04/09). These two approaches yield a range of possible values that I use as lower and upper bounds, as well as our baseline values that are the basis for our main results.

21. According to Robert Morse, "Methodology: Undergraduate Ranking Criteria and Weights," *U.S. News and World Report*, http://www.usnews.com/articles/education/best-colleges/2009/08/19/methodology-undergraduate-ranking-criteria-and-weights.html, the "faculty resources" component represents 20 percent of the total rating. Sixty-five percent of this portion comprises "percent faculty that is full time" (5 percent), "percent faculty with terminal degree in field" (15 percent), "student/faculty ratio" (5 percent), "class size 1–19 students" (30 percent), and "class size 50+ students" (10 percent).

22. Daniel Jacoby, "Effects of Part-Time Faculty Employment on Community College Graduation Rates," *Journal of Higher Education* 77, no. 6 (2006): 1081–1103.

23. National Center for Education Statistics, *Digest of Education Statistics, 2007* (Washington, DC: NCES, 2007), table 237.

24. National Center for Education Statistics, *National Study of Postsecondary Faculty, 2004* (Washington, DC: NCES, 2004).

25. I could not find a nationally representative fringe rate and instead used a rate of 25 percent, using data for public school teachers from U.S. Census, *Public Education Finances*.

26. Edward C. Kokkelenberg, Michael Dillon, and Sean M. Christy, "The Effects of Class Size on Student Grades at a Public University," *Economics of Education Review* 27, no. 2 (2008); the authors find that larger classes lead to lower grade point averages in one U.S. public university. Maria De Paola and Vincenzo Scoppa, "Effects of Class Size on Achievement of College Students" (working paper, Munich Personal RePEc Archive Working Paper #16945, 2009), http://mpra.ub.uni-muenchen.de/16945/; this study examines class size using data from Italy.

27. John Bound, Michael Lovenheim, and Sarah Turner, "Why Have College Completion Rates Declined?" (working paper #15566, National Bureau of Economic Research, Cambridge, MA, 2009).

28. National Center for Education Statistics, *Postsecondary Faculty*.

29. Ronald G. Ehrenberg and Liang Zhang, "Do Tenured and Tenure-Track Faculty Matter?" (working paper #10695, National Bureau of Economic Research, Cambridge, MA, 2004). The study does not utilize college fixed effects, as would be necessary

to characterize this as an interrupted times series or quasi-experiment. The authors indicate that there was insufficient variation to use such an approach with their data. Instead, they simply aggregate data across years.

30. Jacoby, "Effects."
31. Not all the evidence on part-time faculty is so negative; Eric Bettinger and Bridget Terry Long (forthcoming), using a quasi-experimental technique, find that adjuncts increase interest in subsequent course enrollment, relative to full-time faculty.
32. David Myers, Rob Olsen, Neil Seftor, Julie Young, and Christina Tuttle, *The Impacts of Regular Upward Bound: Results from the Third Follow-up Data Collection* (Washington, DC: Mathematica Policy Research, 2004). Amy Albee, "A Cost Analysis of Upward Bound and GEAR UP" (unpublished manuscript, Florida State University, Tallahassee, FL, 2005).
33. Neil S. Seftor, Arif Mamun, and Allen Schirm, *The Impacts of Regular Upward Bound on Postsecondary Outcomes 7–9 Years After Scheduled High School Graduation* (Washington, DC: Mathematica Policy Research, Inc., 2008).
34. Alan Nathan and Douglas N. Harris, "Does Upward Bound Have an Effect on Student Educational Outcomes? A Reanalysis of the Horizons Randomized Controlled Trial" (paper presented at the annual meeting of the Society for Research on Educational Effectiveness, Washington, DC, March 8, 2013).
35. Upward Bound increased postsecondary enrollment or completion rates for the 20 percent of eligible students who had lower educational expectations (no expectation of earning a bachelor's) at baseline. However, because being eligible for Upward requires a considerable degree of disadvantage to begin with, those students who also have low educational expectations are extremely disadvantaged. Therefore, for comparability with other program ECRs in this study, I use the 2 percentage point impact as the baseline. The focus on overall impacts is also preferable because Upward Bound does not limit access based on college expectations nor is likely to do so in the future.
36. Jill M. Constantine et al., *A Study on the Effect of the Talent Search Program on Secondary and Postsecondary Outcomes in Florida, Indiana, and Texas* (Washington, DC: U.S. Department of Education, Office of Planning, Evaluation, and Policy Development, 2006).
37. Ibid.
38. Thurston Domina, "What Works in College Outreach: Assessing Targeted and School-wide: Interventions for Disadvantaged Students," *Educational Evaluation and Policy Analysis* 31, no. 2 (2009): 127–152.
39. Susan Dynarski, "Loans, Liquidity, and Schooling Decisions" (unpublished working paper, University of Michigan, Ann Arbor, MI, 2003), 21, http://www.nber.org/dynarski/Dynarski_loans.pdf.
40. I am aware of no direct evidence on the credit histories of students or their parents (who usually cosign on the loans). Dynarski's one-third subsidy figure assumes that the market interest rate is 7 percent, which she describes as the rate for borrowers with excellent credit histories. She writes that the rate for borrowers with poor credit histories was 9 percent. For market rates of 7, 8, and 9 percent, and a (subsidized) Stafford loan interest rate of 6 percent, the present discounted value to students of the reduced interest charges is 37 percent, 57 percent, and 77 percent (respectively). The first figure most closely matches Dynarski's assumptions. The estimates incorporate both the lower interest rate and the fact that the government pays all interest while students are in school. I assumed a ten-year repayment schedule and two years of time in college

with complete government subsidy. While interest rates have been lower recently, this is unlikely to continue, and I view the chosen market rates as more realistic. I therefore use the middle figure as our cost estimate, which I believe best represents the average student; however, the correct rate certainly varies across individuals.

41. Sara Goldrick-Rab, Douglas N. Harris, Robert Kelchen, and James Benson, *Need-Based Financial Aid and College Persistence: Experimental Evidence from Wisconsin* (Madison, WI: Institute for Research on Poverty, 2012).

42. This calculation ignores nonsubsidized loans as these costs are borne entirely by students. It also ignores changes in work study because (a) the budgetary implications are ambiguous, and (b) the change in work study was very small.

43. Goldrick-Rab et al., *Need-Based Financial Aid.*

44. I arrived at this as follows: the largest persistence effect reported anywhere in the paper is +4.1 for persistence to the second year in a particular subset of colleges (based on instrumental variables estimation). The most optimistic estimate of the fadeout comes from the second cohort, where the persistence effect drops by half from the second to the third year. (In the first cohort, the effect reverses sign—that is, the persistence effect is negative.) Therefore, if we assume the persistence effect of aid received also drops by half, then the persistence effect goes from +4.1 to +2.05. This is the effect reported in the text and figure 3.2. This also assumes that the instrumental variables estimate (i.e., the "local average treatment effect") applies to all the aid changes, which is probably not the case.

45. The cost calculation is complicated by the estimation method of the maximum effect, which is why the costs reported in the second column of table 3.1 are so different for the WSLS minimum effect. The estimation method yields an estimate of the effect per thousand dollars of additional total aid, which combines loans and grants. I therefore adjusted the total aid cost downward because, as noted in the text, loans are less expensive than grants to the government and colleges that provide them. If all aid were grants, then this would be reported as \$100,000 (\$1,000 per student), but the adjustment reduces this by the share of aid that is in the form of loans. This yields: $1((0.67 \times 1.0) + (0.33 \times 0.6)) = \$86,800$. This figure was then multiplied by 3.55, the estimated number of years these students would receive funding.

46. Lashawn Richburg-Hayes et al., *Rewarding Persistence: Effects of a Performance-Based Scholarship Program for Low-Income Parents* (New York: MDRC, 2009).

47. Ibid.

48. Joshua Angrist, Daniel Lang, and Philip Oreopoulos, "Incentives and Services for College Achievement: Evidence from a Randomized Trial," *American Economic Journal: Applied Economics* 1 (2009).

49. Joshua Angrist, Daniel Lang, and Philip Oreopoulos, "Lead Them to Water and Pay Them to Drink: An Experiment with Services and Incentives for College Achievement" (working paper #12790, National Bureau of Economic Research, Cambridge, MA, 2006).

50. David Deming and Susan Dynarski, "Into College, Out of Poverty? Policies to Increase the Postsecondary Attainment of the Poor" (working paper #15387, National Bureau of Economic Research, Cambridge, MA, 2009).

51. Here are the two main exceptions: Suzanne Louise Reyes, "Educational Opportunities and Outcomes: The Role of the Guaranteed Student Loan" (unpublished manuscript, Harvard University, Cambridge, MA, 1995); Dynarski, "Loans."

52. The apparently larger ECR for loans could be due to the estimates being biased (especially in the case of loans where there is much less evidence). Alternatively, students face

minimum thresholds for funds to cover the most basic college costs (e.g., tuition), and it may be that the loans, which are used only after grants and scholarships have been exhausted, are more typically bumping students over that threshold.

53. Douglas A. Webber and Ronald G. Ehrenberg, "Do Expenditures Other Than Instructional Expenditures Affect Graduation and Persistence Rates in American Higher Education?" *Economics of Education Review* 29, no. 6 (2010).

54. Like the financial aid studies, the costs here are already expressed in dollar terms, so there was no need for additional analysis. The IPEDS categories are instructional, academic support (libraries, museums, academic computing), research, and student services.

55. Eric Bettinger and Rachel Baker, "The Effects of Student Coaching: An Evaluation of a Randomized Experiment in Student Advising" (unpublished manuscript, Stanford University School of Education, Stanford, CA, 2011).

56. Ibid.

57. Bettinger and Baker, "Student Advising"; Bettinger and Baker, "Student Mentoring."

58. Paco Martorell and Isaac McFarlin, "Help or Hindrance? The Effects of College Remediation on Academic and Labor Market Outcomes," *Review of Economics and Statistics* 93, no. 2 (2011): 436–454; Brooke D. Terry, *The Costs of Remedial Education* (Austin: Texas Public Policy Foundation, 2007).

59. Martorell and McFarlin, "Help or Hindrance." A similar study in Florida finds the same results: Juan Carlos Calcagno and Bridget Terry Long, "The Impact of Postsecondary Remediation Using a Regression Discontinuity Approach: Addressing Endogenous Sorting and Noncompliance" (working paper #14194, National Bureau of Economic Research, Cambridge, MA, 2008).

60. Alicia C. Dowd and Laura M. Ventimiglia, "A Cost Estimate of Standards-Based Remediation in a Community College Developmental Education Program" (unpublished manuscript, University of Southern California, Los Angeles, CA, and North Shore Community College, Danvers, MA, 2008).

61. Paul Attewell et al., "New Evidence on College Remediation," *Journal of Higher Education* 77, no. 5 (September/October 2006): 886–924; Calcagno and Long, "Impact of Postsecondary Remediation"; Martorell and Martorell, "Help or Hindrance."

62. Eric P. Bettinger and Bridget Terry Long, "Addressing the Needs of Under-Prepared Students in Higher Education: Does College Remediation Work?" (working paper #11325, National Bureau of Economic Research, Cambridge, MA, 2005). Bettinger and Long specifically use an instrumental variable (IV) that takes advantage of the fact that (a) different colleges in Ohio have different remediation policies, and (b) different students are located in closer proximity to, and are therefore more likely to attend, colleges with policies that affect whether they are placed in remediation.

63. The point estimates in Martorell and McFarlin's "Help or Hindrance?" are a fraction of the size of Bettinger and Long's in "Addressing the Needs," so even if we ignored statistical significance the ECR based on the Martorell and McFarlin estimate would be close to zero.

Chapter 4

1. "Fast Facts: Do You Have Information on Postsecondary Enrollment Rates?" National Center for Education Statistics, http://nces.ed.gov/fastfacts/display.asp?id=98.

2. "Fast Facts: What Are the Graduation Rates for Students Obtaining a Bachelor's Degree?" National Center for Education Statistics, http://nces.ed.gov/fastfacts/display.asp?id=40.

3. InsideTrack's mission is to improve student engagement, persistence, and success. Since

2001, the organization has coached more than three hundred fifty thousand students across a broad range of universities, including Columbia University, Penn State University, University of Dayton, and Florida State University. InsideTrack coaching is a methodology that has been proven to have a measurable impact on long-term student success. Similar to executive coaching, InsideTrack coaches work one-on-one with students on a regular basis to clarify where they want to go to college and beyond, map out a plan for getting there, and provide guidance along the way. Coaches also support students in identifying and overcoming the obstacles that can hinder their success. InsideTrack coaching has been proven to improve graduation rates by an average of 15 percent in more than fifty-five controlled studies.

4. http://www.whitehouse.gov/issues/education.

5. "$4.5 Billion in Earnings, Taxes Lost Last Year Due to the High U.S. College Dropout Rate," American Institutes for Research, http://www.air.org/news/index.cfm?fa= viewContent&content_id=1405.

6. Complete College America, *Remediation: Higher Education's Bridge to Nowhere* (Washington, DC: Complete College America, 2012), http://www.completecollege.org/docs/CCA-Remediation-final.pdf.

7. For example, see Vincent Tinto, "Dropout from Higher Education: A Theoretical Synthesis of Recent Research," *Review of Educational Research* 45, no. 1 (1975): 89; Vincent Tinto, "Colleges as Communities: Taking Research on Student Persistence Seriously," *Review of Higher Education* 21, no. 2 (1998): 167–177; Sara Goldrick-Rab, "Challenges and Opportunities for Improving Community College Student Success," *Review of Educational Research* 80, no. 3 (2010): 437; Eric P. Bettinger and Rachel Baker, *The Effects of Student Coaching in College: An Evaluation of a Randomized Experiment in Student Mentoring* (Stanford, CA: Stanford University School of Education, 2011), http://ed.stanford.edu/sites/default/files/bettinger_baker_030711.pdf.

8. The Delta Cost Project is an initiative to help higher education understand and optimize its spending. For more information, see http://www.deltacostproject.org/.

9. Cesare Mainardi, "How to Cut Costs—Strategically," interview by Paul Michelman, 2013, http://www.booz.com/global/home/what_we_think/ccgs/hbp_interview.

10. For an example, see First Analysis Securities Corporation's June 27, 2012, research note on Bridgepoint Education, Inc., entitled "Good Relative Fundamentals & Focus on Improving Outcomes Merit a Higher Multiple," http://www.research-driven.com/pdffiledir/BPI_Good_relative_fundam_06_27_2012.pdf.

11. "State of College Admission," NACAC, http://www.nacacnet.org/research/Publications Resources/Marketplace/research/Pages/StateofCollegeAdmission.aspx.

12. "Education and Training," BMO Capital Markets, http://research-us.bmocapitalmarkets.com/documents/2012/reports/EducationandTraining2012.pdf.

13. Neal A. Raisman, "Retain Students Retain Budgets: A How-To Primer for Colleges and Universities," http://www.universitybusiness.com/article/retain-students-retain-budgets-how.

14. Ibid.

15. "State of College Admission."

16. Jeffrey M. Silber and Paul Condra, *Education and Training* (New York: BMO Capital Markets, 2012).

17. Kenneth C. Green, Scott Jaschik, and Doug Lederman, *The 2011–12 Inside Higher Ed Survey of College and University Chief Academic Officers* (Washington, DC: Inside Higher Ed, 2012), 17, http://www.insidehighered.com/download?file=finalCAOsurveyreport.pdf.

18. See, for example, www.starfish.com.

19. "Yesterday's Nontraditional Student is Today's Traditional Student," Center for Post-secondary and Economic Success, http://www.clasp.org/admin/site/publications/files/Nontraditional-Students-Facts-2011.pdf.

20. Advisory Committee on Student Financial Assistance, *Pathways to Success: Integrating Learning with Life and Work to Increase National College Completion: A Report to the U.S. Congress and Secretary of Education* (Washington, DC: Advisory Committee on Student Financial Assistance, 2012).

21. Complete College America, *Remediation*.

22. "Promising Practices Supporting Low-Income, First-Generation Students at DeVry University," Pell Institute, http://www.pellinstitute.org/downloads/publications-Promising_Practices_at_DeVry_University_May_2011.pdf.

23. http://admission.brandman.edu.

24. "Academic Annual Report 2010–2011," DeVry University Keller Graduate School of Management, http://newsroom.devry.edu/images/20004/2010-2011AcademicAnnual Report_lo%20res_FINAL.pdf.

25. With the exception of InsideTrack, we are not familiar with any large-scale, randomized controlled studies validating the impact and cost-effectiveness of these solutions. We encourage institutions considering these and other solutions to conduct detailed analyses of their payback period and overall return on investment. These analyses should not only evaluate the initial impact of the intervention, but also the persistence of that impact and the level of proof (controlled studies, etc.) available to support the analyses.

26. "About InsideTrack," http://www.insidetrack.com/about/welcome/.

27. Stanford University, "Stanford Study Shows College Student Coaching Improves Retention and Graduation Rates" (press release, March 10, 2011, http://ed.stanford.edu/spotlight/stanford-study-shows-college-student-coaching-improves-retention-and-graduation-rates).

28. "Review of the Report *The Effects of Student Coaching in College: An Evaluation of a Randomized Experiment in Student Mentoring*," What Works Clearinghouse, http://ies.ed.gov/ncee/wwc/SingleStudyReview.aspx?sid=179.

29. For more information, see http://www.smarthinking.com/explore/.

30. "Study Shows Smarthinking's Positive Impact on Learning," Smarthinking, http://www.smarthinking.com/explore/success-stories/florida-college-system/.

31. "Success Stories," Smarthinking, http://www.smarthinking.com/explore/success-stories/all-stories/.

32. "What Customers Say," Smarthinking, http://www.smarthinking.com/explore/what-customers-say/.

33. Learn more at http://www.uboost.com/education/higher-education/.

34. Learn more at http://www.inigral.com.

35. "Impacting Retention," Inigral, http://www.inigral.com/data/retention/index.php.

36. "School Apps: From Orientation to Graduation at Arizona State University," Inigral, http://www.inigral.com/successstories/Arizona-State-University/.

37. During a panel session entitled "Driving Outcomes and Valuation Through Measurement and Transparency," Corey Greendale of First Analysis Securities Corporation said that a good rule of thumb is that a 100-basis-point improvement in retention results in a 100-basis-point improvement in return on invested capital (ROIC).

Chapter 5

1. "Budget Update: 5% State Budget Cuts for Next Fiscal Year," University of North Carolina at Chapel Hill, Office of the Chancellor, http://www.unc.edu/chan/chancellors/thorp_holden/090319-budget_update.php.
2. Andrew Harrell, "Budget Cuts Reach $60 Million," *Daily Tar Heel*, November 13, 2009.
3. University of North Carolina at Chapel Hill's Office of Institutional Research and Assessment, http://oira.unc.edu/.
4. Joe Templeton, telephone interview by Jeffrey J. Selingo, May 4, 2012, and May 14, 2012.
5. Jeff Denneen, telephone interview by Jeffrey J. Selingo, May 1, 2012.
6. "Trends in College Spending 1999–2009," Delta Cost Project, http://deltacostproject.org/resources/pdf/Trends2011_Final_090711.pdf.
7. For a more extensive description of the history of consultants in higher education, see Daniel H. Pilon, "Emerging Needs for Consultants in Higher Education," *New Directions for Higher Education*, spring 1991, no. 73.
8. Ibid.
9. Holden Thorp, telephone interview by Jeffrey J. Selingo, May 4, 2012.
10. Alisha Azevedo, "Operational Excellence: An Overview as Implementation Begins," *Daily Californian,* August 25, 2011.
11. Ronald G. Ehrenberg, telephone interview by Jeffrey J. Selingo, May 15, 2012.
12. Ibid.
13. Joanne M. DeStefano, telephone interview by Jeffrey J. Selingo, May 23, 2012.
14. Frank Yeary, telephone interview by Jeffrey J. Selingo, May 15, 2012.
15. "The 2010 Best Firms: 1. Bain & Company," *Consulting Magazine*, August 23, 2010, http://consultingmagazine.com/article/ART649699?C=pvBCvR3OI5wydD97.
16. Michael Mankins, telephone interview by Jeffrey J. Selingo, April 5, 2012.
17. Jeff Denneen, interview by Jeffrey J. Selingo, Washington, DC, January 18, 2012.
18. This section was compiled from interviews with Bain consultants, campus administrators, and the final reports from the University of North Carolina and the University of California at Berkeley.
19. Denneen, May 2012 interview.
20. Jay P. Greene, Brian Kisida, and Jonathan Mills, *Administrative Bloat at American Universities: The Real Reason for High Costs in American Higher Education* (Phoenix: Goldwater Institute, 2010), http://goldwaterinstitute.org/article/administrative-bloat-american-universities-real-reason-high-costs-higher-education.
21. Denneen, January 2012 interview.
22. Denneen, May 2012 interview.
23. "Operational Excellence," University of California at Berkeley, http://oe.berkeley.edu.
24. Michael Stratford, "Cornell Hires Outsiders to Ease Budget Woes," *Cornell Daily Sun*, September 2, 2009.
25. "Administrative Streamlining Program," Cornell University, http://asp.dpb.cornell.edu.
26. Tamar Lewin, "Universities Turn to Consultants to Trim Budgets," *New York Times*, November 19, 2009.
27. "Carolina Budget Information," University of North Carolina at Chapel Hill, http://universityrelations.unc.edu/budget/.
28. Edward Pickup, "UNC's Carolina Counts Faculty Initiative Tells Board of Visitors It's on Target to Meet 5-Year Goals," *Daily Tar Heel*, October 17, 2011.
29. Personal e-mail communication from Tom Schnetlage to Jeffrey J. Selingo, May 24, 2012.

30. Denneen, January 2012 interview.

31. Final Bain report to UNC.

32. Andrew Szeri, telephone interview by Jeffrey J. Selingo, May 14, 2012.

33. Denneen, January 2012 interview.

34. Jeff Denneen and Tom Dretler, "The Financially Sustainable University" (white paper, Bain & Company/Sterling Partners, 2012).

35. David Skorton, telephone interview by Jeffrey J. Selingo, May 30, 2012.

36. Goldie Blumenstyk, "Business Advice Meets Academic Culture," *Chronicle of Higher Education*, April 29, 2012.

37. "University of North Texas at Dallas and Bain & Company in $1 Million, Multi-Year Pro Bono Service Partnership to Develop Strategic Vision for Universities of the 21st Century" (press release), http://www.bain.com/about/press/press-releases/university_north_texas_and_bain_partnership.aspx.

38. Mark Gottfredson, telephone interview by Jeffrey J. Selingo, April 5, 2012.

39. John Ellis Price, interview by Jeffrey J. Selingo, Washington, DC, May 10, 2012.

40. Denneen and Dretler, "The Financially Stable University."

Chapter 6

1. Robert Reich, "The Commencement Address That Won't Be Given," http://robertreich.org/post/23301640941robertreich.org, May 18, 2012.

2. Morley Safer, "Dropping Out: Is College Worth the Cost?" *60 Minutes*, May 20, 2012.

3. Clayton M. Christensen, Michael B. Horn, Louis Soares, and Louis Caldera, *Disrupting College: How Disruptive Innovation Can Deliver Quality and Affordability to Postsecondary Education* (Washington, DC, and Mountain View, CA: Center for American Progress and Innosight Institute, 2011), http://www.americanprogress.org/wp-content/uploads/issues/2011/02/pdf/disrupting_college.pdf.

4. http://en.wikipedia.org/wiki/Bloom%27s_Taxonomy.

5. Matt Burns, "Apple Announces iBooks 2, a New Textbook Experience for the iPad," *TechCrunch*, January 19, 2012, http://techcrunch.com/2012/01/19/apple-announces-ibook-2-a-new-textbook-experience-for-the-ipad/.

6. Tamar Lewin, "Instruction for the Masses Knocks Down Campus Walls," *New York Times*, March 4, 2012, http://www.nytimes.com/2012/03/05/education/moocs-large-courses-open-to-all-topple-campus-walls.html?pagewanted=all&_r=0.

7. George Anders, "So Long Stuffy Lecture Halls: Coursera Just Tripled Its Digital Campus," *Forbes*, July 17, 2012, http://www.forbes.com/sites/georgeanders/2012/07/17/coursera-boom/.

8. Alexia Tsotsis, "OpenStudy Wants to Turn the World into 'One Big Study Group,'" *TechCrunch,* June 8, 2011, http://techcrunch.com/2011/06/08/openstudy-wants-to-turn-the-world-into-one-big-study-group/.

9. Joshua Foer, *Moonwalking with Einstein: The Art and Science of Remembering Everything* (New York: Penguin Press, 2011).

10. Steve Kolowich, "Khan Academy Ponders What It Can Teach the Higher Education Establishment," *Inside Higher Ed*, December 7, 2011, http://www.insidehighered.com/news/2011/12/07/khan-academy-ponders-what-it-can-teach-higher-education-establishment.

11. Alexandra Rice, "To Monitor Online Testing, Western Governors U. Gives Students Webcams," *Wired Campus* (blog), *Chronicle of Higher Education*, November 2, 2011, http://chronicle.com/blogs/wiredcampus/to-monitor-online-testing-western-

governors-u-gives-students-webcams/34099.

12. Steve Kolowich, "Recommended for You," *Inside Higher Ed*, March 16, 2012, http://www.insidehighered.com/news/2012/03/16/university-builds-course-recommendation-engine-steer-students-toward-completion.

13. Personal conversation with the author.

14. David Blake, "Jailbreaking the Degree," *TechCrunch*, May 5, 2012, http://techcrunch.com/2012/05/05/jailbreaking-the-degree/.

15. Dana Oshiro, "Where Is Entrepreneurship Really Taught?" *ReadWriteWeb*, February 8, 2010, http://readwrite.com/2010/02/08/where-is-entrepreneurship-real.

16. Derek Bok, *Our Underachieving Colleges* (Princeton, NJ: Princeton University Press, 2007).

17. Randall Stross, "The Algorithm Didn't Like My Essay," *New York Times*, June 9, 2012, http://www.nytimes.com/2012/06/10/business/essay-grading-software-as-teachers-aide-digital-domain.html.

18. Personal conversation with the author.

19. Blake Boles, *Better Than College: How to Build a Successful Life Without a Four-Year Degree* (Loon Lake, CA: Tells Peak Press, 2012).

Chapter 7

1. Unless otherwise noted, all quotations are from in-person interviews by the author. Names of interviewees, in the order they appear in the text, and dates of interviews are as follows: Greg von Lehmen, senior vice president of External Relations and Initiatives, University of Maryland University College (UMUC), June 7, 2012; Cynthia Davis, acting dean of the Undergraduate School, UMUC, June 7, 2012; Sharon Biederman, interim associate provost, Instructional Services and Support, UMUC, June 7, 2012; Richard Schumaker, director of Faculty Professional Development and Training, UMUC, June 7, 2012; Alan Carswell, chair of the Department of Cybersecurity and Information Assurance at UMUC's Graduate School of Management and Technology, June 7, 2012; Emily Medina, acting director, Course Development, UMUC, June 7, 2012; Kim Stott, executive director, UMUC's Center for Teaching and Learning, June 7, 2012; Keith Williams, interim director, UC Online, June 22, 2012; Mary-Ellen Kreher, director of Course Design and Development, June 22, 2012; David Stavens, president and chief operating officer, Udacity, June 20, 2012; David Evans, vice president of education, Udacity, and associate professor of computer science, University of Virginia, June 26, 2012.

2. Greg von Lehman, private remarks at "Stretching the Higher Education Dollar" workshop, American Enterprise Institute, Washington, DC, February 2, 2012.

3. Christopher Edley Jr., "Online Learning Matches UC's Mission," *San Francisco Chronicle*, July 18, 2010, http://www.sfgate.com/education/article/Online-learning-matches-UC-s-mission-3181054.php.

4. "UC Online Education: Frequently Asked Questions," University of California, http://www.ucop.edu/uconline/_files/uc_online_fact_sheet.pdf.

5. "Press Room: Online Education," University of California, http://qa.universityofcalifornia.edu/press-room/current-issues/online-education.

6. Tamar Lewin, "Instruction for Masses Knocks Down Campus Walls," *New York Times*, March 4, 2012, http://www.nytimes.com/2012/03/05/education/moocs-large-courses-open-to-all-topple-campus-walls.html?pagewanted=all.

7. Ibid.

8. Ibid.

9. Nick DeSantis, "Stanford Professor Gives Up Teaching Position, Hopes to Reach 500,000 Students at Online Start-Up," *Wired Campus* (blog), *Chronicle of Higher Education*, January 23, 2012, http://chronicle.com/blogs/wiredcampus/stanford-professor-gives-up-teaching-position-hopes-to-reach-500000-students-at-online-start-up/35135.

10. http://sloanconsortium.org/news_press/january2013_new-study-over-67-million-students-learning-online.

Chapter 8

1. "Business Intelligence and SAS Analytics Software," UC Berkeley Extension, http://extension.berkeley.edu/spos/sas.html.

2. Neera Grover, telephone interview by Steve Kolowich, n.d.

3. Tamar Lewin, "Education Site Expands Slate of Universities and Courses," *New York Times*, September 19, 2012, http://www.nytimes.com/2012/09/19/education/coursera-adds-more-ivy-league-partner-universities.html.

4. David L. Chandler, "MIT and Harvard Launch a 'Revolution in Education'," *MIT News*, May 2, 2012, http://web.mit.edu/newsoffice/2012/edx-launched-0502.html.

5. Steve Kolowich, "Advancing the Open Front," *Inside Higher Ed*, December 12, 2011, http://www.insidehighered.com/news/2011/12/20/planned-mit-courses-may-advance-front-elite-open-education.

6. Ibid.

7. Molly Bloom, "Computers Grade Essays Fast . . . but Not Always Well," *NPR*, June 7, 2012, http://www.npr.org/2012/06/07/154452475/computers-grade-essays-fast-but-not-always-well.

8. Steve Kolowich, "Elite Universities' Online Play," *Inside Higher Ed*, April 18, 2012, http://www.insidehighered.com/news/2012/04/18/princeton-penn-and-michigan-join-mooc-party.

9. Tamar Lewin, "College of Future Could Be Come One, Come All," *New York Times*, November 19, 2012, http://www.nytimes.com/2012/11/20/education/colleges-turn-to-crowd-sourcing-courses.html?pagewanted=all&_r=0.

10. "Udacity in Partnership with Pearson VUE Announces Testing Centers," *Udacity Blog*, June 1, 2012, http://blog.udacity.com/2012/06/udacity-in-partnership-with-pearson-vue.html.

11. Jeffrey R. Young, "A Conversation with Bill Gates About the Future of Higher Education," *Chronicle of Higher Education*, June 25, 2012, http://chronicle.com/article/A-Conversation-With-Bill-Gates/132591/.

12. Steve Kolowich, "American Council on Education Recommends 5 MOOCs for Credit," *Chronicle of Higher Education*, February 7, 2013, http://chronicle.com/article/American-Council-on-Education/137155/.

13. Katherine Mangan, "A First for Udacity: A U.S. University will Accept Transfer Credit for One of Its Courses," *Chronicle of Higher Education*, September 6, 2012, http://chronicle.com/article/A-First-for-Udacity-Transfer/134162/.

14. Paul Fain, "As California Goes?" *Inside Higher Ed*, January 16, 2013, http://www.insidehighered.com/news/2013/01/16/california-looks-moocs-online-push.

15. Tamar Lewin, "Instruction for Masses Knocks Down Campus Walls," *New York Times*, March 4, 2012, http://www.nytimes.com/2012/03/05/education/moocs-large-courses-open-to-all-topple-campus-walls.html?pagewanted=all.

16. Ibid.

17. "Courses," Stanford University, http://ai.stanford.edu/~ang/courses.html.

18. William G. Bowen, Matthew M. Chingos, Kelly A. Lack, and Thomas I. Nygren, *Interactive Learning Online at Public Universities: Evidence from Randomized Trials* (New York: Ithaka S&R, 2012), http://www.sr.ithaka.org/research-publications/interactive-learning-online-public-universities-evidence-randomized-trials.

19. Kevin M. Guthrie, "Barriers to the Adoption of Online Learning Systems," *Educause Review Online*, July 18, 2012, http://www.educause.edu/ero/article/barriers-adoption-online-learning-systems.

20. Marsha Lovett, Oded Meyer, and Candace Thille, "The Open Learning Initiative: Measuring the Effectiveness of the OLI Statistics Course in Accelerating Student Learning," *Journal of Interactive Media in Education*, May 2008, http://jime.open.ac.uk/2008/14.

21. Marsha Lovett, Oded Meyer, and Candace Thille, "In Search of the 'Perfect' Blend Between an Instructor and an Online Course for Teaching Introductory Statistics" (paper presented at the Eighth International Conference on Teaching Statistics, Ljubljana, Slovenia, July 15, 2010), http://www.stat.auckland.ac.nz/~iase/publications/icots8/ICOTS8_9G2_LOVETT.pdf.

22. Paul Fain, "College Credit Without College," *Inside Higher Ed*, May 7, 2012, http://www.insidehighered.com/news/2012/05/07/prior-learning-assessment-catches-quietly.

23. Ibid.

24. "A Stronger Nation Through Higher Education," Lumina Foundation, http://www.luminafoundation.org/publications/A_stronger_nation.pdf.

25. "Fueling the Race to Postsecondary Success," Council for Adult and Experiential Learning, http://www.cael.org/pdfs/PLA_Fueling-the-Race.

26. Fain, "College Credit."

27. Ibid.

28. Ibid.

29. Ibid.

30. Ibid.

31. David Moldoff, telephone interview by Paul Fain, n.d.

32. Ibid.

33. "About the American Council on Education," American Council on Education, http://www.acenet.edu/about-ace/Pages/default.aspx.

34. John Ebersole, telephone interview by Paul Fain, n.d.

35. "Hamburger University: McDonald's Center of Training Excellence," McDonald's Corporation, http://www.aboutmcdonalds.com/mcd/corporate_careers/training_and_development/hamburger_university.html.

36. Paul Fain, "Online Classes. Low Prices. Every Day," *Inside Higher Ed*, May 8, 2012, http://www.insidehighered.com/news/2012/05/08/walmart-and-american-public-u-chart-new-ground-partnership.

37. Ebersole, interview.

38. Doug Lederman, "Credit Hour (Still) Rules," *Inside Higher Ed*, April 30, 2012, http://www.insidehighered.com/news/2012/04/30/wgu-example-shows-chilly-policy-climate-competency-based-education.

39. Tamar Lewin, "Official Calls for Urgency on College Costs," *New York Times*, November 29, 2011, http://www.nytimes.com/2011/11/30/education/duncan-calls-for-urgency-in-lowering-college-costs.html?_r=0.

40. Tamar Lewin, "A Way to Speed the Pace," *New York Times*, August 25, 2011, http://

www.nytimes.com/2011/08/25/education/25future_straight.html.

41. Rebecca Klein-Collins, *Strategies to Produce New Nurses for a Changing Profession* (Chicago: CAEL, 2011), http://www.excelsior.edu/c/document_library/get_file?uuid= a70d70c8-60ca-4466-b10b-3d0e1172672f&groupId=78666.

42. Ebersole, interview.

43. Karen Herzog, "Some College Graduates Turn to Tech School for Job Training," *Milwaukee Journal Sentinel*, May 28, 2012. http://www.jsonline.com/news/education/ some-college-graduates-turn-to-tech-school-for-job-training-055hg7u-155158985.html.

44. Stephen Morse, "What Will the Future Bring for Coursera and Online Learning?" *Atlantic*, September 24, 2012, http://www.theatlantic.com/sponsored/bank-of-america/ archive/2012/09/what-will-the-future-bring-for-coursera-and-online-learning/262803.

45. Steve Kolowich, "Learning from One Another," *Inside Higher Ed*, August 30, 2012, http://www.insidehighered.com/news/2012/08/30/first-humanities-mooc-professors- road-test-courseras-peer-grading-model.

Chapter 9

1. Tamar Lewin, "Instruction for the Masses Knocks Down Campus Walls," *New York Times*, March 4, 2012. See also: Tamar Lewin, "Harvard and MIT Team Up to Offer Free Online Courses," *New York Times*, May 2, 2012.

2. Clayton Christensen, *The Innovator's Dilemma: When New Technologies Cause Great Firms to Fail* (Boston: Harvard Business School Press, 1997).

3. On student outcomes in online learning, see U.S. Department of Education, *Evaluation of Evidence-Based Practices in Online Learning: A Meta-Analysis and Review of Online Learning Studies*, Washington, DC: U.S. Department of Education, Office of Planning, Evaluation, and Policy Development, 2010). On cost-effectiveness of hybrid delivery, see the research conducted by the National Center for Academic Transformation (www.thencat.org) on course redesign. For example, see Carol Twigg, "The Math Emporium: Higher Education's Silver Bullet," *Change: The Magazine of Higher Learning*, May–June 2011.

4. Clayton Christensen and Henry B. Eyring, *The Innovative University: Changing the DNA of Higher Education from the Inside Out* (New York: Jossey-Bass, 2011).

5. Clayton Christensen, *The Innovator's Solution: Creating and Sustaining Successful Growth* (Boston: Harvard Business Press, 2002).

6. Jennifer Epstein, "Express Lane to a B.A.," *Inside Higher Education*, March 11, 2010, http://www.insidehighered.com/news/2010/03/11/threeyears.

7. On mission creep in higher education, see David A. Longanecker, *Mission Differentiation vs. Mission Creep: Higher Education's Battle Between Creationism and Evolution* (Boulder, CO: Western Interstate Commission on Higher Education, 2008), http:// www.wiche.edu/info/gwypf/dal_mission.pdf.

8. It is important to note that it can also introduce the discomfort of using technology for some adults (being introduced to wikis, blogs, and tweets, for example), but adults choosing online learning tend to be self-selecting, and good providers tend to offer 24/7 tech support and other easy-to-access guidance.

9. Richard Arum and Josipa Roksa, *Academically Adrift: Limited Learning on College Campuses* (Chicago: University of Chicago Press, 2011).

10. Christensen, *Innovator's Dilemma*.

11. Angela Gonzales, "Enrollment Declines Hit Apollo Group's Bottom Line," *Phoenix Business Journal*, June 25, 2012, http://www.bizjournals.com/phoenix/news/2012/

06/25/enrollment-declines-hit-apollo-groups.html.

12. "Happy families are all alike; every unhappy family is unhappy in its own way."

13. Bill Gates, *The Road Ahead* (New York: Penguin, 1995).

Chapter 10

1. "Annual Report 2001: Financial Review," United States Postal Service, http://about .usps.com/who-we-are/financials/annual-reports/fy2001/welcome.htm.

2. Ibid.

3. "School Enrollment," United States Census Bureau, http://www.census.gov/hhes/ school/data/cps/historical/index.html.

4. Peter Smith, *Harnessing America's Wasted Talent* (San Francisco: Jossey-Bass, 2010), 96.

5. "School Enrollment"; "Historical National Population Estimates: July 1, 1900 to July 1, 1999," United States Census Bureau, http://www.census.gov/population/estimates/ nation/popclockest.txt.

6. Russ Poulin, "Should Online Courses Charge Less? It Doesn't Just Happen," *WCET Learn* (blog), March 22, 2012, http://wcetblog.wordpress.com/2012/03/22/should-online-courses-charge-less/.

7. Clayton Christensen, *The Innovator's Dilemma* (Cambridge, MA: Harvard Business Press, 1997).

8. "Yesterday's Nontraditional Student Is Today's Traditional Student," Center for Law and Social Policy, http://www.clasp.org/admin/site/publications/files/Nontraditional-Students-Facts-2011.pdf.

9. Anne Ryman, "ASU Seizing Online Future," *Arizona Republic*, June 5, 2011, http:// www.azcentral.com/arizonarepublic/news/articles/2011/06/05/20110605arizona-state-online-classes.html.

10. Marc Parry, "Online Venture Energizes Vulnerable College," *Chronicle of Higher Education*, August 28, 2011, http://chronicle.com/article/How-Big-Can-E-Learning-Get-At/128809.

11. Jay Greene, *Administrative Bloat at American Universities: The Real Reason for High Costs in Higher Education* (Phoenix: Goldwater Institute, 2010).

12. Course Redesign is a set of principles that colleges can use to redesign high enrollment courses. For more information, contact the National Center for Academic Transformation (www.thencat.org).

13. "Governor's Budget 2012," State of Massachusetts, http://www.mass.gov/bb/h1/ fy12h1/brec_12/dpt_12/hhe2.htm.

14. "A Portrait of Part-Time Faculty Members: A Summary of Findings on Part-Time Faculty Respondents to the Coalition on the Academic Workforce Survey of Contingent Faculty Members and Instructors," Coalition on the Academic Workforce, http://www .academicworkforce.org/survey.html.

15. Daniel Wagner, "Colleges' Bank Deals Saddle Students with Big Fees," *Yahoo! News*, May 31, 2012, http://news.yahoo.com/colleges-bank-deals-saddle-students-big-fees-152242593—finance.html.

Conclusion

1. "Tuition Inflation," FinAid!, http://www.finaid.org/savings/tuition-inflation.phtml.

2. "Remarks by the President in the State of the Union Address," Office of the White

House Press Secretary, http://www.whitehouse.gov/the-press-office/2012/01/24/ remarks-president-state-union-address.

3. Russ Poulin, "Should Online Courses Charge Less? It Doesn't Just Happen," *WCET Learn* (blog), March 22, 2012, http://wcetblog.wordpress.com/2012/03/22/should-online-courses-charge-less/.

4. Michael Stratford, "Independent Colleges are Keen on Affordability Goals, but Wary of How to Achieve Them," *Chronicle of Higher Education*, January 31, 2012, http://chronicle.com/article/Keen-on-College-Affordability/130593/.

5. Kevin Kiley, "What Will $10,000 Get Me?" *Inside Higher Ed*, May 9, 2012, http://www.insidehighered.com/news/2012/05/09/10000-degree-push-has-led-innovation-pricing-not-cost-control.

6. Ben Wildavsky, Andrew Kelly, and Kevin Carey, eds., *Reinventing Higher Education: The Promise of Innovation* (Cambridge, MA: Harvard Education Press, 2011).

7. "Six States Selected to Participate in NGA Policy Academy to Improve Performance Measures for Higher Education," National Governors Association, http://www.nga.org/cms/home/news-room/news-releases/page_2011/col2-content/main-content-list/six-states-selected-to-participa.html.

8. Tamar Lewin and John Markoff, "California to Give Web Courses a Big Trial," *New York Times*, January 15, 2013, http://www.nytimes.com/2013/01/15/technology/california-to-give-web-courses-a-big-trial.html?_r=0.

9. *Innovations in College Affordability, Before the Senate Committee on Health, Education, Labor and Pensions*, 112th Cong., 2d sess. (2012) (testimony by Kevin Carey).

10. Will Oremus, "In Victory for Common Sense, Minnesota Will Allow Free Online Courses After All," *Future Tense* (blog), *Slate*, October 19, 2012, http://www.slate.com/blogs/future_tense/2012/10/19/minnesota_coursera_ban_state_won_t_crack_down_on_free_online_courses_after.html.

11. Vance Fried, "Venturing to Affordability" (paper presented at the Stretching the Higher Education Dollar conference, American Enterprise Institute, Washington DC, August 2, 2012).

Acknowledgments

In the midst of the recent economic downturn, America's leaders have turned to the nation's higher education system as the engine to drive our economic recovery. The nation has embarked upon an ambitious "completion agenda" premised on the idea that the country will need to produce more postsecondary credentials to meet labor market demand in the years to come. And yet, the same economic forces that have made higher education more vital than ever before have also threatened to put it out of reach for American families. The recession hit colleges as well, leading to cuts in state support at public institutions and reduced endowment earnings at private ones. In response, most colleges and universities have increased tuition prices at a feverish pace. And while the federal government has traditionally maintained affordability via generous investments in student aid, tight budgets in Washington mean that these investments simply cannot keep pace with increases in tuition. Policy makers, researchers, and journalists have come to recognize that improving affordability in the absence of additional subsidies will require a search for lower-cost models of postsecondary education.

In early 2012, we set out to examine this neglected side of the college affordability question. Texas Governor Rick Perry had provided the country with a reference point, challenging his state universities to create a $10,000 bachelor's degree. Using Perry's challenge as a touchstone, we began to discuss whether such a dramatic reduction in the price of college was possible, and how we might get there. From the start, we took pains to draw the necessary distinction between "cost" (what it actually costs to deliver postsecondary education) and "price" (what students pay), a distinction that is often missed in the conventional coverage of "college costs."

To kick off the project, we held a private gathering in February 2012 with prominent academics, university leaders, and entrepreneurs in the higher education space to discuss current trends, opportunities for cost containment, and the potential for innovation to reduce the cost of delivery.

What followed was a lively conversation that helped inform our thinking on the opportunities for reform and the obstacles therein. We also walked away with a sense that reform energies must be dedicated to both containing costs at existing colleges and universities and to the creation of a new and decidedly different higher education market made up of new ventures and unbundled service providers.

From this, we proceeded to commission ten pieces of new research that sketched the case for reform, explored the opportunities and barriers at existing institutions, highlighted how a new crop of entrepreneurs are lowering prices by "unbundling" a college degree, and closed with implications for leaders and policy makers. Most of these essays were first presented at a public conference at the American Enterprise Institute (AEI) in August 2012. The final, revised versions of those essays, along with an additional chapter, are collected in this volume.

We would like to thank the authors for their excellent contributions as well as their patience during the editing process. We would also like to thank the following discussants for their invaluable feedback on the draft papers at the August 2012 conference: Robert B. Archibald, College of William & Mary; Zakiya Smith, White House Domestic Policy Council; Wally Boston, American Public University System; Andrew Delbanco, Columbia University; Ann Kirschner, Macaulay Honors College, City University of New York; Amy Laitinen, New America Foundation; Arthur M. Hauptman, public policy consultant; and Raymund A. Paredes, Texas Higher Education Coordinating Board.

We are also indebted to the steadfast support of AEI and its president, Arthur Brooks, and of the New America Foundation and its president, Steve Coll. The Bill & Melinda Gates Foundation generously provided the financial support for this project. We are particularly thankful to the Foundation's former senior economic and data advisor, Marguerite Roza, for her early support of this effort, and our program officer, Matthew Joseph, for helping shepherd this project to completion. The staff at AEI deserves our appreciation for coordinating the conference and editing the contributions. In particular, we thank Daniel Lautzenheiser for his role managing the project, as well as KC Deane, Taryn Hochleitner, Allison Kimmel, Lauren Aronson, and Chelsea Straus for their assistance. Finally, we express our continued gratitude to the Harvard Education Press team, particularly publisher Doug Clayton and editor-in-chief Caroline Chauncey, whose advice and support made this volume a reality.

About the Editors

Andrew P. Kelly is a resident scholar in education policy studies at AEI. His research focuses on higher education policy, innovation in education, the politics of education reform, and consumer choice in education. Previously, he was a research assistant at AEI, where his work focused on the preparation of school leaders, collective bargaining in public schools, and the politics of education. His research has appeared in *Teachers College Record, Educational Policy, Policy Studies Journal, Education Next,* and *Education Week,* as well as popular outlets such as *Inside Higher Ed, Forbes, The Atlantic, National Review,* and *The Huffington Post.* He is coeditor of *Getting to Graduation: The Completion Agenda in Higher Education* (Johns Hopkins University Press, 2012); *Carrots, Sticks, and the Bully Pulpit: Lessons from A Half-Century of Federal Efforts to Improve America's Schools* (Harvard Education Press, 2012); and *Reinventing Higher Education: The Promise of Innovation* (Harvard Education Press, 2011). In 2011, Kelly was named one of sixteen "Next Generation Leaders" in education policy by *Education Week*'s Policy Notebook blog.

Kevin Carey is director of the education policy program at the New America Foundation. An expert on preK–12 and higher education issues, Carey has published articles on education and other topics in magazines including *The New Republic, Washington Monthly, The American Prospect,* and *Democracy.* He writes monthly columns on education for *The Chronicle of Higher Education* and *The New Republic* and edits the annual Washington Monthly College Guide. Carey's research topics include higher education reform, college graduation rate improvement, college rankings, community colleges, and the Elementary and Secondary Education Act. His writing was anthologized in *Best American Legal Writing 2009* and received an Education Writers Association award for commentary in 2010. He appears frequently on media outlets including CNN, C-SPAN, and NPR. Before joining New America, Carey worked as the policy director of Education Sector and at the Education Trust. Previously, he worked as an analyst in the Indiana Senate and as Indiana's assistant state budget director. He also teaches education policy at Johns Hopkins University.

About the Contributors

Ari Blum is chief executive officer of InsideTrack, an organization dedicated to improving outcomes for students and the universities that serve them. His career has included leadership roles in a broad range of mission-driven, rapidly growing, and successful businesses. Before joining InsideTrack, Blum was with Niman Ranch, the nation's leading brand for natural meats of exceptional quality, integrity, and sustainability. He has experience in early-stage venture investing with Investors' Circle and in investment banking with Houlihan, Lokey, Howard, and Zukin. Since joining InsideTrack as chief financial officer in 2006, Blum has been responsible for the company's strategic direction and growth.

Paul Fain is a senior reporter with online trade publication *Inside Higher Ed*, where he covers community colleges, for-profit institutions, the nontraditional student market, and the completion agenda. Previously, Fain was a senior reporter with the *Chronicle of Higher Education*, where from 2004 to 2011, he wrote broadly about college leaders, finance, and governance. Fain is regularly asked to speak at conferences and events and has been widely cited in the news media. Before joining the *Chronicle*, Fain reported for *C-VILLE Weekly*, a newspaper in Charlottesville, Virginia. He has also written for *The New York Times*, *Philadelphia City Paper*, *Washington City Paper*, and *Mother Jones*. Fain has done two stints in public relations, most recently in the higher education practice of Widmeyer Communications. Fain's writing has won numerous awards, including the 2008 Dick Schaap Excellence in Sports Journalism Award.

Douglas N. Harris is an associate professor of economics and the University Endowed Chair in Public Education at Tulane University. Harris has been at the forefront of research attempting to identify policies that improve teacher effectiveness. His book, *Value-Added Measures in Education: What Every Educator Needs to Know* (Harvard Education Press, 2011) was nominated for the national Grawemeyer Award in Education. He is also branching out into two new areas. In his position at Tulane, he is creating a research consortium to study New Orleans school choice and "portfolio district" reforms. Harris has also created two of the first randomized trials of college financial aid, the Wisconsin Scholars Longitudinal Study (WSLS) and the Milwaukee College Access Project for Success (M-CAPS). He has been the principal investigator on more than $6 million in research grants, and the results of this work have been published in the journal *Science*, *The Journal of Public Economics*, and dozens of academic publications. His education research is frequently cited in national media such as *The New York Times*, *Washington Post*, CNN, and NPR, and he consults widely on policy matters with elected officials, state departments of education, and organizations such as the National Council of State Legislators, National Governors Association, and National Academy of Sciences. Until recently, he was associate professor of educational policy and public affairs at the University of Wisconsin–Madison, where he remains an affiliate of the Wisconsin Center for the Advancement of Postsecondary Education (WISCAPE) and Institute for Research on Poverty.

Dave Jarrat is the vice president of marketing at InsideTrack. Jarrat leads InsideTrack's marketing, research, and industry relations activities. In addition to engaging prospective university partners and building InsideTrack's brand through thought leadership and research activities, he also manages the Inside-Track advisory board and the company's relationships with key associations and policy bodies. Prior to joining InsideTrack, Jarrat spent a decade as a marketing executive, building a track record of success opening new markets and growing revenues for businesses in environmental and information technology.

Anya Kamenetz is a senior writer at *Fast Company* magazine. She is the author of four books that explore the future of education and give an in-depth analysis of the many factors influencing higher education. Her book *Generation Debt* (Riverhead, 2006) addresses student loans, generational economics, and politics, while her book *DIY U: Edupunks, Edupreneurs, and the Coming Transformation of Higher Education* (Chelsea Green Publishing, 2010) investigates the roots of the cost, access, and quality crises in higher education and offers innovative ideas to address these crises. She has also written two e-books, including *The Edupunks' Guide*, which was funded by the Bill & Melinda Gates Foundation, and *Learning, Freedom and the Web*, produced in collaboration with the Mozilla community. Both books were released in 2011. In 2010, Kamenetz was named Game Changer in Education by *The Huffington Post*. In 2010 and 2009, she received two national awards for education reporting from the Education Writers Association. Kamenetz was also nominated for a Pulitzer Prize in Feature Writing by *The Village Voice* in 2005. She gives speeches across the country and provides commentary on NPR, CNN, and other news networks.

Steve Kolowich is a reporter for *The Chronicle of Higher Education*, returning after a three-year stint with *Inside Higher Ed*. During his time at *The Chronicle*, he was awarded the David W. Miller Award for Young Journalists. Kolowich is also a freelance music writer.

Paul J. LeBlanc became president of Southern New Hampshire University (SNHU) in 2003 after having served as president of Marlboro College from 1996 to 2003. In the ten years under LeBlanc's direction, SNHU has more than doubled in size and has become the largest provider of online higher education in New England. In 2012, the university was number 12 on *Fast Company* magazine's World's Fifty Most Innovative Companies list and was the only university included. SNHU has been recognized by the Bill & Melinda Gates Foundation as a "Beating the Odds" school for its innovative programming to increase graduation rates and productivity. It has also been on *The Chronicle of Higher Education*'s Best Colleges to Work For list every year since the list was created and, in 2011, was named to the Honor Roll. In 2010, SNHU earned a Carnegie Foundation Community Engagement classification and moved from Tier 3 to Tier 1 for regional universities in *U.S. News & World Report*'s ranking. LeBlanc has been asked to speak on innovation, online learning, and higher education reform by the New England Board of Higher Education, the Lumina Foundation, Rhode Island's Board of Higher Education, Harvard University's Schools of Business and Education, IBM, and the CTO Forum, among others. LeBlanc won a New England Higher Education Excellence Award in 2012 and was named one of New Hampshire's Most Influential People by *The New Hampshire Business Review*. Before joining Marlboro College, he was vice president for new technology at Houghton Mifflin Company. He also served as chair of the humanities department at Springfield College in Massachusetts. An authority on technology and education, LeBlanc is also the author or editor of three books.

Robert E. Martin is professor emeritus of economics at Centre College, where he has held a Boles Professorship since 1996. Martin began his teaching career at Louisiana State University Student Union, where he taught graduate microeconomic theory and mathematical economics for thirteen years. Following that position, he served for a time at the University of Texas at Arlington, where he was a professor and interim dean of the business school. In 2005, he received the Kirk Award for Excellence in Teaching at Centre College, where he completed his teaching career in 2008. Martin has also worked as a corporate development manager and served as a senior executive in a publicly held firm, where he was responsible for financial planning, budgeting, mergers, and acquisitions. He has also published two books and over forty articles on the diverse topics of behavior under risk and uncertainty, recycling, externality regulation, medical economics, franchising, enrollment management, and tuition discounting. The bulk of these publications are in academic journals such as *The American Economic Review*, *The Journal of Public Economics*, *Economic Inquiry*, *Southern Economic Journal*, *Applied Economics*, and *The Journal of Comparative Economics*. Martin continues to pursue an active higher education research agenda.

Jeffrey J. Selingo has been the vice president and editorial director of *The Chronicle of Higher Education* since August 2011. Selingo is a leading authority on higher education worldwide, campus leadership, college and university governance, fundraising and trustees, executive compensation, and state-government policy and politics. He writes a regular blog and column for *The Chronicle* and *The Huffington Post* called "Next," where he explores innovation in higher education and offers insights on the future of college. Before coming to *The Chronicle*, Selingo covered environmental issues as a reporter for *The Wilmington Star-News* (1995–1997) and worked for *The Ithaca Journal* (1994–1995). As a recipient of a Pulliam Journalism Fellowship, he covered business technology for *The Arizona Republic*. For the past fifteen years, Selingo has worked in a variety of roles at *The Chronicle*, including as editor from 2007 to 2011. His work has been honored with awards from the Education Writers Association, the Society of Professional Journalists, and the Associated Press. He was a finalist for the Livingston Award for Young Journalists. He has been a featured speaker before dozens of national higher education groups and appears regularly on regional and national radio and television programs, including NPR, PBS, ABC, MSNBC, and CBS. His writing has also appeared in *The New York Times* and *The Washington Post*. Selingo is currently working on his first book, *College (Un)Bound: The Future of Higher Education and What It Means for Students*, which will be published by Amazon and Houghton Mifflin Harcourt in the spring of 2013.

Burck Smith is the CEO of StraighterLine, which he founded in 2009. Ten years before launching StraighterLine, he cofounded SMARTHINKING, the largest online tutoring provider for schools and colleges. Smith has written chapters for two books on education policy for AEI. Before starting SMARTHINKING, Smith worked as an independent consultant, contracting with for-profit and nonprofit educational organizations, including clients such as the Bill & Melinda Gates Foundation, Microsoft, Computer Curriculum Corporation, the CEO Forum on Education and Technology, the Milken Exchange on Education and Technology, Teaching Matters Inc., and *Converge* magazine, among others. As an education and technology issues writer, Smith has been published by *Wired* magazine, *Wired News*, *Converge* magazine, *University Business* magazine, and the National School Boards Association. In the early

1990s, he wrote articles on a variety of subjects, including the creation of community telecommunication networks, electronic access to political information, telecommunications deregulation, and the ability of utilities to serve as telecommunications service providers.

Michael Staton is founder and CEO of Inigral. An educator turned Internet entrepreneur, he has led Inigral through three rounds of investment and brought on ninety partner institutions. Inigral is considered the leading company in developing social software for student recruitment and retention in higher education. It has also been named one of the top ten innovative companies in education by *Fast Company* magazine and has attracted a program-related venture investment from the Bill & Melinda Gates Foundation. As the leader of Inigral's strategic direction, Staton thinks about the transformation of institutions to adapt to the coming wave of technology and disruptive market forces. Staton has been a panelist and speaker at the Arizona State University Innovation in Education Summit, South by Southwest, Internet Week, National College Access Network, the White House, and the President's Council on the Advancement of Science and Technology. He tries to help other education entrepreneurs get off the ground and functions as an adviser to various startups in the education space, including the New Schools Venture Fund Seed Fund. Before starting Inigral, he was an innovative educator and curriculum designer focused on building a college-readiness curriculum framework.

Ben Wildavsky is a senior scholar in research and policy at the Kauffman Foundation and a guest scholar at the Brookings Institution. He is the author of *The Great Brain Race: How Global Universities Are Reshaping the World* (Princeton University Press, 2010), which won the Frandson Award for Literature in the Field of Continuing Higher Education and is being translated into Chinese, Vietnamese, and Arabic. He is also coeditor of *Reinventing Higher Education: The Promise of Innovation* (Harvard Education Press, 2011). Before joining the Kauffman Foundation in 2006, Wildavsky was the education editor of *U.S. News & World Report*, where he was the top editor of America's Best Colleges and America's Best Graduate Schools. Before joining *U.S. News*, he was a budget, tax, and trade correspondent for *National Journal*, a higher education reporter for *The San Francisco Chronicle*, and executive editor of *The Public Interest*. His writing has also appeared in *The Washington Post*, *The Wall Street Journal*, *Foreign Policy*, and *The New Republic*, among other publications. He is a guest blogger for *The Chronicle of Higher Education*. As a consultant to national education reformers, he has written several influential reports, including "A Test of Leadership" for the secretary of education's Commission on the Future of Education. He appears regularly in the media, including on CNN, in *The New York Times*, and on American Public Media's *Marketplace*. He has spoken to dozens of audiences in the United States and abroad, including at Google, Harvard University, the London School of Economics, the Organisation for Economic Cooperation and Development, *The Economist*'s Human Potential conference, the American College of Greece, and the University of Melbourne.

Index